The Heart Of Pittsburgh

D1360008

Sacred Heart Elementary School

Parent Teacher Guild

♥

Pittsburgh, Pennsylvania

By the Parent Teacher Guild of

Sacred Heart Elementary School

Additional copies may be obtained at the cost of $17.95,

plus $2.50 postage and handling, each book.

Pennsylvania residents add $1.26 sales tax, each book.

Send check or money order, along with your name and address to:

Sacred Heart Elementary School PTG

c/o Cookbook Committee

325 Emerson Street

Pittsburgh, PA 15206

———❤———

Proceeds from the sale of

The Heart of Pittsburgh

benefit the construction and ongoing development of the

Library/Media Center of Sacred Heart Elementary School

Copyright © 1998, Sacred Heart Elementary School PTG

Pittsburgh, Pennsylvania

First Printing, April, 1999–2,500 copies
Second Printing, August, 1999–3,000 copies
Third Printing, March, 2000–5,000 copies

ISBN 0-9667438-0-6

LCCCN 98-061264

Printed in the USA by
WIMMER
The Wimmer Companies
Memphis
1-800-548-2537

The Heart of Pittsburgh is a collection of more than 300 kitchen-tested recipes submitted by the families and friends of Sacred Heart Elementary School. Inspired by our school's 125th Anniversary serving the East End of Pittsburgh, PA, the book is a celebration of our city's cultural diversity, our rich ethnic heritage, and most of all, our food!

From its impressive skyline to the more than 500 bridges spanning three rivers, Pittsburgh has a wealth of opportunities and experiences to offer. Industry, business, higher education, the arts, museums, libraries, hospitals, research facilities, festivals and sports all help to enrich our lives. Especially enticing from the heart of our city is the selection of available foods. With eighty-eight culturally diverse neighborhoods, a vast array of ethnic and American cuisine can be found. Sample this fare at a sidewalk stand, an ethnic church or synagogue's food festival, a cafe or bistro. One may also lunch within a museum, nosh while listening to local musicians, dine waterside or cliffside, or spend the night at a bed & breakfast and enjoy scrumptious fare in the morning.

The Heart of Pittsburgh contains 13 sections, each introduced by a brief historical sketch of one of the many neighborhoods that make Pittsburgh so special. We've included our friends' and families' favorite hors d'oeuvres, beverages, marinades, sauces, breads, soups, salads, entrees, side dishes, vegetables and desserts. As an added feature, we have included some "Uniquely Pittsburgh" recipes in the final section of our book. We hope you will enjoy these recipes as much as we have enjoyed testing them, and that perhaps some day one of them will make its way into your family's culinary heritage.

Our cookbook has taken over two years to prepare, but it has been a labor of love. We thank Bishop William J. Winter, pastor of Sacred Heart Parish, and Sister Patricia Laffey, principal of Sacred Heart Elementary School, for their unfailing support; the Sacred Heart Parent Teacher Guild for their guidance; and our many financial benefactors for helping us to get up and get going.

We dedicate *The Heart of Pittsburgh* to all the families and friends of Sacred Heart — past, present, and future.

The Cookbook Committee

*C*ommittee Acknowledgments

Co-chairs: Karen Raffensperger and Mary Roberge

Editorial Staff:
Betty Austin · Robert DeBartolo · Diane DeNardo · Sonja Hissom-Braun · Anne McCafferty
Nicole Owens · Karen Raffensperger · Mary Roberge · Raymond Roberge

Graphic Design: McGuire Anderson Design
Historical Copy Editor: Anne McCafferty
Legal Advisor: Margaret K. Sitko, Attorney-at-Law
Marketing Coordinator: Diane DeNardo
Photography: Karen Raffensperger

Committee:

Betty Austin	Maria DePasquale	Marcella McGuire
Beverly Beisgen	Diane DeNardo	Joanne Redondo
Mary Bernacki	Regina Frey	Sylvia Stehlik
Donna Caligiuri	Kim Goldman	Danielle Tallman
Lynn Cauley	Sonja Hissom-Braun	Angela Walker
Pamela D'Alessandro	Donna Linnelli	William Walker
Sandra DeBartolo	Anne McCafferty	Patty Walters
Autumn DeMauro	Deborah McCarthy	Tina Zeigler

The committee wishes to extend its sincere thanks to the following people for their contribution of time and effort in assisting us with the monumental task of testing our recipes:

Lisa Anselmo	Ellen Gunnell	Janet Peterson
Dorianne DiGregorio	Gregory Heisler	Margaret Procario
Kathy Fine	Mary Ann Lasky	Megan Procario
Betty Gaston	Lynn Maola	Dorothy Van Wassen
Anne Franks Gillespie	Mary Anne Murphy	Gregory Welsh

The committee also acknowledges the many local establishments and persons that have made the "Uniquely Pittsburgh" section of our book a reality. The foodwriter's, chef's and establishment owner's contribution of time and talents in the production of this section are greatly appreciated.

Sincere thanks are extended to the Pittsburgh Neighborhood Alliance and Wendell Jordon, under whose leadership numerous community leaders created the *Pittsburgh Neighborhood Atlas*, Pittsburgh, PA, originally published in 1976. This book provided all of the neighborhood historical data for our cookbook.

Finally, we wish to commend the children of Sacred Heart Elementary School for their tremendous effort in assisting the committee with the collection of recipes. Their eagerness helped to fuel our enthusiasm!

Contributors

♥

Platinum Level
Federated Investors, Inc.
Raymond J. Roberge, M.D.
Shehady's Carpets and Oriental Rugs
The Western Pennsylvania Hospital Foundation

Gold Level
John Raffensperger, M.D.
Lewis A. Storb, D.M.D., M.S.
The Towers Family

Silver Level
Fuel and Fuddle Brick Oven Bar and Restaurant
Andrea and John Leavitt
Storb, Stockton, Hillenburg & Associates
The Sweeney Family

Bronze Level
Beth Shalom Catering
Café Baci
Goldman's Amoco
Carolyn Morris, Associate Broker
Oakland Catholic High School
Perform, Inc.
Pittsburgh Green Tree Marriott
Salon de Stefino
J. Matthew Stacey Jr., D.D.S., M.D.S.
William and Angela Walker

Patrons

Antiques of Shadyside	The Honorable Joyce Lee Itkin
Appletree Bed & Breakfast	Johnston the Florist
Central Catholic High School	Kelly and David Meade
Club One	Philip Pelusi Salons
Del's Restaurant	Pulmonary Consultants of Pittsburgh
Dunnings Grill	Rosebud's Gifts & Accessories
Councilman Jim Ferlo	Sacred Heart Women's Guild
Steele William Filipek, M.D.	Anne Scholle
Fraser-O'Loughlin Bed & Breakfast	*In Memory* — George J. Storb
Gulliver's Travels	Wayne and Patri DeVargas-Walker

$\mathcal{E}$lementary education is a cornerstone in the development of every child, serving as the foundation for so many of life's important endeavors. Born in 1873 of the educational and spiritual needs of the predominantly Irish immigrants of Pittsburgh's East End, Sacred Heart Elementary School has been dedicated to developing moral and academic excellence for more than 125 years.

The first Sacred Heart Church, situated on what is now Centre Avenue, originally served as both church and school. The school opened in 1873 under the direction of parishioners Misses Barry and White, and moved into its own four-room brick building adjacent to the church in 1874. The first year enrollment of 204 students grew rapidly and in December, 1894, seven Sisters of Charity came from Altoona, Pennsylvania, to staff the school. The sisters and lay teachers have provided guidance and tutelage to our students ever since.

Responding to continued parish growth, a three-story school building was completed in 1884, and Sacred Heart High School was established in one room of that building in 1913. A new eight-room school building on Sheridan Avenue was completed in 1923. The following year, construction of a new church on Shady and Walnut streets was begun, and, in 1947, the current Sacred Heart Elementary School, on Walnut and Emerson streets, was dedicated. Sacred Heart High School moved to the new Alder Street location in 1950, where it served the East End until 1989.

Today, Sacred Heart Elementary School provides an academically enriched program that includes reading and English, mathematics, algebra, science, religion, social studies, health and physical education, Spanish, music, art, and computer applications. Because of well-developed study habits and the involvement of parents and dedicated teachers, our students consistently demonstrate significant achievement in language and mathematics that is well above the national average. As one of the largest elementary schools in the Roman Catholic Diocese of Pittsburgh, our school continues to offer our students the highest caliber of education and moral guidance.

After 125 years of existence, Sacred Heart Elementary School is a stellar example of the adage, "Great beginnings last a lifetime."

The Cookbook Committee

Table of Contents

East Liberty

*E*ast Liberty began in 1758 when Brigadier General John Forbes built a roadway through the area for his expedition against Fort Duquesne. The French were routed from the Point (where the three rivers meet), and East Liberty's fertile land was farmed to produce food for the British garrison at Fort Pitt.

Alexander Negley, known as the "Father of East Liberty," settled in the area with his wife and five children. His son Jacob bought more land and laid out the local roads, including Penn Avenue. East Liberty was named after a farm that his wife had inherited. A "liberty" was land set aside for cattle grazing outside of London and Dublin.

Through much of the 1800's, East Liberty had a rural charm which attracted many of Pittsburgh's wealthy families. The Mellon, Larimer, King, Roup and Baum families all built their homes there. East Liberty became part of the city's "Classic East End" following its annexation in 1868.

Further development of East Liberty began with the construction of avenues and rail lines that serviced the great estates and transformed the neighborhood into the crossroads of the East End. The East Liberty Passenger Rail opened in 1860, bringing public transit to the wealthy and to the German-speaking immigrants living along Penn and Fifth Avenues.

Stockyards were built along Penn Avenue between Fifth Avenue and Denniston Street; houses, hotels and amusement centers followed. By 1920, seven movie theaters occupied Penn and Highland Avenues. Many grocery, drug, furniture, jewelry and shoe stores made East Liberty one of the major retail centers of Pittsburgh.

Once known as Pittsburgh's second downtown, East Liberty experienced urban renewal problems in the 1960's. Nonetheless, the neighborhood has generated significant revitalization through the efforts of East Liberty Development, Inc. and other local community groups. The success of the Penn-Highland Building project, which created a new commercial/office building along with many jobs, was a major milestone in East Liberty's recovery. Plans for additional residential housing and national retail stores are testimony to East Liberty's commitment to remaining a vital city neighborhood. ♥

Sangría

750 milliliters (3 cups plus 1 ounce) Spanish Rioja (red wine)
3 cups plus 1 ounce Five Alive (orange, tangerine, lemon-lime and grapefruit blended fruit juice)
1 ounce dark rum
Sliced fresh oranges, apples and strawberries, for garnish

Mix all ingredients together. Serve within 2 hours of adding the fruit; chill in refrigerator.

Yield: 2 quarts

José Ettedgui

Bloody Mary

2 (32-ounce) bottles Clamato juice
9 ounces vodka
4 tablespoons lime juice
½ cup Worcestershire sauce
Celery salt, to taste

In a 3½ to 4-quart container, combine Clamato juice, vodka, lime juice and Worcestershire. Sprinkle with a generous amount of celery salt. Stir. Serve in tall glasses with celery sticks as a garnish.

Note: Best when made ahead and refrigerated overnight.

Yield: 3 quarts

Raymond Roberge

"Stucco" Tea Syrup

8 cups water
1 cup loose tea
4½ cups sugar
12 ounces lemonade concentrate
16 ounces orange juice concentrate

Boil water. Add tea and steep for 10 minutes; strain. Add sugar and concentrates. For 2 quarts of tea, mix 6 cups water to 1½ cups syrup. Add ice and serve. Stucco work creates quite a thirst. This tea quenches it!

Note: Refrigerate unused syrup.

Yield: 11½ cups syrup; 10 (2-quart) servings

Marcia Storb

11

Fruit Smoothies Milkshake

1 apple, peeled, cored and diced
1 banana, sliced
4 ounces vanilla or lemon yogurt
2 cups apple juice
8-10 ice cubes

Place all ingredients in blender. Blend until smooth. Enjoy all summer long!

Yield: 4 to 6 servings

Antoinette Marra

Hot Buttered Rum

Batter:
1 pound dark brown sugar
½ pound salted butter
1 teaspoon ground nutmeg
1 teaspoon ground cinnamon
1 teaspoon ground cloves
1 teaspoon ground white
    cardamom
1 teaspoon vanilla

Premium dark rum

Place all batter ingredients in a blender or food processor. Blend well. Store in refrigerator or freezer. To prepare drink, use 1 to 2 tablespoons batter mixed with 1 to 2 ounces dark rum. Add both to a mug filled ¾ full with very hot water. Mix well.

Variation: Omit rum for a non-alcoholic treat.

Yield: 1½ pounds batter

Ellen Gunnell

Sherbet Punch

46 ounces orange juice, chilled
46 ounces pineapple juice, chilled
46 ounces apricot juice, chilled
1 quart ginger ale, chilled
2 oranges, sliced
1 (10-ounce) jar maraschino
    cherries, drained
1 quart orange sherbet

Combine juices in punch bowl. Add ginger ale; stir. Add orange slices and cherries. Place sherbet container under warm water until loosened. Place frozen sherbet in bowl.

Yield: 34 (5-ounce) servings

Peg Kalinowski

Frozen Daiquiris

1 (6-ounce) can frozen limeade,
  thawed, undiluted
¾-1 cup light rum
Ice cubes

Combine limeade and rum in blender. Blend for 30 seconds. Add enough ice to bring mixture to a 4-cup level. Blend until slushy. Pour into a quart-size container; freeze. To serve, let mixture stand at room temperature until slushy (about 20 minutes). Stir and serve immediately. Great for summertime picnics!

Note: Recipe may be doubled, tripled, quadrupled and so on! Can prepare up to 1 month in advance and freeze.

Yield: 8 (4-ounce) servings

Mary Roberge

Lime Cooler

1 cup lime sherbet
6 ounces frozen limeade
  concentrate
2 (7-ounce) bottles ginger ale,
  chilled
2 cups water

Place sherbet in bowl or pitcher and stir to soften. Stir in remaining ingredients. Ladle or pour into glasses and enjoy!

Yield: 6 servings

Betty Laufman

Orange and Spice Hot Mulled Wine

4 cups red table wine
4 orange and spice herbal tea bags
½ cup light brown sugar
1 bay leaf

Place wine in medium saucepan and heat to simmer. (Do not boil.) Add tea bags and let sit over low heat for 30 minutes. Remove tea bags; add sugar and bay leaf. Stir until sugar is dissolved. Let wine sit over low heat another 10 minutes; remove bay leaf. Serve hot in mugs.

Yield: 8 (4-ounce) servings

Eileen Wilson

13

Whiskey Sours

6 ounces frozen lemonade
   concentrate
6 ounces whiskey
Ice cubes
Grenadine
1 quart club soda
Orange slices
Maraschino cherries

Place concentrate and whiskey in blender. Add an equal amount of ice to liquid. Adding small amounts of grenadine, blend until foamy and light pink in color. (Mixture will be slushy.) Fill 6 (6-ounce) cocktail glasses ½ full of mixture. Add club soda until glasses are ¾ filled. Fill with ice. Garnish with orange slice and maraschino cherry.

Yield: 6 servings

John Raffensperger

Wassail

Liquid mixture:
2 quarts Newcastle Dark Brown
   Ale
2 quarts premium hardened cider
1½ quarts sherry
2 cups brandy
2 cups spiced rum
6 cups brown sugar

Spice mixture:
2 cups lemon juice
1½ tablespoons nutmeg
1 tablespoon ginger
1 teaspoon mace
9-10 whole cloves
1½ sticks cinnamon
2 allspice berries

Combine all liquid ingredients in a 2½-gallon (or larger) pot. Set aside. In medium saucepan, combine all spice mixture ingredients and heat to 200 degrees, stirring continuously. When spice mixture is hot, and spices have largely dissolved, combine with liquid mixture; heat until sugar dissolves and wassail is warm. (Do not overheat, as alcohol will evaporate!) A traditional Celtic drink to celebrate Calan Gaeaf (December 21st, the eve of the winter solstice).

Note: Recipe can be doubled.

Yield: 1½ gallons

Richard and Michele Griffiths

Roquefort Yogurt Dressing

1 cup mayonnaise
½ cup plain yogurt
2-3 tablespoons buttermilk
⅓ cup crumbled Roquefort cheese
1 tablespoon white wine vinegar
2 cloves garlic, minced
1 teaspoon salt
½ teaspoon fresh ground black
    pepper
¼ teaspoon cayenne pepper
¼ cup chopped chives

Combine all ingredients except chives in blender or food processor. Blend until smooth. (If thinner dressing consistency is desired, add an additional 1 tablespoon of buttermilk.) Stir in chives. Chill until ready to use.

Yield: 2 cups

Tony DiLembo

Creole Sauce for Eggs

¼ cup finely chopped green
    pepper
¼ cup finely chopped onion
2 tablespoons butter
1¼ cups chopped (canned or
    fresh) tomatoes
¼ teaspoon Tabasco sauce
½ teaspoon sugar
½ teaspoon salt

In medium skillet, sauté pepper and onion in butter until tender. Do not brown. Add tomatoes and seasonings. Cook over low to medium heat for ½ hour. Sauce will thicken. Delicious served over an omelet or scrambled eggs!

Variation: Olive oil may be substituted for butter.

Yield: Approximately 1 cup

Lorraine Raffensperger

Creole Mayonnaise

1 cup mayonnaise
2 teaspoons fresh lemon juice
½ teaspoon dill weed
½ teaspoon celery seed
½ cup chopped fresh parsley
1 teaspoon Creole seasoning
Black pepper, to taste

Combine all ingredients in a small bowl. Mix thoroughly. Serve over Pasta Chicken Salad (found in the Salads section) or be creative!

Yield: 1½ cups

Charlotte Broome

15

Clarified Butter

½ cup butter

Over low heat, allow butter to melt completely. Remove from heat; let stand 3 to 5 minutes until settling occurs. Using a flat spoon, skim foam from top and discard. Strain the remaining liquid into a container to save or serve. Discard strained solids.

Yield: 7/16 cup

Lisa Raffensperger

A Very Hearty Pasta Sauce

1½ pounds bulk Italian sausage
3 cups sliced fresh mushrooms
½ cup chopped carrots
½ cup chopped green peppers
½ cup chopped onions
1 (28-ounce) can crushed tomatoes
1 (15-ounce) can tomato sauce
1 (6-ounce) can tomato paste
½ cup grated Parmesan cheese
½ cup beef broth or red wine
¾ teaspoon aniseed
¾ teaspoon seasoned salt
¾ teaspoon pepper
¾ teaspoon garlic powder
¾ teaspoon brown sugar
¾ teaspoon dried basil
¾ teaspoon dried oregano
4 cups coarsely chopped fresh
   spinach, cleaned and drained
2 cups shredded mozzarella cheese

In Dutch oven or large heavy pot, crumble and brown sausage. Add mushrooms, carrots, green peppers and onions. Sauté for 5 minutes. Add crushed tomatoes, tomato sauce and tomato paste. Stir in Parmesan cheese, broth and all seasonings. Cover and simmer for 1 hour. Add spinach; heat thoroughly. Serve over your favorite cooked pasta. Top with mozzarella cheese.

Yield: Approximately 2 quarts

Carole Annis

Ed's Pesto Sauce

½ cup pine nuts
¼ cup walnuts
1¼ cups olive oil, divided
2 cups fresh basil leaves, washed
    and patted dry
1 clove garlic
¼ cup fresh parsley sprigs
1 tablespoon fresh oregano
3 tablespoons balsamic vinegar
¾ cup freshly grated imported
    Parmesan cheese
¼ cup freshly grated imported
    Romano cheese
¼ teaspoon red pepper flakes
Freshly ground black pepper, to
    taste

Sauté pine nuts and walnuts in ¼ cup of the olive oil over low-medium heat until golden. Combine nuts, basil, garlic, parsley and oregano in bowl of food processor and chop. With motor running, add the remaining 1 cup of olive oil and vinegar in a slow steady stream. Turn motor off; add cheeses and peppers. Process to just combine; scrape pesto into bowl and cover until ready to use.

Note: Add more olive oil depending on desired consistency. If using a blender, divide recipe in half and blend in 2 batches. Pesto can be made ahead and stored in the refrigerator for up to 2 weeks.

Yield: 2 cups; enough for 2 pounds of pasta.

Ed D'Alessandro

Basic Tomato Sauce

3 tablespoons vegetable oil
3 shallots or 1 medium onion,
    peeled and finely chopped
2 cloves garlic, minced
1 (12-ounce) can tomato paste
2 (15-ounce) cans tomato sauce
1 (28-ounce) can crushed tomatoes
2 bay leaves
3-5 fresh leaves or 1 tablespoon
    dried basil
2 carrots, peeled and cut in half
5-6 cups water
2 tablespoons grated Parmesan
    cheese

Heat oil over low heat in large stock pot. Simmer shallots, stirring occasionally, until tender. Add garlic, tomato paste, tomato sauce, crushed tomatoes, bay leaves, basil, carrots and water. Stir until well-blended. Heat thoroughly, about 1 hour. Stir occasionally. Add Parmesan cheese and continue cooking for at least 1 hour longer, stirring occasionally. Remove carrot halves and bay leaves before serving.

Yield: 8 cups

Virginia Gatto

"Italian Gourmet" Marinara Sauce

3 medium white onions, quartered
1 medium carrot, quartered
1 rib celery, quartered
3 cloves garlic
2 tablespoons olive oil
1 (28-ounce) can plum tomatoes, chopped
1 (15-ounce) can tomato sauce
1 teaspoon dried or 2-3 teaspoons fresh minced basil
1 tablespoon minced fresh parsley
1 teaspoon dried oregano
½ teaspoon salt
2 teaspoons red pepper flakes
1 teaspoon freshly ground black pepper
1½ cups Italian red wine, divided
1 cup freshly grated Parmesan cheese, divided

By hand or using a food processor, finely chop the onion, carrot, celery and garlic. In a large sauté pan, heat olive oil over medium heat. Add chopped vegetables; sauté until onions are soft. Transfer to a large pot. Add plum tomatoes, tomato sauce, basil, parsley, oregano, salt, red pepper, black pepper, ¾ cup of the wine and ½ cup of the Parmesan cheese. Stir vigorously and bring to a boil. Let boil for 2 minutes; reduce heat. Simmer, uncovered, for 45 minutes, stirring occasionally. Stir in remaining wine and cheese. Cover and simmer an additional 45 to 50 minutes, stirring occasionally.

Note: Store in refrigerator in an airtight container for up to 1 week. When ready to use, reheat, adding a small amount of water or red wine to thin.

Yield: Sauce for 16 large servings of pasta.

Joanne Redondo

Asian Barbecue Marinade

½ cup peanut oil
¼ cup Hoisin sauce
¼ cup soy sauce
½ cup rice or distilled white vinegar
¼ cup rice wine or dry sherry
½ teaspoon hot chili oil
1 teaspoon dark sesame oil
2 whole scallions, minced
2 whole shallots, minced
2 cloves garlic, minced
3 tablespoons minced fresh ginger

Whisk all ingredients together. Pour over meat or poultry. Marinate overnight, turning once. Discard marinade.

Yield: 2½ cups

Joanne Redondo

Marinade for Fowl

1 cup olive oil
¼ cup dry sherry
1 garlic bulb, divided and peeled
2 teaspoons ground black pepper
½ cup chopped fresh thyme
½ cup chopped fresh rosemary
Salt, to taste

Mix all ingredients together in a blender. Rinse fowl and pat dry. Place bird in a large plastic bag. Rub marinade over entire bird. Fill cavity with excess marinade. Tie bag securely. Place into a second plastic bag. Tie second bag securely. Marinate in refrigerator for 1 to 2 days; discard marinade before roasting.

Yield: Enough marinade for 1 (10 to 12-pound) turkey or other fowl.

Patti Hanley

Marinade for Fish

½ teaspoon finely grated lemon
   peel
⅓ cup lemon juice
⅓ cup olive oil
1 tablespoon prepared
   horseradish
½ teaspoon kosher salt
¼ teaspoon dried basil
¼ teaspoon dried oregano
⅛ teaspoon pepper

Put fish in a plastic bag and place in large bowl. Combine all marinade ingredients and pour into bag. Seal bag tightly. Refrigerate 2 to 3 hours, turning bag frequently. Baste fish with marinade while cooking. Discard marinade after use.

Yield: Enough marinade for 2 pounds of fish.

Michele Chaballa

Marinade for Flank Steak

¾ cup Burgundy wine
¾ cup olive oil
1 clove garlic, crushed
1 tablespoon grated onion
1 teaspoon kosher salt
¼ teaspoon black pepper
½ teaspoon dried or 1½ teaspoons
   chopped fresh oregano
½ teaspoon dried or 1½ teaspoons
   chopped fresh basil

Mix all ingredients together in a 9x13-inch glass baking dish. Mix well. Place steak in marinade. Cover tightly. Refrigerate; let marinate overnight, turning once. Grill or broil steak to desired doneness. Discard marinade after use.

Yield: Enough marinade for a 1 to 2-pound flank steak.

Jack Gaston

19

Easy Hollandaise Sauce

¾ pound butter (no substitutions)
4 egg yolks
2 tablespoons water
½ teaspoon fresh lemon juice
Dash ground white pepper
Dash ground cayenne pepper

Melt butter in a small saucepan over low heat until bubbling. Place egg yolks, water, lemon juice and peppers in a blender. Blend at high speed until smooth. Immediately add hot butter in a steady stream; stop blender. Delicious served on top of cooked asparagus garnished with pimento slices.

Note: This recipe contains raw eggs.

Yield: 1¾ cups

Mary Roberge

Barbecue Sauce

1 teaspoon paprika
½ teaspoon ground pepper
4 teaspoons sugar
1 teaspoon dry mustard
1 tablespoon butter or margarine
½ cup chopped onions
4 teaspoons Worcestershire sauce
½ cup ketchup
¼ cup vinegar
¼ cup water

Combine paprika, pepper, sugar and mustard. Set aside. In a medium saucepan, melt butter. Sauté onion until opaque. Add Worcestershire, ketchup, vinegar and water. Cook over low-medium heat, stirring often, for 3 to 5 minutes. Add dry seasonings to sauce and cook another 3 to 5 minutes. Use as a basting sauce for chicken or ribs. Use with hamburger or shaved pork for delicious barbecued sandwiches.

Yield: 1 cup

Betty Gaston

Highland Park

*H*ighland Park's name is a play on words, indicating both the original surveyor's name—Hilands—and the area's elevation. Highland Park was annexed to the City of Pittsburgh in 1868.

Part of Highland Park was once a 300-acre land grant farm owned by Alexander Negley. Negley had come from Philadelphia in 1788 and built his home on what is now the basin of the Highland Park Reservoir. Negley Circle, a family burial ground located on a knoll above Serpentine Road, is the resting place of some fifty of this valley's settlers. Highland Park's "farm house" was built in 1840 as part of a dairy farm on the original Negley land grant. Over the next century, it served as a clubhouse for the Highland Park Country Club and later as a picnic shelter, office and public amenities station.

Highland Park opened in 1893. The park's 366 acres are a result of over 110 land acquisitions obtained at a cost of $905,508. Edward Manning Bigelow, the "Father of Pittsburgh's Parks," was responsible for the development of the beautiful green space. As the City Engineer (today's Director of Public Works), Bigelow's plans were not always appreciated by City Council members and Pittsburgh taxpayers. As a result, he sometimes resorted to devious techniques to obtain money for park expansion. Often not revealing that his land purchases were for the park, he was known, on occasion, to have had property condemned when people refused to sell. Removed from his position at City Hall in 1900, Bigelow was re-appointed in 1903, only to be ousted again in 1906.

In the late 19th century, the Highland Park neighborhood included the estate of T.P. Barnsdale, an oil pioneer and prominent landowner. H. Frederick Mercer, a noted lawyer, bought the estate in the 1920's and gave it his name. The Mercer mansion was demolished in 1948 making way for the development of 144 housing units.

Highland Park is home to the Pittsburgh Zoo which has been in existence for over 100 years. Today, Highland Park is noted for the rich variety of architectural styles that make up its housing stock, a strong sense of community, and its attractiveness to families who value its close proximity to all of Pittsburgh's amenities. ♥

Roasted Portobello Appetizer

4 large portobello mushrooms
½ cup Italian-style salad dressing
1 (4-ounce) jar sun-dried
   tomatoes, drained and diced
4 ounces goat cheese, crumbled

Clean mushrooms with a wet paper towel; remove stems. Place mushroom caps and stems in a 7x11-inch baking dish. Pour Italian dressing over mushroom pieces. Marinate overnight in refrigerator. Preheat oven to broil. Place mushroom caps on broiling pan. Discard marinade. Broil for 5 minutes on each side; remove from oven. Decrease oven temperature to 350 degrees. Chop mushroom stems coarsely; toss with tomatoes in small bowl. Return mushroom caps to baking dish. Top with tomato mixture and goat cheese. Bake for 15 minutes, until portobellos are tender.

Yield: 4 servings

Rebecca Lando

Chinese Tea Eggs

6 eggs
2 tea bags
1 tablespoon salt
1 teaspoon-size star anise (seed
   pod)

Hard boil eggs; cool. Crack shells all over; do not peel. Place eggs, tea bags, salt and star anise in a medium saucepan with enough water to cover eggs. Heat to a boil and simmer for 1 hour. Remove from heat; allow eggs to cool in the liquid. Keep eggs in liquid; refrigerate overnight. When ready to serve, peel eggs and cut each into 4 wedges, lengthwise. Serve cold. This unique appetizer has the appearance of marbleized eggs with a mild taste of anise.

Note: Star anise (seed pod) can be found in most Asian food stores.

Yield: Serves 6 to 12

Anne Franks Gillespie

Mushroom Turnovers with Cream Cheese Pastry

Pastry Shell:
2 (8-ounce) packages cream
    cheese, softened
1 cup margarine
3 cups flour

Filling:
3 tablespoons margarine
3 tablespoons finely minced
    shallot
½ pound mushrooms, finely
    minced
½ teaspoon salt
¼ teaspoon nutmeg
2 tablespoons flour
½ cup sour cream

1 egg, beaten

To prepare pastry shell, combine all ingredients; mix well; divide in half. Wrap pastry halves in waxed paper and refrigerate at least 1 hour or overnight. To prepare filling, melt margarine in a skillet. Sauté shallots and mushrooms until tender. Stir in salt, nutmeg and flour. Blend in sour cream; cool. Bring pastry dough to room temperature. Preheat oven to 450 degrees. Roll out ½ of dough on a floured board. Roll thin and cut out 2-inch circles with a cookie or biscuit cutter. Brush edges of circles with beaten egg. Place ½ teaspoon of the mushroom mixture in center of pastry circle; fold in half. Press edges together with fork and prick tops of pastry. Place on ungreased baking sheet; bake for 12 to 15 minutes.

Note: Freeze turnovers after baking for an enhanced flavor. To re-heat, bake, unthawed, 7 to 9 minutes in a pre-heated 450 degree oven. Serve immediately.

Yield: Approximately 6 dozen

Coleen Powell

Cucumber Dip

1 large cucumber
¼ cup shredded carrots
¼ cup shredded radish (optional)
¼ cup minced onion (optional)
½-1 teaspoon celery seed, to taste
1 tablespoon dried, crushed
    parsley
1 cup mayonnaise
½ cup sour cream

Peel and seed cucumber. Shred coarsely; drain well on paper towels. In a medium bowl, mix remaining ingredients together. Combine with drained cucumber; refrigerate until use. Serve with assorted crackers or fresh vegetables.

Yield: 3 to 4 cups

Diane Alexander

Baked Artichoke Dip

2 (13¾-ounce) cans artichoke
    hearts, drained and chopped
2 tablespoons lemon juice
1 cup mayonnaise
1½ cups Parmesan cheese
¼ teaspoon garlic powder

Preheat oven to 350 degrees. Place artichokes in small bowl; sprinkle with lemon juice. In a separate bowl, combine mayonnaise, Parmesan and garlic powder. Add to artichokes, mixing well. Place in baking dish; bake for 30 minutes or until golden brown. Serve with crackers.

Note: Can be made ahead of time. Store in refrigerator until ready to bake.

Yield: 10-12 servings

Autumn DeMauro

Hummus

1 (20-ounce) can chick peas
2 cloves garlic, minced
⅓ cup fresh lemon juice
½ cup tahini
6 tablespoons olive oil, divided

Drain chick peas in colander, reserving ¼ cup of liquid. Place garlic, lemon juice and reserved liquid in food processor. Process for 30 seconds. Alternately add chick peas and tahini. Process 30 seconds after each addition. With food processor running, add 4 tablespoons of the olive oil in a steady stream. Purée to a smooth consistency. Transfer to a shallow serving bowl. Cover and refrigerate 6 to 8 hours. Prior to serving, float a skim coat of the remaining 2 tablespoons olive oil on top of hummus. Serve with pita bread wedges or fresh vegetables.

Note: Must be made at least 6 to 8 hours ahead.

Yield: Approximately 2 cups

Natalie Barry

Skordalia

Greek-Style Garlic Sauce

3-4 medium potatoes
3 tablespoons minced garlic
1 cup olive oil
⅓ cup white wine vinegar
¼ cup cold water, if needed
1-2 teaspoons salt, to taste
1 teaspoon white pepper

Peel and boil potatoes until soft. Drain. Blend garlic and drained potatoes together using a blender or food processor. Add olive oil and vinegar; continue to blend. If mixture is dry or thick, add cold water, a little at a time, until a smooth and creamy consistency is achieved. Add salt and pepper; blend an additional 20 seconds. Serve with pita wedges or any good crusty bread.

Yield: 2 to 3 cups

Marcella Karvellis McGuire

Rumaki

2 (8-ounce) cans whole water
chestnuts, halved
1 (12-ounce) can pineapple
chunks, juice reserved
1½ pounds thick sliced bacon,
slices halved
1 (20-ounce) jar Major Grey
chutney

Preheat oven to 350 degrees. Layer 1 water chestnut half and 1 pineapple chunk atop each bacon slice. Wrap bacon slices around water chestnuts and pineapples; secure with tooth-picks. Place on broiler rack (allowing fat to drain while baking). Bake for 40 minutes. Turn each piece; bake an additional 20 minutes, or until crispy. Remove from oven; dip each piece in the chutney. (Reserved juice may be used to thin chutney.) Place all pieces on a well-greased baking sheet. Bake an additional 20 to 30 minutes.

Note: Can freeze after first baking. Freezes well up to 2 months. Thaw before dipping in chutney; proceed with final baking of 20 to 30 minutes at 350 degrees.

Yield: Approximately 40 Rumakis

Kim Ogle

Hot Tuna!

1 cup mayonnaise
2 tablespoons lemon juice
2 tablespoons grated onion
½ teaspoon salt
2 (6½-ounce) cans tuna, drained
2 cups chopped celery
1 cup slivered almonds
½ cup grated sharp Cheddar
    cheese

Preheat oven to 400 degrees. In a large bowl, mix mayonnaise, lemon juice, onion and salt together. Add tuna, celery, almonds and cheese. Pour into a greased 1½-quart casserole. Bake for 15 minutes. Serve on bread as a hot sandwich or in a chafing dish with crackers.

Variation: Substitute 2 cups shredded crab meat or chicken for the tuna.

Yield: 4 to 6 servings

Joanne Mast Dalrymple

Spinach Balls with Dipping Sauce

Spinach Balls:
1 (10-ounce) package frozen
    chopped spinach, thawed and
    well-drained
1 cup herb-seasoned stuffing mix
½ cup Parmesan cheese
2 eggs, lightly beaten
⅓ cup butter or margarine,
    melted
1 teaspoon minced onion
⅛ teaspoon nutmeg

Sauce:
½ cup mayonnaise
¼ cup sour cream
1 tablespoon fresh lemon juice
1 teaspoon sugar
1 teaspoon Dijon mustard
Dash Tabasco sauce

Mix all spinach ball ingredients together in a large bowl. Roll into 1 to 1½-inch balls. Arrange on baking sheet and place in freezer for 15 minutes. Preheat oven to 350 degrees. Bake 10 to 15 minutes, until lightly golden brown. In a small serving bowl, combine sauce ingredients; blend well. Use as a dip for spinach balls.

Variation: Substitute thyme for nutmeg.

Yield: 2 dozen

Cathy Gleason and Jane Steineck

Whatevers

1 (8-ounce) can crab meat,
   drained and picked through
½ cup butter or margarine,
   softened
7 ounces sharp, processed cheese
   spread
2 tablespoons mayonnaise
½ teaspoon salt
½ teaspoon garlic salt
6 whole English muffins, split

In a medium bowl, mix together crab meat, butter, cheese spread, mayonnaise, salt and garlic salt. Spread on muffin halves; place on baking sheet and freeze for 30 minutes. Pre-heat broiler. Cut each half in half again. Broil 3 to 5 minutes until puffy.

Note: Can be prepared ahead; freezes well for up to one week.

Yield: 24 Whatevers

Cathy Gleason

Nippy Shrimp

¾ pound medium shrimp, cooked,
   peeled and deveined
½ clove garlic, minced
½ cup chili sauce
10-12 slices bacon, cut in half

Combine shrimp and garlic in a medium bowl. Pour chili sauce over top. Cover and refrigerate 2 to 4 hours; stir occasionally. Fry bacon until partially cooked; drain well. Preheat broiler. Wrap each shrimp in 1 piece of bacon; secure with wooden toothpicks. Broil 2 to 3 inches from heat until bacon is crisp.

Yield: 20 to 24 appetizers

Coleen Powell

North Carolina Caviar

2 (15-ounce) cans black-eyed peas,
   drained and rinsed
½ green pepper, finely chopped
½ red pepper, finely chopped
1 red onion, finely chopped
⅛ cup vegetable oil
⅛ cup (apple cider or red wine)
   vinegar
2 dashes of Tabasco sauce, or to
   taste
Salt and pepper, to taste

Mix all ingredients together and chill overnight. Serve with corn chips or other sturdy chips. A New Year's Day tradition!

Yield: Approximately 4 cups

Susan Dawson

Keftaidakia

Greek Cocktail Meatballs

**2 slices white bread, crusts
  removed**
¼ cup water
1 pound lean ground beef
1 medium onion, finely chopped
**2 tablespoons chopped fresh
  parsley**
1 tablespoon chopped fresh mint
**1 tablespoon chopped fresh
  oregano**
1 egg
½ teaspoon salt
¼ teaspoon pepper
2 cloves garlic, minced
¾ cup flour
5 tablespoons olive oil

Soak bread briefly in water. Squeeze out excess water. In a large mixing bowl, combine bread and ground beef. Add onion, parsley, mint, oregano, egg, salt, pepper and garlic; mix well. Roll into 1½-inch meatballs. Roll each meatball in flour to coat; fry in hot oil until brown and cooked through. Serve hot or at room temperature.

Note: Can be made ahead.

Yield: 1½ to 2 dozen

Marcella Karvellis McGuire

Salsa Caliente

1 cup chopped onion
**1 cup seeded, minced serrano or
  jalapeño peppers**
2-4 cloves garlic, chopped, to taste
**1 (28-ounce) can plum tomatoes,
  drained, ½ of liquid reserved**
**Juice of 1 lemon or lime, or to
  taste**
**2 tablespoons minced, fresh
  cilantro (optional)**

In a large bowl, combine onion, peppers and garlic. Coarsely chop tomatoes; add to bowl. Add lemon juice and cilantro. Add reserved tomato liquid, if necessary, to thin salsa. Refrigerate 2 to 3 hours before serving. Serve with tortilla chips. Not a wimpy salsa!

*Note: Best if made in advance. Keeps for
1 week refrigerated.*

Yield: 5 to 6 cups

Anne Franks Gillespie

Horseradish Guacamole

2-3 ripe avocados
3 tablespoons light mayonnaise
½ tablespoon salt, or to taste
½ tablespoon pepper, or to taste
½ tablespoon Tabasco sauce
½ tablespoon Worcestershire
  sauce
½ tablespoon horseradish
4 plum tomatoes, diced

Cut avocados in half; remove pit. Scoop avocado into a medium bowl; mash with a fork. Mix in mayonnaise. Add salt, pepper, Tabasco, Worcestershire and horseradish; blend well. Fold tomatoes in gently. Cover and refrigerate for 1 hour. Stir before serving. Serve with tortilla chips.

Variation: Substitute 2 tablespoons mild salsa for horseradish.

Yield: 4 servings

JoAnn Willey

Baked Brie Bread

1 round loaf of French bread
2 tablespoons butter
1 clove garlic, minced
1 small onion, finely chopped
1 small shallot, finely chopped
8 ounces Brie cheese, cubed
1 (8-ounce) package cream cheese,
  cubed
8 ounces sour cream
1 tablespoon brown sugar
1½ teaspoons Worcestershire
  sauce

Preheat oven to 350 degrees. Cut top off bread loaf; set aside. Hollow out center of loaf, 1 inch from edges and 3 inches deep; tear bread center into 2-inch pieces; set aside. In large skillet, heat butter over medium heat. Sauté garlic, onion and shallot until soft (do not brown). Reduce heat to low. Add cheese cubes to skillet. Heat, stirring, until cheese melts. Remove from heat; add sour cream, brown sugar and Worcestershire. Stir until creamy. Pour into bread shell; replace top. Wrap bread shell in foil; place on baking sheet. Bake for 45 minutes. Serve hot with reserved bread pieces for dipping.

Yield: Serves 6 to 8

Ellen Gunnell

Chili Brie in Sourdough

1 teaspoon chili powder
½ teaspoon dry mustard
½ teaspoon garlic powder
½ teaspoon sugar
1 (1-pound) round loaf of
  sourdough bread
1 tablespoon butter, softened
1 (8-ounce) wheel Brie cheese

Preheat oven to 350 degrees. In a small bowl, combine chili powder, mustard, garlic powder and sugar; set aside. Cut top off bread; set aside. Hollow out bread center, 1 inch from sides and 3 inches deep. Tear bread center into 2 inch pieces; set aside. Spread inside of bread shell with butter; sprinkle with 2 teaspoons of spice mixture. Using a serrated knife, make 2-inch cuts around top edge of bread shell at 1-inch intervals. Remove rind from cheese and discard. Place cheese in bread shell. Sprinkle remaining spice mixture into shell. Replace top of bread. Place bread on baking sheet; bake 20 to 30 minutes until cheese is melted. Serve hot with reserved bread pieces for dipping.

Yield: Serves 6 to 8

Patty Schlicht (Quinn)

Pesto Cream Cheese Spread

6-8 sun-dried tomatoes, divided
1 (8-ounce) package cream cheese,
  unsoftened
1 (6-ounce) jar pesto with pine
  nuts, divided

Boil tomatoes in water for 2 minutes to soften. Cool and coarsely chop all but 2 tomatoes. Slice the remaining 2 tomatoes; set aside. Place cream cheese on its side; cut through lengthwise to form 2 rectangular halves. Place 1 half on a serving plate. Spread ½ of the pesto over top of cream cheese. Cover pesto with chopped tomatoes. Top with second cream cheese half. Spread remaining pesto over top of second half. Lay sliced tomatoes over pesto to garnish. Serve cheese spread whole or sliced with French bread or table crackers.

Yield: 16 ounces cheese spread; serves 20

Louise Sciannameo

Lucia's Boursin

1 (8-ounce) package cream cheese,
   softened
4 tablespoons butter, softened
4 teaspoons heavy cream
¼ teaspoon garlic powder
⅛ teaspoon dried oregano
⅛ teaspoon dried thyme
⅛ teaspoon dried marjoram
⅛ teaspoon dried dill
⅛ teaspoon dried basil
⅛-¼ cup coarsely cracked
   peppercorns

With an electric mixer, beat together cream cheese, butter and heavy cream, on low speed, until well blended. Add herbs; blend on low speed. Remove both ends of a clean tuna fish can to use as a mold. Place on waxed paper; fill completely with cheese mixture, leveling top of can. Chill in mold for at least one hour; remove mold and roll in peppercorns. Serve boursin with crackers.

Yield: 6 to 10 servings

Ann Kelly

Korean Pork

½ cup soy sauce
3 tablespoons sugar
2 tablespoons minced onion
2 cloves garlic, minced
2 teaspoons ground ginger
¾ cup toasted sesame seeds
2 pork tenderloins, center-cut
2 tablespoons oil

Combine soy sauce, sugar, onion, garlic, ginger and sesame seeds together in a large bowl; add pork and coat with mixture. Cover and marinate for at least 3 hours in refrigerator; turn pork occasionally. Preheat oven to 375 degrees. Coat a roasting pan with the oil. Transfer pork to pan; roast for 45 minutes. Heat marinade in small saucepan over medium heat for 5 to 7 minutes. Thinly slice pork; place in serving bowl. Pour marinade over top. Serve with bread on the side.

Yield: Serves 6 to 8

Mary Claire Kasunic

Chinese Meatballs

Meat Mixture:
1 pound ground beef
1 teaspoon salt
1 teaspoon pepper
¼ cup water
1 egg
2 tablespoons chopped onion
1½ cups bread crumbs

Sauce:
3 tablespoons cornstarch,
    dissolved in small amount of
    cold water
3 tablespoons vinegar
1 tablespoon vegetable oil
1 tablespoon soy sauce
½ cup sugar
1½ cups pineapple juice
4 pineapple slices, cut into chunks
½ green pepper, sliced
½ red pepper, sliced

Preheat oven to 375 degrees. Combine all meat mixture ingredients in a large bowl; mix well by hand. Form into 36 (1½-inch) balls. Place meat balls on baking sheet. Bake 10 minutes. Mix together all sauce ingredients in a medium saucepan. Cook over medium heat for approximately 10 minutes, until thickened. Transfer meatballs to serving dish; pour on sauce and serve warm.

Variation: Serve with rice as a main dish.

Yield: 36 meatballs

Mary Bernacki

Kielbasy Appetizer

2 pounds kielbasy
1 large onion, chopped
1 (16-ounce) jar applesauce
1 (1-pound) box brown sugar

Preheat oven to 250 degrees. Place kielbasy in a 9x13-inch baking dish. Bake for 45 minutes. Remove from oven; pierce with fork and drain grease. Cut kielbasy into bite-size pieces; return to baking dish. Spread onion over kielbasy; set aside. Increase oven temperature to 350 degrees. In large bowl, mix applesauce with brown sugar. Pour evenly over kielbasy and onion. Bake for 1½ hours. Serve with decorative toothpicks for a festive look.

Yield: 15 to 20 servings

Ann M. Kelly

Spicy Glazed Pecans

½ cup sugar
3 tablespoons water
1 teaspoon salt
½ teaspoon cayenne pepper
2 cups pecan halves

Preheat oven to 350 degrees. Butter a large heavy baking sheet. Combine first 4 ingredients in small heavy saucepan. Stir over medium heat until sugar dissolves. Increase heat; boil 2 minutes. Add pecans slowly; stir until coated, about 1 minute. Transfer pecans to prepared baking sheet, spreading evenly. Bake until pecans are just beginning to brown, about 13 minutes. Transfer pecans to a baking sheet lined with waxed paper. Separate into single layer using a fork. Cool completely. Store in an airtight container.

Note: Can be prepared 1 week in advance.

Variation: Add Spicy Glazed Pecans and chunks of blue cheese to a salad; top with an oil and vinegar dressing.

Yield: 2 cups

Allison DeBartolo

Vegetable Pizza

2 (8-ounce) packages refrigerated
  crescent roll dough
1 (16-ounce) container sour cream
2 (8-ounce) packages cream
  cheese, softened
1 (1-ounce) package ranch-
  flavored dip mix
1 bunch broccoli florets
1 bunch cauliflower florets
1 pound carrots, shredded
8 ounces shredded Cheddar or
  mozzarella cheese

Preheat oven to 400 degrees. Place rolls, sides touching, on an ungreased baking sheet. Using hands, flatten rolls to cover entire sheet; pinch edges together. Bake for 10 to 15 minutes, until golden. In a medium bowl, mix together sour cream, cream cheese and dip mix; spread over crust. Crumble broccoli and cauliflower florets into small pieces. Spread vegetables, including carrots, evenly over cheese layer. Top with shredded cheese. Slice into squares with a pizza cutter and serve.

Yield: 12 servings

Lisa Anselmo

Stuffed Mushrooms

1 pound of mushrooms
4 tablespoons butter, divided
⅓ cup chopped onion
1 small clove garlic, minced
⅓ cup coarsely chopped
    pepperoni
⅓ cup shredded mozzarella cheese
½ teaspoon Italian seasoning
1⅓ cups seasoned bread crumbs

Preheat oven to 350 degrees. Clean mushrooms. Remove stems; chop and set aside. Melt 2 tablespoons of the butter. Dip mushroom caps in melted butter to coat. Place caps in a 9x13-inch baking dish. Sauté onion, garlic and mushroom stems in remaining 2 tablespoons of the butter until tender; remove from heat. Add pepperoni, cheese, seasoning and bread crumbs; mix well. Spoon mixture into mushroom caps. Bake for 15 minutes, until hot.

Note: Extra filling can be baked around mushroom caps. Use as a side dish to accompany a meal.

Yield: 30 appetizers

Karen Graziano

Hot Crab Dip

1 (6½-ounce) can crab meat,
    picked through
1 cup mayonnaise
1 cup finely chopped onions
1 cup shredded extra-sharp white
    Cheddar cheese
1 tablespoon grated Parmesan
    cheese
½ teaspoon paprika

Preheat oven to 350 degrees. In a large bowl, combine crab meat, mayonnaise, onion and cheese. Place in an 8x8-inch baking dish. Mix together Parmesan cheese and paprika. Sprinkle over top of crab mixture. Bake for 40 to 60 minutes until bubbly. Serve with crackers.

Variation: Double recipe; do not top with Parmesan cheese and paprika. Place in a 9x13-inch baking dish. Bake for 40 minutes in a pre-heated 350 degree oven. Hollow out a round loaf of Italian bread, reserving center bread pieces. Spoon baked dip into bread shell. Top with Parmesan cheese and paprika mixture. Bake an additional 10 minutes. Serve with reserved bread pieces.

Yield: Serves 10 to 12

Diane Soehner and Terri Williams

35

Bruschetta

1½ baguettes of bread (French or
   Italian)
¼ cup olive oil

Paste Mixture:
1 cup pitted black olives
2 tablespoons balsamic vinegar
1½ teaspoons small capers,
   drained
1 teaspoon olive oil
2 cloves fresh garlic

Tomato Mixture:
1 cup diced fresh red tomatoes
⅓ cup finely sliced scallions
1 tablespoon olive oil
½ cup finely chopped fresh basil
   or oregano
Freshly ground black pepper, to
   taste

3 tablespoons Parmesan cheese

Preheat oven to 425 degrees. Slice baguettes into 1-inch thick slices; arrange on a large ungreased baking sheet. Brush both sides of bread with olive oil. Bake until light and crispy, approximately 1 to 2 minutes. Place all paste mixture ingredients into food processor. Process until mixture becomes a coarse paste, scraping sides of bowl frequently. Spread paste evenly on bread slices. Combine all tomato mixture ingredients. Spread 1 rounded teaspoon of tomato mixture on top of each bread slice. Sprinkle Parmesan cheese lightly over top. Bake for an additional 2 to 3 minutes.

Note: Recipe can be partially made 1 day ahead. Slice, oil, and bake the bread; set aside to cool. Place in a plastic bag overnight. Prepare paste and tomato mixtures; refrigerate in individual containers overnight. To serve, assemble bruschetta, sprinkle with Parmesan cheese and bake 2 to 3 minutes in a pre-heated 425 degree oven.

Yield: 35 to 40 slices

Natalie Barry

Soups & Breads

Polish Hill

*P*olish Hill is named for the first people who settled the area around 1885. The Polish immigrants called their community "Polskie Gory" or "Polish Hill." A steady influx of Polish families continued through 1900.

Following the pattern of many Southern and Eastern European ethnic groups, Polish immigrants centered their lives around the church. In 1906, Polish men in the neighborhood, most of whom were highly skilled from their work in the foundries, steel mills and glass factories, assisted in the construction of Immaculate Heart of Mary Roman Catholic Church. The design for the church was based on St. Peter's, the masterpiece in Rome. In 1922, the parish had a membership of 1000 families and by 1945 the number had grown to 1350.

Pittsburgh's first Polish Lyceum, located on Phelan Way, was developed on the site of the old West Penn Hospital which had originally been the University of Pittsburgh's medical building.

President Jimmy Carter brought national prominence to Polish Hill in 1976 by making a highly publicized visit to the neighborhood during his presidential election campaign. Discovering that the story of Polish Hill made good copy, journalists, commentators, urban policy makers and researchers began to use Polish Hill as a symbol of the many ethnically rich city neighborhoods around the nation that were threatened by urban decay. Polish Hill was used as an example in bringing the issue to national attention.

Recognizing the need to preserve their neighborhood history and accomplishments, residents formed the Polish Hill Civic Association. The association promotes economic development as well as housing development projects to ensure that Polish Hill continues to thrive as one of the city's historically diverse communities. ♥

Kielbasa Soup

48 ounces water
48 ounces chicken broth
¾ pound kielbasa, cut into ¼ to ½-inch slices
2 bay leaves
1 tablespoon black peppercorns
½ cup sliced carrots
¾ cup diced celery
4 ounces medium egg noodles

In a large soup pot, bring water and broth to a boil. Add kielbasa, bay leaves and peppercorns. Simmer for 1 hour. Add carrots and celery. Simmer an additional 45 minutes. Remove bay leaves and strain out peppercorns. Add noodles cooked according to package directions and serve.

Yield: 3 quarts

Gregory Heisler

The Classroom's Roasted Carrot and Potato Soup

3 pounds Idaho potatoes
1 pound carrots
6 cloves garlic
3 ribs celery
1 medium onion
½ cup butter, melted
Salt and freshly cracked pepper, to taste
1 quart chicken stock
1 pint heavy cream

Preheat oven to 400 degrees. Peel and coarsely cut potatoes, carrots, garlic, celery and onion; place in roasting pan. Coat with butter, season with salt and pepper and mix thoroughly. Roast until vegetables brown slightly, about 30 to 45 minutes. Reduce oven temperature to 325 degrees and roast until tender, about ½ hour longer. (Stir frequently to prevent scorching.) Remove pan from oven; purée vegetables and juices in a blender or food processor. (If purée is too thick, add small amounts of chicken stock.) Place purée in soup pot and add remaining stock. Bring to a simmer. Add heavy cream; season with salt and pepper. Stir frequently.

Note: For a full-flavored robust soup, use a hearty chicken stock. Soup can be made a day ahead. Re-heat slowly in a crock pot. This recipe was published in the Pittsburgh Post-Gazette, *11-6-94, highlighting a Peters Township Restaurant, The Classroom.*

Yield: 8 to 10 generous servings

The Dickson Family

French Onion Soup

**8 slices uncooked bacon, cut into
  small pieces**
**3 pounds onions, sliced ¼-inch
  thick**
8 cups beef broth
**½ tablespoon fresh or ½ teaspoon
  dried thyme**
**1½ cups fresh grated Parmesan or
  Gruyère cheese (optional)**

In a large skillet, cook bacon until crisp. Drain all but 2 tablespoons of the bacon fat. Add onions to skillet; cook over medium heat until onions caramelize, about 10 to 15 minutes. Transfer bacon and onion to a soup pot. Add broth and thyme; simmer ½ hour. Pour into individual mugs or bowls. Top with cheese; heat in microwave on high for 30 seconds *or* pour into oven-proof crocks and place under broiler until cheese is melted and lightly browned.

Yield: 6 servings

Marner Family

Hot Italian Sausage-Clam Soup

12 ounces hot Italian sausage
1 cup chopped clams
**½ pound fresh mushrooms,
  chopped**
3 cups tomato sauce
**1 (16-ounce) can chopped
  tomatoes**
1 (8-ounce) bottle clam juice
1 teaspoon dried basil
2 teaspoons minced garlic
1 tablespoon dried parsley

In a large skillet, cook and crumble sausage; drain well. Combine sausage and remaining ingredients in a 4-quart pot. Simmer for at least 30 minutes. Serve hot.

Yield: 6 servings

Lorraine Raffensperger

Tex-Mex Tostada Soup

½ pound ground beef
1 small onion, chopped
1 (14-ounce) can pinto or light red
  kidney beans, drained
1 (14-ounce) can chopped
  tomatoes
1 (8-ounce) can tomato sauce
1 cup picante sauce, mild or
  medium
1 cup water
1 tablespoon ground cumin

Topping:
½-1 cup crushed tortilla chips
½-1 cup shredded lettuce
½-1 cup shredded Cheddar or
  Mexican-style cheese
4 ounces sour cream or plain
  yogurt

In a large soup pot, brown the meat. Add onion and cook until soft. Drain fat. Add beans, tomatoes, tomato sauce, picante sauce, water and cumin to pot. Bring to a low boil; reduce heat to simmer and cook 10 minutes. Ladle soup into individual bowls. Top each bowl with tortilla chips, lettuce, cheese and a dollop of sour cream. Serve soup with warm flour tortillas.

Yield: 4 servings

Lynn Murray-Coleman

Spanish Lentil Soup

2 tablespoons cooking oil
2 tablespoons paprika
2 cups lentils
1 ham hock
1 tomato, quartered
1 green pepper, quartered and
  seeded
1 onion, quartered
1 carrot, peeled and chopped
2 potatoes, coarsely chopped
1 clove garlic, minced
3 teaspoons salt

Heat oil and paprika in a large soup pot. Swirl until oil turns orange in color. Add lentils. Stir until lentils become orange in color. Add all other ingredients and enough water to cover. Bring to a boil. Decrease heat and simmer, covered, until lentils become tender, approximately 2 hours. Add water, as needed, to maintain desired consistency. Stir frequently.

Note: Vegetables breakdown while cooking, making this a thick and hearty soup.

Variation: Use ½ pound Chorizo, fried and drained, in place of ham hock.

Yield: 6 to 8 servings

Frederick Dawson

Butternut Squash Soup

1½ pounds butternut squash
2 large onions, chopped
2 large potatoes, peeled and cubed
4 cups water
2 cubes chicken bouillon
Salt and pepper, to taste
8 ounces sour cream
½ cup chopped fresh chives

Peel, seed and cut squash into 2-inch cubes. Place squash, onions and potatoes into a large soup pot and add water. Cook on high heat; bring to a boil. Add bouillon. Decrease heat, cover and simmer until squash and potatoes are tender. Remove pot from heat; allow to cool for 15 minutes. Using a blender or food processor, purée small batches of the soup until smooth. Season with salt and pepper. Re-warm soup; serve in individual bowls with a dollop of sour cream and fresh chives.

Variation: Toast squash seeds and serve on or with soup.

Yield: 8 servings

Beverly Varnay

Pasta Fagioli

1 tablespoon olive oil
1 clove garlic, minced
2 cups coarsely chopped canned
  plum tomatoes, with juice
2 tablespoons chopped fresh
  or 1 teaspoon dried basil
Freshly ground black pepper, to
  taste
¼ teaspoon red pepper flakes
2 cups canned cannellini beans,
  with liquid
4 ounces ditalini, cooked and
  drained
¼ cup chopped fresh parsley
Freshly grated Romano or
  Parmesan cheese

Combine oil and garlic in a 2-quart casserole. Microwave on high for 35 seconds. Add tomatoes, basil, black pepper and red pepper flakes. Cover with waxed paper and microwave on high until boiling, 5 to 8 minutes. Stir in beans with liquid. Re-cover and cook at 50% power for 10 to 12 minutes. Serve over pasta in individual bowls. Sprinkle with parsley. Serve with freshly grated cheese.

Note: Another type of pasta may be substituted.

Yield: 4 servings

Joan Grattan

Hearty Mushroom and Beef Soup

4 tablespoons vegetable oil,
  divided
1 pound fresh mushrooms, sliced
2 pounds boneless chuck, cut into
  ¼-inch cubes
1 cup chopped onion
6 cups beef broth
1 (28-ounce) can crushed tomatoes
1¾ teaspoons salt
1½ teaspoons oregano leaves,
  crushed
1¾ teaspoons minced garlic
1 bay leaf
¾ cup sliced carrots
3 tablespoons cornstarch
½ cup cold water
1 cup cooked rice
½ cup red Burgundy wine

In a large saucepan or soup pot, heat 2 tablespoons of the oil. Add mushrooms and sauté until golden. Remove mushrooms and set aside. Add remaining 2 tablespoons of oil to saucepan and re-heat. Add ½ of the beef; brown on all sides. Remove beef; set aside. Add onions and remaining beef to saucepan. Sauté until meat is browned and onions are golden. Return all meat to pot. Add broth, tomatoes, salt, oregano, garlic and bay leaf. Bring to a boil; reduce heat and simmer, covered, until meat is tender, about 1 hour and 20 minutes. Add carrots and simmer, covered, until carrots are almost tender, about 7 minutes. Mix cornstarch with water; stir until smooth. Add cornstarch, rice and mushrooms to saucepan. Cook and stir until soup is slightly thickened and mushrooms and rice are heated through, about 2 minutes. Stir in wine; heat 2 minutes longer. Remove bay leaf before serving.

Yield: 12 cups

Pam D'Alessandro

Vichyssoise

French Potato Soup

1 cup thinly sliced leeks (white
  part only)
1 tablespoon butter or margarine
4 cups peeled and thinly sliced
  potatoes (approximately
  1½ pounds)
3 cups chicken broth
⅛ teaspoon nutmeg (optional)
2½ cups low-fat milk
Salt and pepper, to taste

In a large pot, sauté leeks in butter until tender. Do not brown. Add potatoes, broth and nutmeg. Bring to a boil; reduce heat and simmer, partially covered, for 30 minutes. Purée soup in blender or food processor. Pour into a serving bowl and add milk. Season with salt and pepper. Serve warm or chilled.

Note: Keeps for 2 to 3 days in the refrigerator.

Yield: 6 servings

Lisa Hlavatovic

43

French-Canadian Pea Soup

1 pound whole yellow dry peas
9 cups water
1 ham bone
2 tablespoons finely chopped fresh
 parsley
2 tablespoons chopped onion
1 teaspoon salt
⅛ teaspoon pepper

Rinse peas and place in pan. Cover with water to 2 inches above level of peas; soak overnight. Drain peas and place in soup pot. Add the 9 cups of water and all remaining ingredients. Simmer slowly until peas are tender, approximately 2 to 2½ hours. Remove bone and serve. A favorite wintertime soup in Quebec.

Note: Requires advance preparation.

Yield: 8 servings

Claire Roberge

Zucchini Bread

2½ cups flour
2 teaspoons baking soda
1 teaspoon baking powder
1 teaspoon salt
1 teaspoon cinnamon
3 eggs, beaten
2 cups sugar
1 cup oil
2½ cups grated, unpeeled zucchini
2 teaspoons vanilla extract
1 cup chopped nuts (optional)

Preheat oven to 350 degrees. Grease and flour 2 (5x9x3-inch) loaf pans. In a medium bowl, sift together flour, baking soda, baking powder, salt and cinnamon. Set aside. In large mixing bowl, combine eggs, sugar and oil. Alternately, add dry ingredients and zucchini. Mix well. While mixing, add in vanilla and nuts. Pour batter into prepared pans. Bake 45 to 60 minutes until cake tester inserted in center comes out clean. Cool bread in pans before removing.

Note: Zucchini can be grated ahead and frozen in 2½ cup batches. Defrost in colander before using in recipe.

Yield: 2 loaves

Catherine Rosfeld

Cranberry Nut Bread

2½ cups flour
1 cup sugar
1½ teaspoons baking powder
1 teaspoon salt
½ teaspoon baking soda
2 large egg whites, lightly beaten
1 large egg, lightly beaten
1 cup fresh orange juice
¼ cup vegetable or canola oil
2 tablespoons grated orange zest
2 cups fresh or frozen cranberries
½ cup coarsely chopped pecans

Preheat oven to 350 degrees. Lightly grease a 5x9x3-inch loaf pan. In large mixing bowl, sift together flour, sugar, baking powder, salt and baking soda. In small bowl, whisk egg whites, egg, orange juice, oil and orange zest. Add to dry ingredients, mixing until just combined. Do not over-stir. Fold in cranberries and pecans. Pour batter into prepared pan. Bake for 50 to 60 minutes or until cake tester inserted in center of bread comes out clean.

Yield: 1 loaf

Terry Laskowski

Poppy Seed Bread

Bread:
3 cups flour
2½ cups sugar
1½ cups milk
1 cup plus 1 tablespoon vegetable oil
1½ tablespoons poppy seeds
1½ teaspoons baking powder
1½ teaspoons vanilla extract
1½ teaspoons almond extract
1½ teaspoons salt
3 eggs

Glaze:
½ cup sugar
2 tablespoons butter, melted
½ teaspoon vanilla extract
½ teaspoon almond extract
¼ cup orange juice

Preheat oven to 350 degrees. Grease and flour 2 (5x9x3-inch) loaf pans. In large mixing bowl, mix all bread ingredients together. Beat for 3 minutes. Pour into prepared pans. Bake for 1 hour. In small bowl, mix all glaze ingredients together using a spoon. Do not beat. While loaves are still hot in pans, drizzle glaze over tops.

Yield: 2 loaves

Sylvia Stehlik

Date and Nut Loaves

1 pound dates, chopped
1½ cups walnuts, chopped
2 cups sugar
6 level tablespoons shortening
2½ cups boiling water
4 cups flour
3 teaspoons baking soda
½ teaspoon salt
1½ teaspoons vanilla
4 eggs, beaten

Preheat oven to 375 degrees. Grease and flour 2 (5x9x3-inch) loaf pans and line with waxed paper. In a large bowl, combine dates, walnuts, sugar and shortening. Pour boiling water over ingredients; stir until shortening is mostly dissolved. Add flour, baking soda, salt and vanilla. Mix thoroughly by hand. Stir in eggs. Pour batter into prepared pans. Bake for 70 minutes in electric oven or 80 minutes in gas oven. Loaves will rise considerably and may appear burnt on top; this does not mean they are overdone. Cool in pans for 15 minutes before removing to racks. Delicious with cream cheese. My Irish Grandmother's oldest recipe.

Note: Freezes well.

Yield: 2 loaves

Margaret Procario

Irish Brown Bread

5 cups whole wheat flour
3 cups all-purpose flour
3 teaspoons baking soda
1 teaspoon salt
2 tablespoons sugar
½ cup butter
3½ cups buttermilk
2 eggs

Preheat oven to 375 degrees. In a large bowl, mix all dry ingredients together. Cut butter into flour mixture. In small bowl, whisk buttermilk and eggs together. Make a well in flour; add buttermilk mixture. Stir well. Divide dough in half. Knead each half about 10 times. Place in 2 ungreased 8-inch round cake pans. Cut an X shape on top with a floured knife. Bake for 15 minutes. Decrease oven temperature to 350 degrees and bake for an additional 30 minutes.

Yield: 2 loaves

Kathy Cauley

Apple Raisin Bread

1¼ cups vegetable oil
4 eggs, beaten
1 tablespoon plus 1 teaspoon
   vanilla extract
3 cups flour
2½ cups sugar
1 teaspoon baking powder
1½ teaspoons baking soda
1 teaspoon ground cloves
2 teaspoons cinnamon
1½ teaspoons salt
⅔ cup raisins
½ cup chopped nuts
3 cups chopped, unpared apples

Preheat oven to 325 degrees. Generously grease bottoms of 2 (5x9x3-inch) loaf pans. Using an electric mixer, combine oil, eggs and vanilla in a large bowl. Add flour, sugar, baking powder, baking soda and spices. Mix on low speed for 1 minute, scraping bowl continuously. Beat at medium speed for 1 minute. Fold in raisins, nuts and apples. Pour batter into prepared pans. Bake for 1 hour, or until a toothpick inserted in middle of bread comes out clean.

Yield: 2 loaves

Betty Austin

Pumpkin Bread

3 cups sugar
4 eggs
1 cup vegetable or canola oil
1 teaspoon cinnamon
1 teaspoon nutmeg (optional)
1½ teaspoons salt
1 cup pumpkin
2 teaspoons baking soda
⅔ cup water
3 cups flour

Preheat oven to 350 degrees. Grease and flour 3 (1-pound) coffee cans or 2 (5x9-inch) loaf pans. In a large mixing bowl, combine sugar, eggs, oil, cinnamon, nutmeg and salt. Add pumpkin, baking soda, water and flour. Mix well. Pour into prepared pans. Bake for 1 hour. Immediately remove from pans. Cool on wire racks.

Note: Freezes well.

Yield: 2 to 3 loaves

Mary Gehman

Homemade Croutons

1 loaf day-old bakery bread,
    unsliced
3 tablespoons vegetable or olive oil
1 teaspoon salt
1 teaspoon pepper

Preheat oven to 200 degrees. Cut bread into 1-inch cubes. Toss with oil, salt and pepper. Place bread on baking sheet and toast for 10 minutes. Cool. Serve with your favorite salad.

Yield: 5 to 6 cups

Mary Frances Egyed

Stollen

Filling:
½ cup golden raisins
¼ cup rum
¾ cup mixed candied fruit
½ cup flour

Yeast Dough:
½ cup lukewarm milk
1 package, or 1 tablespoon, active
    dry yeast
½ cup butter, softened
½ cup sugar
¼ teaspoon nutmeg
3 eggs
4 cups flour, divided
½ cup ground almonds
1 tablespoon grated lemon peel

4 tablespoons butter, melted
½ cup cinnamon-sugar

To prepare filling, mix raisins with rum. Set aside and let stand for 1 hour. Drain and reserve rum. Toss candied fruit with flour. (Flour will keep fruit from sticking together.) Chop coarsely. Set aside. To prepare yeast dough, pour milk into large bowl. Sprinkle with yeast; let stand 5 minutes or until surface is frothy. Stir in reserved rum. Beat in butter, sugar, nutmeg and eggs. Add 2 cups of the flour, candied fruit mixture, almonds and lemon peel. Gradually add the remaining flour. Knead until smooth. Knead in raisins last. Place batter in a greased bowl, cover and let rise in a warm place for 1½ hours. Punch down. Use whole or divide dough in half. On a floured surface, gently roll into a long oval which is thinner in the middle than at the edges. Spread with melted butter and sprinkle with cinnamon sugar. Fold dough into thirds to form the traditional Stollen shape. Place dough on greased baking sheet and let rise until almost double, about 1 hour. Preheat oven to 375 degrees. Bake for 40 to 45 minutes or until a rich golden brown.

Yield: 2 small or 1 large Stollen

Anna Laufer

Irish Scones

4 cups flour
1 cup sugar
4 teaspoons baking powder
1 teaspoon baking soda
½ cup butter or margarine
1 cup raisins
2 eggs, beaten
1½ cups buttermilk, divided

Preheat oven to 400 degrees. In large bowl, mix dry ingredients together. Cut in butter. Add raisins. Add eggs and 1 cup of the butter- milk. Mix, adding remaining buttermilk as needed, until dough is workable. Roll or pat dough to 1-inch thickness on a floured surface. Cut with floured biscuit cutter or glass rim. Bake on ungreased baking sheets until golden brown, 10 to 15 minutes.

Yield: 2 dozen

Mary Anne McGuire

Beignes Délicieux

Delightful Doughnuts

4¾ cups sifted flour
4 teaspoons baking powder
1 teaspoon salt
½ cup shortening or soft
  margarine
1 cup granulated sugar
3 eggs
1 teaspoon vanilla
1 cup milk
3 pounds lard or shortening for
  frying
Granulated sugar and cinnamon
  mixture (optional)

Sift flour, baking powder and salt together in large bowl. Set aside. Using an electric mixer at medium speed, blend together the shorten- ing and sugar. Add eggs and continue beating until light and fluffy. With mixer at low speed, add flour mixture, vanilla and milk; blend until smooth. Refrigerate 1 hour or longer. Place lard in a 5-quart Dutch oven (or large, 5-inch deep pan). Heat lard to 370 degrees, or until a cube of bread dropped into heated lard browns in 60 seconds. On a floured board, roll dough out to ¼-inch thick. Cut out with floured doughnut cutter. Drop into heated lard, a few at a time. Fry until golden brown, turning over once with a long handled fork. Remove and cool on a wire rack. Roll doughnuts in sugar and cinnamon mixture. These old-fashioned cake doughnuts are popular in French-Canadian homes.

Note: Doughnut holes can be fried or re-rolled to cut additional doughnuts.

Yield: 3 to 3½ dozen

Mathilda Roberge

49

Fastnacht Keukles

A German Pastry

3-4 cups flour, divided
1 package dry yeast
½ teaspoon salt
¼ cup sugar
1¾ cups milk
4 tablespoons butter or margarine
1 large egg
Oil or shortening for deep frying
Granulated or powdered sugar
(optional)

Mix 1½ cups of the flour with yeast, salt, and sugar in a large bowl. Heat milk and butter in a saucepan until warm; add to dry ingredients. Using an electric mixer, beat for 2 minutes at medium speed. Add egg and ½ cup of the flour; beat for 2 minutes at high speed. Stir in enough remaining flour to make a soft dough. Cover and let rise for 1½ hours. Knead and roll dough to about ½-inch thick. Cut with round biscuit cutter and let rise 10 to 20 minutes. To form keukles, rub cooking oil on fingertips, take each cut-out dough form and stretch so that the center part becomes thin and the outer edges rounder and thicker. Deep fry keukles, turning over once, until lightly brown. Center part of keukle will puff up as it fries and the keukle will resemble a hat. Place on paper towels to drain. When cooled, sprinkle with granulated or powdered sugar.

Variation: Dough can be used to make a raised coffee cake. Preheat oven to 375 degrees. After first rising, form dough into small balls, 2-inches in diameter. Dip in melted butter and roll in a cinnamon-sugar mixture. Place dough balls side-by-side in a greased 9x13-inch baking pan; let rise an additional 20 minutes. Bake for about 30 minutes. Ingredients may be added to dough: 1 tablespoon chopped orange or lemon zest, 1 cup chopped walnuts or pecans, 1 cup raisins or 1 teaspoon vanilla, etc.

Yield: 2 to 3 dozen

Ruth (Wehrle) Staudacher

German Pancake

4 tablespoons butter, divided
2 eggs
½ cup milk
½ cup flour
2 apples, pared and sliced
½-1 teaspoon cinnamon, to taste
Whipped cream (optional)

Preheat oven to 425 degrees. Place 3½ tablespoons of the butter in a 10 to 12-inch cast iron skillet or round glass baking dish. Place in oven until butter is melted. In small bowl, mix eggs, milk and flour. Place mixture in hot pan and return to oven. Bake for 20 minutes. Pancake will rise and turn golden brown. While pancake is baking, use medium skillet to sauté apple slices in the remaining ½ tablespoon butter until soft. Sprinkle with cinnamon. Serve with apples on top of pancake and top with whipped cream.

Variation: Substitute 1 cup sliced strawberries for apples. Place strawberries in microwaveable bowl. Sprinkle with 2 tablespoons sugar. Microwave 45 seconds on high until soft.

Yield: 4 servings

Straker Carryer

Zucchini Pancakes

⅓ cup biscuit baking mix
¼ cup grated Parmesan cheese
Salt and pepper, to taste
2 eggs, lightly beaten
2 cups unpared, shredded
**   zucchini**
2 tablespoons butter

In a medium bowl, mix together biscuit mix, Parmesan cheese, salt and pepper. Stir in eggs until mixture is just moistened. Do not overstir. Fold in zucchini. Melt butter in skillet. Over medium heat, drop batter by tablespoonfuls; cook 2 to 3 minutes on each side until browned. Serve as a side dish in place of potatoes or pasta.

Yield: 6 servings

Mary Jane Driscoll Kelly (In Memory)

Pineapple Stuffing

¼ cup butter, softened
1 cup sugar
4 eggs
1 (20-ounce) can crushed
  pineapple, undrained
1 loaf of French or Italian bread,
  cut in 2-inch cubes

Preheat oven to 350 degrees. In a small bowl, beat butter and sugar until light and creamy. Set aside. In a large mixing bowl, beat eggs until frothy. Add butter mixture to eggs; mix well. Stir in pineapple with juice. Fold in bread until completely moistened. Place in a greased 3-quart casserole or baking dish. Bake, uncovered, for 45 to 60 minutes. A great accompaniment to fresh baked ham.

Variation: Substitute 12 slices white bread, cubed. Use 1 (8-ounce) can pineapple.

Yield: 6 servings

Betty Gaston

Grandma Limegrover's Stuffing

2 loaves day-old (French or
  Italian) bakery bread, without
  preservatives
1½ cups unsalted butter
1 tablespoon salt
⅛ teaspoon pepper
4 tablespoons chopped fresh sage
4 tablespoons chopped fresh
  parsley
1 onion, chopped

Cut bread, including crusts, into 1-inch cubes. Place in large mixing bowl(s). Melt butter in a medium saucepan; add salt, pepper, sage, parsley and onion. Simmer for 1 minute. Add seasoned butter to bread; mix well. Stuff turkey loosely with ½ of the stuffing; roast turkey as usual. Bake remaining stuffing in a greased 2-quart casserole for 30 minutes in a pre-heated 350 degree oven. This is a German recipe which has been a Thanksgiving tradition for more than seven generations.

Variation: Mix together crunchy stuffing from casserole and moister stuffing from turkey for a delicious combination.

Yield: 8 to 10 servings

Laurie Klatscher (Lehane)

Oakland

$\mathcal{O}$akland received its name from the farm of one of its early settlers, William Eichbaum, whose property held many oak trees. By the early 1800's, Oakland was owned by a few businessmen and landowners, including Neville B. Craig, editor of the *Pittsburgh Gazette* from 1829 to 1841, whose farm was named "Bellefield."

After the Great Fire of 1845 in Downtown Pittsburgh, Oakland developed rapidly as people moved out to what was then a suburban territory. In 1850, William Dithridge, a glass manufacturer, bought Neville Craig's "Bellefield" and started to develop housing in the area. By 1860, passenger rail service had encouraged residential growth as far as Bates and North Bellefield Streets and commercial development along Fifth Avenue. Oakland Township was incorporated in 1866 and was annexed to the city two years later.

In 1889, Mary Croghan Schenley gave the city 300 acres in Oakland for a park. City officials bought another 100 acres from her to establish Schenley Park. Later, Schenley gave another gift of land for Schenley Plaza. Here, Andrew Carnegie built a library, museum and concert hall complex which opened in 1895. Businessman Frank Nicola built the Schenley Hotel on Forbes Street at the turn of the century and developed the Schenley Farms area in 1905, spending $1.5 million on utilities, streets and landscaping. Oakland was well on its way to becoming a civic center.

Development in many fields — education, entertainment and medicine — came in rapid succession. Carnegie Institute of Technology, now Carnegie Mellon University, opened in 1905. The western University of Pennsylvania, now the University of Pittsburgh, relocated to Oakland in 1907. In 1909, Forbes Field was built and became the original home of the Pittsburgh Pirates. Work began on the Cathedral of Learning in 1925 and upon completion it was the tallest educational building in the world.

Oakland is perhaps the most ethnically diverse of all Pittsburgh's neighborhoods. Italians, African-Americans, Jews, Syrians and Poles have long been permanent residents. University students reflect the diversity of backgrounds that create the cultural tapestry of Pittsburgh, with approximately 98 foreign countries being represented in Oakland's student body. ♥

Spring Salad

Dressing:
1⅛ cups balsamic vinegar
1½ teaspoons salt
6 tablespoons brown sugar
3 tablespoons Dijon mustard
1½ cups vegetable oil
1½ cups olive oil

Salad:
1 pound baby spinach, washed
   and drained
1 head Boston lettuce, washed and
   drained
1 head Romaine lettuce, washed
   and drained
1 head red leaf lettuce, washed
   and drained
1 pound Spring mix, washed and
   drained
1½ cups diced celery
2 large red onions, thinly sliced
2 cups pecans, toasted and
   chopped
2½ cups dried cranberries
6 pears, sliced just prior to serving

In a medium bowl, mix together all dressing ingredients; whisk vigorously. Store in a sealed container; refrigerate. To prepare salad, tear up greens and place in a large salad bowl. Mix in celery and onions. Add pecans, cranberries and pears just prior to serving. Pour dressing over salad and toss. Serve immediately.

Note: Buy pears several days ahead to allow for ripening.

Yield: Serves a crowd! 4½ cups dressing

Franny Capozzi-Alvin

Wilted Leaf Lettuce Salad

1 pound leaf lettuce
6 strips bacon
4 tablespoons red vinegar
Salt and pepper, to taste

Wash lettuce; set aside to drain. In a large skillet, fry bacon until crisp; reserve drippings in skillet. Remove bacon; drain on paper towels and crumble. Add vinegar to hot bacon drippings. Tear lettuce into pieces; place in serving bowl. Toss with crumbled bacon and hot skillet mixture. Season with salt and pepper. Serve immediately.

Yield: 6 to 8 servings

Michelle Battocchi

55

Chinese Salad

2 heads Napa cabbage, coarsely
    chopped
6 green onions, finely chopped
½ cup margarine
2 (3-ounce) packages Ramen
    noodles, crushed in package
½ cup sesame seeds
1 (8-ounce) package slivered
    almonds

Dressing:
½ cup rice vinegar
1 cup sugar
2 tablespoons soy sauce
¼ teaspoon pepper
1 cup vegetable or canola oil

In large mixing bowl, combine cabbage and onion. Refrigerate several hours. Melt margarine in large skillet. Remove and discard seasoning packet from crushed noodles. Add noodles, sesame seeds and almonds to skillet. Sauté until browned, stirring frequently. Drain on paper towels. Combine noodle mixture with cabbage and onion. In a covered carafe, mix together ingredients for dressing. Shake well. Add dressing to cabbage just before serving.

Yield: 10 to 12 servings

Lisa Cornack

Tri-color Pasta Salad

1 (1-pound) package tri-color
    spiral pasta
1 tablespoon olive oil
1 (8-ounce) bottle Caesar salad
    dressing, divided
1 red pepper, julienned
1 green pepper, julienned
1 (6-ounce) jar artichoke hearts,
    drained and coarsely chopped
4-6 ounces Monterey Jack cheese,
    cubed
Sliced Bermuda onion, to taste
    (optional)
1 avocado, cut into chunks

Prepare pasta according to package directions. Remove from heat. Drain. Place in a large bowl. Toss with olive oil. Cool. Add ½ bottle of the salad dressing, peppers, artichokes, cheese and onion. Marinate in the refrigerator for 4 hours. Before serving, add remaining dressing and avocado. Toss.

Note: Recipe must be made ahead.

Yield: 8 servings

Janet Peterson

Spinach Salad with Fresh Strawberries

Dressing:
½ cup sugar
2 tablespoons sesame seeds
2 tablespoons poppy seeds
1 small onion, minced (optional)
1 scant teaspoon paprika
1 teaspoon Worcestershire sauce
½ cup vegetable or canola oil
¼ cup apple cider vinegar

Salad:
10 ounces fresh spinach, stemmed, washed and drained
2 pints fresh strawberries, hulled

In a blender or using a wire whisk, blend all dressing ingredients until thickened. To prepare salad, place spinach and strawberries in a large salad bowl. Toss with dressing. Serve immediately.

Note: Larger strawberries can be halved or quartered.

Yield: 4 to 6 servings

Laura Grimm

Chicken Pasta Salad

3 whole chicken breasts, cooked and chopped
¼ cup balsamic vinegar
1½ teaspoons salt
1 (16-ounce) package rotini pasta
1 tablespoon olive oil
1 cup chopped celery
1 red bell pepper, chopped
3 tablespoons chopped green onion
1 cup Creole Mayonnaise (see Note)

Place chicken in a large bowl and sprinkle with balsamic vinegar and salt. Cover and chill for 2 to 3 hours. Cook pasta according to package directions; toss with olive oil. Add pasta, celery, pepper and onion to chicken. Coat with Creole Mayonnaise. Chill salad for an additional 2 hours or overnight.

Note: Recipe for Creole Mayonnaise can be found in the Beverages, Sauces and Marinades section.

Variation: Substitute 1 (15-ounce) can chickpeas (drained and rinsed) for chicken and add 1 cup small pitted black olives, halved.

Yield: 10 servings

Charlotte Broome

Taco Salad

1 pound ground beef
1 (16-ounce) can kidney beans,
   drained
1 onion, chopped
1 head of lettuce, chopped
3 tomatoes, chopped
¼ pound Cheddar cheese, grated
½ cup Italian dressing
1 (1-ounce) package ranch-
   flavored dressing, prepared
1 (14½-ounce) bag tortilla chips

In a large skillet, brown ground beef; drain and discard fat. Return beef to skillet; add beans, stirring until heated. In large bowl, mix onions, lettuce, tomatoes, cheese, Italian and ranch dressings. Add beef and beans to bowl. Mix well. Serve over tortilla chips.

Note: May be served warm or cold.

Yield: 6 to 8 servings

Babs Carryer

Thai Papaya Salad

¾ cup pine nuts, divided
1 tablespoon unsalted butter
1 tablespoon peanut oil
1 small clove garlic, minced
2½ teaspoons minced ginger,
   divided
1 pound bay scallops
3 tablespoons fresh lime juice
2 tablespoons packed light brown
   sugar
1 tablespoon light soy sauce
½ teaspoon Chinese chili sauce
2 scallions, minced
1 tablespoon minced fresh
   coriander
1½ ripe papayas, peeled, seeded
   and cut into ½-inch pieces
1 medium red bell pepper, cut into
   ½-inch pieces
1 small cucumber, cut in half
   lengthwise, seeded and cut into
   ½-inch pieces
1 pound fresh spinach, stemmed

Preheat oven to 325 degrees. Place pine nuts on a baking sheet; toast until golden brown, about 10 minutes. In a large skillet, melt butter, oil, garlic and ½ teaspoon of the ginger, over moderately high heat. Add scallops and cook, stirring, until firm and opaque, about 2 minutes. Using a slotted spoon, transfer scallops to small bowl; let cool. Cover and refrigerate until use. In a medium jar, combine lime juice, brown sugar, soy sauce, chili sauce, the remaining 2 teaspoons of the ginger, scallions and coriander. Cover tightly and shake vigorously to blend and dissolve sugar. In large bowl, combine papayas, red pepper and cucumber. Add dressing, scallops and all but 2 tablespoons of the pine nuts. Toss well to coat. Divide spinach among chilled dinner plates. Spoon scallop mixture over spinach. Sprinkle the remaining 2 tablespoons of the pine nuts over salads and serve.

Variation: 2 tablespoons fish sauce can be substituted for soy sauce.

Yield: 4 to 6 servings

Lori Bennett

Eggless Caesar Salad

1 clove garlic, peeled and halved
½ cup olive oil
Juice of 1 lemon
3 heads, hearts of Romaine lettuce
½ cup grated Romano cheese
Homemade Croutons (see Note)
Freshly ground black pepper, to
    taste

Marinate garlic in olive oil for 8 hours or longer. Strain olive oil; discard garlic. Mix oil with lemon juice; set aside. Wash, drain and tear lettuce; place in salad bowl and toss with oil. Add cheese and croutons; toss lightly. Season with pepper and serve.

Note: Salad must be partially made ahead. Recipe for Homemade Croutons can be found in the Soups and Breads section.

Yield: 4 to 6 servings

Mary Frances Egyed

Pignolia, Hearts of Palm and Gorgonzola Salad

Dressing:
¼ cup plus 2½ tablespoons
    balsamic vinegar
2 tablespoons water
1 (¾-ounce) package Italian salad
    dressing mix
⅓ cup plus 1 tablespoon vegetable
    or canola oil

Salad:
1 large or 2 small heads red leaf
    lettuce
½ pound Gorgonzola cheese,
    crumbled
¾ cup pignolia nuts
8 ounces mushrooms, sliced
2 medium carrots, grated
1 (14-ounce) can hearts of palm,
    drained, cut into ¼-inch slices
2½ cups shredded red cabbage

In a 1-cup container, mix together all dressing ingredients; cover tightly and shake. Store in refrigerator. Wash, drain and tear lettuce; arrange in large salad bowl. Add cheese, nuts, mushrooms, carrots, palm and red cabbage. Toss salad with prepared dressing just before serving.

Variation: Substitute Boston Bibb lettuce or baby mixed greens for red leaf lettuce. Add sliced, grilled chicken breast for a heartier salad.

Yield: 4 to 6 servings

Joanne Redondo

Pink Cole Slaw

1 medium head of cabbage
1 small fresh beet, peeled and
  finely shredded
1 small onion, finely grated
  (optional)
2-3 carrots, coarsely shredded
1 teaspoon sugar
1 teaspoon salt
¾ cup mayonnaise
¾ cup sour cream
2 tablespoons lemon juice
⅛ teaspoon pepper

Quarter and core cabbage; slice thinly and place in large bowl. Cover with ice water; refrigerate 1 hour. Drain well. Add beet, onion, carrots, sugar and salt. Toss gently. Combine mayonnaise, sour cream, lemon juice and pepper in small bowl; stir well. Pour over cabbage mixture and toss to coat. Cover; refrigerate 3 to 4 hours.

Note: Can be made a day in advance.

Yield: 6 to 8 servings

Sharon Lyles

Tomato and Cucumber Salad

6 cucumbers or 15 pickling
  cucumbers, peeled
½ cup olive oil
¼ cup red wine vinegar
1 teaspoon salt
½ teaspoon pepper
2 large ripe tomatoes, seeded and
  coarsely chopped
1 medium red onion, diced

Cut cucumbers in half lengthwise (if using large cucumbers, remove seeds). Slice across width in ¼-inch slices. Mix oil, vinegar, salt and pepper together in large bowl. Add tomatoes, cucumbers and onion. Toss well; chill for 4 to 6 hours. A perfect use for summer cucumbers!

Yield: 4 to 6 servings

Sandra DeBartolo

Curry Chicken Salad

1 chicken breast, cooked and
  minced
2 ribs celery, chopped
1 apple, peeled and finely chopped
¼ cup raisins
4 tablespoons mayonnaise
2 tablespoons milk
2 teaspoons curry powder

In a medium bowl, combine chicken, celery, apple and raisins. In a small bowl, mix together mayonnaise and milk until smooth; stir in curry powder. Combine curry mixture with chicken; mix well. Serve mounded on lettuce, with crackers or stuffed into small pita pockets.

Yield: 2 cups

Shelley Hall

Tomato and Green Bean Salad

½ cup olive oil
3 tablespoons balsamic vinegar
1 teaspoon salt
1 teaspoon pepper
2 pounds fresh green beans
8 large tomatoes, cut into wedges
¾ cup kalamata olives (optional)
¼ cup chopped green onions
¼ cup chopped fresh basil
1 (4-ounce) package feta cheese,
    crumbled

In a small container, whisk together olive oil, vinegar, salt and pepper. Cover tightly and refrigerate until use. Cook beans in boiling water for 5 to 6 minutes or until crisp but tender. Rinse with cold water; drain and place in large bowl. Add tomatoes, olives, onions, basil and feta cheese. Cover and chill. Pour dressing over salad just before serving. Toss gently.

Yield: 12 servings

Camille Bloodworth

Polynesian Chicken Salad

4 cups diced cooked chicken,
    chilled
1 cup diced celery
1 (8-ounce) can pineapple chunks,
    drained
1 cup grapes, halved
¾ cup slivered almonds, toasted
1 cup mayonnaise
Salt and pepper, to taste

Mix chicken, celery, pineapple, grapes and almonds in large bowl. Add mayonnaise; mix well. Season with salt and pepper. Serve over lettuce on individual plates.

Variation: Top with shredded coconut for a tasty change.

Yield: 6 to 8 servings

Rebecca Lando

Tahitian Salad

2 cups cubed, cooked chicken
½ pound cooked shrimp, peeled
    and deveined
½ teaspoon salt
1 (8-ounce) can pineapple tidbits,
    drained
1 (11-ounce) can Mandarin
    oranges, drained
4 slices bacon, cooked and
    crumbled
1 cup white seedless grapes
1 (8-ounce) bottle sweet and sour
    dressing
Salad greens

In a large bowl, mix together all ingredients except dressing. Just before serving, toss with dressing. Serve on your choice of salad greens.

Yield: 4 to 6 servings

Lorraine Raffensperger

Mandarin Salad

Dressing:
¼ cup olive oil
2 tablespoons chopped fresh parsley
2 tablespoons sugar
2 tablespoons cider vinegar
Dash of Tabasco

Salad:
½ cup sliced almonds
3 tablespoons sugar
½ head leaf lettuce
½ head Romaine lettuce
1 cup sliced celery
2-3 whole green onions, chopped
1 (11-ounce) can Mandarin
    oranges, drained
Pepper, to taste

To prepare salad dressing, combine all dressing ingredients in a carafe or 1-cup sealed container. Shake vigorously to blend. Store in refrigerator until use. In small skillet, combine almonds and sugar. Stir, over medium heat, until almonds brown. Let cool; crumble and set aside. Wash, drain and tear lettuce. In salad bowl, combine lettuce, celery and onion. Just before serving, toss with almond mixture, oranges and dressing. Season with pepper and serve.

Yield: 4 servings

Jeanine Sismour

Midsummer Salad

Syrup:
¾ cup sugar
½ cup water
1 tablespoon grated lemon rind
1 tablespoon grated orange rind
¼ cup lemon juice
3 tablespoons lime juice

Fruit:
½ watermelon
1 large cantaloupe
1 large honeydew melon
1 cup seedless grapes
1 cup strawberries
1 cup canned pineapple chunks,
    drained
Fresh mint leaves (optional)

Mix all syrup ingredients together in a medium saucepan. Stir over medium heat until sugar dissolves. Increase heat; boil 5 minutes, stirring. Let cool. Seed watermelon. Halve and seed cantaloupe and honeydew. Scoop all melon flesh into balls. Halve grapes. Stem and halve strawberries. Place prepared fruit and pineapple chunks in large glass bowl. Gently mix. Pour syrup over top; chill before serving. Garnish with mint leaves.

Yield: 10 to 15 servings

Katie Johnson

Strawberry Pretzel Jello Salad

Crust:
¾ cup margarine, melted
3 teaspoons sugar
2 cups crushed pretzels

Filling:
1 (8-ounce) package cream cheese,
    softened
1 (8-ounce) container frozen
    whipped topping
1 cup sugar

Topping:
1 (6-ounce) package strawberry
    jello
2 cups boiling water
2 (10-ounce) packages frozen
    strawberries

Preheat oven to 400 degrees. To prepare crust, use a fork to blend margarine and sugar together in a medium bowl. Add pretzels; mix well. Press crust mixture firmly into a 9x13-inch baking dish. Bake 8 to 10 minutes; cool. To make filling, mix cream cheese, whipped topping and sugar together in medium bowl. Spread over cooled crust. For topping, dissolve jello in boiling water; add strawberries while stirring. Cool for 10 minutes. Pour over cream cheese mixture. Chill in refrigerator until jello is set. Wonderful on a hot summer evening!

Yield: 16 to 20 servings

Mary Anne McGuire

Cherry Applesauce Jello Mold

Jello Mold:
2 cups frozen dark sweet pitted
   cherries
3 cups apple juice
2 (3-ounce) packages cherry jello
1 cup chunky applesauce
½ cup chopped celery
½ cup walnuts, chopped (optional)
celery leaves (optional)

Sauce:
⅓-½ cup apple juice, to taste
1 (8-ounce) container soft-style
   cream cheese

To prepare jello mold, drain frozen cherries in colander, while thawing at room temperature. In a medium saucepan, heat the 3 cups of apple juice to a boil; remove from heat. Add jello and stir until dissolved. Chill mixture until partially set, approximately 1½ hours. Halve partially thawed cherries. Stir cherries, applesauce, celery and nuts into jello mixture. Pour into a 6 to 7-cup mold. Chill until firm. Loosen from mold onto a serving plate. Garnish with celery leaves. To prepare sauce, blend the ⅓ to ½ cup apple juice with cream cheese to form a smooth consistency. Serve sauce, on the side, with jello mold. This makes a great accompaniment to Thanksgiving dinner.

Yield: 8 to 10 servings

Pam D'Alessandro

Cranberry Relish

1 (12-ounce) bag fresh cranberries
1 apple
1 seedless orange
2 cups sugar

Wash and drain cranberries. Wash, quarter and core the apple, leaving skin intact. Lightly scrub skin of orange. Quarter orange, leaving skin intact. Place all fruits and sugar into large bowl of a food processor. Process until fruit is coarsely chopped. Allow relish to sit, covered, for 1 day in refrigerator before use.

Note: Freezes well for months!

Yield: Approximately 1½ quarts

Karen Raffensperger

Shadyside

$\mathcal{S}$hadyside was the original name of the Pennsylvania Railroad Station in this area. The Railroad had asked David Aiken, donator of the land for the station building, to name it. His wife Caroline suggested "Shady Side," reportedly the title of a book she had been reading. Surrounded by woods and farmland, and replete with shady lanes in the mid-19th century, the neighborhood had been named appropriately.

During the 1700's, George Anshutz bought 286 acres in the area. In 1792, he established an iron furnace near Bayard Street and Amberson Avenue, and later sold some of his land to David Ekin who used the land for farming.

The Ekin Farm lay within what is today Shadyside West. David Ekin married Rachel Castleman, and their daughter married Thomas Aiken. Following Mrs. Aiken's death, Thomas and his son David divided the farm. Thomas took the eastern part from Amberson Avenue to Aiken Avenue and built a home at the corner of Ellsworth Avenue and St. James Street. His son took the western section from Amberson Avenue to Neville Street.

It was not until the opening of the Pennsylvania Railroad to through traffic in 1852, that Shadyside became a desirable suburb. Robert Pitcairn, for whom Pitcairn Street is named, bought land from Thomas Aiken. Another prominent land buyer was Judge Thomas Mellon. Much of Thomas Aiken's farm was divided into residential lots after his death in 1873.

Following its annexation from Peebles Township to the City of Pittsburgh in 1868, Shadyside grew rapidly. Dr. William Beatty served as the minister of Shadyside Presbyterian Church, for which Thomas Aiken had donated land in 1866. In 1869, the church elders built the Pennsylvania College for Women for their daughters. The college is now known as Chatham College.

After the 1920's, professionals, artists, students and apartment dwellers settled in Shadyside. Today, Walnut Street and Ellsworth Avenue are prosperous and popular areas, housing a unique variety of speciality shops and restaurants. ♥

Scrapelles

An Italian Dish

2 cups flour, sifted
½ cup grated Parmesan cheese,
   sifted
½-1 teaspoon salt, to taste
½ teaspoon pepper, or to taste
1½ cups water
6 eggs

In large mixing bowl, combine flour, cheese, salt, pepper and water. Add eggs one at a time, mixing well after each addition. Blend until mixture is smooth and creamy. Rub a non-stick 10-inch skillet with cooking oil and heat on medium. Ladle ½ cup of mixture into skillet, swirling to coat bottom. When liquid disappears from top, cook about 10 seconds, or until there is a hint of brown on underside. Turn, cook about 30 seconds longer, until small bubble marks on underside are lightly browned. Taste first scrapelle to adjust salt and pepper. Cool on wire rack. Roll tightly into logs; cut into 1-inch sections. Serve in individual bowls with hot chicken broth. This "side dish" is an Italian specialty of my mother-in-law's. It soon turns into a main dish, because no one will eat anything else!

Note: Scrapelles should be thin. If uncooked batter thickens, add water, a small amount at a time, to obtain desired consistency.

Yield: 4 servings

Margaret Procario

Easy Quiche Lorraine

3 eggs, slightly beaten
½ cup biscuit baking mix
½ cup melted butter
1½ cups milk
Salt and pepper, to taste
½ cup chopped onions
½ cup cooked, chopped bacon or
   ham
1 cup cubed Swiss cheese

Preheat oven to 350 degrees. In medium bowl, blend eggs, baking mix, butter, milk, salt and pepper. Layer onion, bacon and cheese in a 9 to 10-inch quiche or deep pie pan. Pour egg mixture over top. Bake for 40 minutes.

Note: A baking sheet with sides under pie pan will catch any drips.

Yield: 4 to 6 servings

Mary Claire Kasunic

Ricotta Spinach Pie

1 teaspoon flour
1 (9-inch) unbaked pie crust
  (prepared or homemade)
1 (10-ounce) package frozen
  chopped spinach
3 tablespoons butter
1 medium onion, chopped
½ teaspoon salt
½ teaspoon pepper
¼ teaspoon nutmeg
8 ounces grated mozzarella cheese
1 cup grated Parmesan cheese
1 (15-ounce) container ricotta
  cheese
3 large eggs, beaten

Preheat oven to 350 degrees. Sprinkle flour over pie crust. Place, flour-side down, into a 9-inch glass or ceramic pie dish. Flute edges. Place spinach in colander, allow to thaw and drain thoroughly. Melt butter in large skillet over medium heat. Sauté onion until tender. Add spinach, salt, pepper and nutmeg. Sauté until all liquid evaporates. Combine mozzarella, Parmesan and ricotta cheeses in large bowl. Mix in eggs. Add spinach mixture; blend well. Spoon filling into pie crust. Bake for 40 minutes until filling is set and pie is brown on top. Let stand for 10 minutes before serving.

Yield: 6 to 8 servings

Maggi Sitko-Sweeney

Ham and Cheese Pie

2 tablespoons butter
2 tablespoons flour
½ teaspoon salt
⅛ teaspoon nutmeg
1½ cups milk
1 cup shredded Swiss cheese
3 eggs
1 cup diced ham
1 teaspoon grated onion
1 (9-inch) unbaked pie crust
  (prepared or homemade)

Preheat oven to 425 degrees. Melt butter in large saucepan over low heat. Blend in flour, salt and nutmeg. Add milk, stirring, until mixture is smooth and thickened. Gradually add cheese, stirring until melted. Cool slightly. In a small bowl, beat eggs lightly. Add a small amount of cheese mixture to eggs, stirring to temper. Add egg mixture to saucepan, stirring well. Stir in ham and onion. Place pie crust in pie plate; flute edges. Bake pie crust shell for 15 minutes and remove from oven. Reduce oven temperature to 300 degrees. Pour egg mixture into shell. Bake for 40 minutes until set and lightly browned on top. Knife inserted into center of pie should come out clean.

Yield: 8 servings

Susan Mickens

Egg Brunch Casserole

2 cups plain croutons
1 cup shredded Cheddar cheese
4 eggs, slightly beaten
2 cups milk
½ teaspoon salt
½ teaspoon prepared mustard
½ teaspoon onion powder
⅛ teaspoon pepper
4 slices bacon, cooked and
    crumbled

Preheat oven to 350 degrees. Place croutons and cheese into bottom of greased 9x13-inch baking dish. In a bowl, combine eggs, milk and seasonings. Pour egg mixture over cheese and croutons. Sprinkle bacon over top. Bake for 55 to 60 minutes, or until eggs are set. Garnish with additional crisp, crumbled bacon, if desired.

Note: Recipe can be doubled, tripled, etc., increasing size of baking dish to accommodate.

Yield: 6 servings

Ellen Gunnell

Tortilla Española

Potato Omelette

6-9 tablespoons olive oil, divided
4 medium potatoes, cut into 1-inch
    cubes
6 eggs, separated

Heat 6 tablespoons of the olive oil in large skillet. Cook potatoes until tender. In a separate bowl, whip egg whites until softly peaked. Add egg yolks to egg whites, mixing gently. Remove potatoes from skillet, using a slotted spoon; add to egg mixture. Stir to mix. Reheat olive oil in skillet (adding remaining 2 to 3 tablespoons oil if needed). Place egg and potato mixture in skillet; cook over medium heat until edges appear dry (top will still be moist). Place a large plate over top of skillet and carefully flip tortilla onto plate. Slide tortilla back into skillet, uncooked-side down. Cook until firm.

Yield: 4 servings

Susan Dawson

Huevos Rancheros

Mexican Eggs

4 tortillas
4 eggs
1 cup Mexican-style salsa, divided
½ cup shredded Cheddar cheese,
    divided

Preheat oven to 300 degrees. Place tortillas on broiling pan and warm in oven. While tortillas are warming, fry eggs sunny-side up. Remove tortillas from oven; keep on broiling pan. Increase oven temperature to broil. Top each tortilla with 1 egg. Cover each egg with ¼ cup salsa and ⅛ cup cheese. Place under broiler for 1 to 2 minutes until cheese bubbles. Olé!

Yield: 4 servings

Maura Petrone

Egg Strata

6 tablespoons butter, softened,
    divided
10 slices white or whole grain
    bread, crust removed
8 eggs
4 cups milk
Salt and pepper, to taste
1 bunch scallions, chopped
8 ounces button mushrooms,
    sliced
2 cups broccoli florets, steamed
8 ounces grated sharp Cheddar
    cheese

Grease a 9x13-inch baking dish. Spread butter evenly on bread slices, using approximately 4 tablespoons of the butter. Line bottom of dish with bread, buttered-side down, cutting as necessary to fit. Set aside. Beat eggs and milk in medium bowl. Season with salt and pepper. Set aside. Melt remaining 2 tablespoons of the butter in a small skillet. Sauté scallions until tender. Add mushrooms; sauté until tender. Cover bread with sauté mixture, broccoli and cheese. Pour egg mixture over top. Cover dish; refrigerate overnight. Preheat oven to 325 degrees. Bake, uncovered, 50 to 75 minutes, until eggs are set.

Note: Recipe must be prepared a day ahead.

Yield: 8 servings

Jan Grice

Gougère with Ham and Mushrooms

Pâte à Choux:
(Pastry)
1 cup water
½ cup butter, cut into chunks
1 cup flour
4 eggs
½ cup shredded Cheddar cheese
½ rounded teaspoon summer
    savory

Filling:
4 tablespoons butter
1 large onion, chopped
½ pound mushrooms, sliced
1½ tablespoons flour
¼ teaspoon pepper
1 teaspoon chicken broth granules
1 cup hot water
2 large tomatoes, chopped
1½ cups julienne strips of ham
2 tablespoons chopped fresh
    parsley

Preheat oven to 400 degrees. To prepare pâte à choux, heat water and butter in a medium saucepan until butter melts. Increase heat and bring to a boil. Add flour all at once, stirring vigorously, until mixture forms a ball in center of the pan. Allow mixture to cool 5 minutes. Add eggs one at a time, beating well using a wooden spoon after each addition. (This beating is important as the gougère will not puff otherwise.) Stir in cheese and summer savory. Grease a 10-inch pie pan or shallow baking dish. Spoon the pâte à choux in a ring around edge of the pan leaving center open. To prepare the filling, melt butter in a large skillet. Sauté onion until soft; do not brown. Add mushrooms and continue cooking 2 minutes. Add flour and pepper; cook an additional 2 minutes, stirring often. Add chicken broth granules and water; mix well. Bring to a boil, stirring continuously. Reduce heat; simmer 4 minutes. Remove from heat. Add tomatoes, ham and parsley. Pour filling into center of pâte à choux. Bake for 45 minutes. Serve immediately.

Yield: 6 servings

Anna Laufer

Killer Omelet with Garlic-Onion Potatoes and Bacon

4 potatoes, cut into 1-inch cubes
1 clove garlic, minced
½ medium onion, chopped
1-2 tablespoons olive oil
8 slices bacon
½ red pepper, chopped
½ green pepper, chopped
2 tomatoes, chopped
1 small jalapeño pepper, chopped
8 eggs, at room temperature
¼ cup whipping cream
¼ cup grated sharp Cheddar
   cheese
¼ cup grated Swiss cheese

Preheat oven to 180 degrees. In a large skillet, fry potatoes, garlic and onions in olive oil. Keep warm in oven. Fry bacon; reserve grease. Drain bacon on paper towels. Transfer to plate; keep warm in oven. Lightly fry red and green peppers, tomatoes and jalapeño pepper in a small amount of the reserved bacon grease. Keep warm in oven. Combine eggs and whipping cream in large bowl. Whip until blended. Prepare large skillet (or skillets), by heating a small amount of the bacon grease over medium heat. Pour egg mixture into skillet(s) to a depth of ¼-inch. Cook eggs until set. Place pepper mixture and cheeses in center(s) of egg mixture. Fold egg edges over to cover. Cook until cheeses melt. Serve with potatoes and bacon.

Note: Recipe can be stretched to accommodate any number. Use 2 to 3 eggs per person and adjust whipping cream accordingly.

Yield: 4 servings

Straker Carryer

Spring Vegetable Quiche

¼ cup chopped green pepper
¼ cup chopped broccoli
¼ cup chopped cauliflower
¼ cup chopped zucchini
¼ cup chopped celery
¼ cup chopped onion
2 tablespoons butter
1 pint whipping cream
2 eggs, beaten
1 cup shredded Swiss cheese
1 (9-inch) unbaked pie shell

Preheat oven to 350 degrees. In large skillet, sauté green pepper, broccoli, cauliflower, zucchini, celery and onion in butter until soft. Remove from heat. Beat whipping cream into eggs. Add to skillet. Stir in shredded cheese. Pour into pie shell. Bake, uncovered, for 50 minutes or until set.

Yield: 8 servings

Michelle Bisceglia

Belgian Breakfast Crêpe

½ cup flour
2 tablespoons plus 2 teaspoons
  sugar
⅛ teaspoon salt
½ cup milk
4 large eggs
1 tablespoon vanilla extract
2 tablespoons butter, divided
Brown sugar and butter, to taste

In a medium bowl, mix flour, sugar and salt together. Add milk and stir to make a fluid paste. Using a wire whisk, blend in eggs. Whisk in vanilla. Place 2 teaspoons of the butter in a 10-inch skillet or crêpe pan. Heat until lightly browned. Swirl butter to completely coat bottom of pan. Ladle ½ cup of batter into hot pan and swirl to completely cover bottom of pan. When crêpe begins to look dry, check underside to see if lightly browned. Flip crêpe and cook an additional 15 to 30 seconds until lightly browned. Transfer crêpe to serving plate. Repeat process, beginning with placing 2 teaspoons of the butter into pan before adding new batter. To serve, cut each crêpe into quarters, butter lightly and sprinkle brown sugar on top. While my children were growing up, I made this wonderful crêpe (recipe tripled) almost every Sunday morning for our family brunch.

Yield: 3 to 4 servings

Henry Van Wassen

French Toast Sandwich

2 tablespoons cream cheese,
  softened
2 tablespoons jam plus extra for
  topping
4 slices bread
2 eggs, beaten
2 teaspoons milk

To prepare each sandwich, spread cream cheese and a thin layer of jam on a slice of bread. Top with second slice. Combine egg and milk in a small shallow dish. Dip prepared sandwich in egg mixture. Fry in buttered skillet until golden brown on both sides. Garnish each sandwich with a spoonful of jam.

Yield: 2 servings

Maggi Sitko-Sweeney

73

Cheese and Broccoli Soufflé

4 tablespoons butter
1 small onion, minced
¼ cup flour
1½ cups milk
Pinch of salt
1 pound grated Cheddar cheese
4 egg yolks
1 pound broccoli florets
6 egg whites

Preheat oven to 375 degrees. In large saucepan, melt butter over low heat. Add onion and sauté until opaque. Add flour; whisk until well blended. In separate saucepan, bring milk to a boil. Add milk and salt to onions; stir continuously until thickened. Remove pan from heat; allow to cool for 2 to 3 minutes. Add cheese; stir until melted. Beat in egg yolks, one at a time. Let mixture cool. Add broccoli. In separate bowl, beat the 6 egg whites until they stand in peaks. Fold egg whites into mixture. Gently pour into a greased 3-quart casserole. Bake for 30 to 45 minutes. Very pretty presentation!

Yield: 6 to 8 servings

Anonymous

Bloomfield

*B*loomfield's name is most likely derived from the many wildflowers that bloomed in the area's fields years ago.

In 1850, Bloomfield had only 13 houses, with truck gardens and dairies nearby. Joseph Conrad Winebiddle, a German immigrant and prominent landowner, developed this farmland into residential lots from 1870 to 1905. Winebiddle Street is named for him.

German families, mostly millworkers in nearby Lawrenceville, purchased the lots from Winebiddle and constructed row houses and businesses in the style of their homeland. The homes, designed for single families, were small and narrow with garden plots in the rear.

Businesses in turn-of-the-century Bloomfield bore German names. Hinnebusch and Mentzer's Shoe Store, Kuenzig's Confectionery, Fink's Poultry and Geschwender's Steam Sausage and Pudding Works could all be found in the neighborhood's shopping district along Liberty Avenue.

St. Joseph's Catholic Church, also on Liberty Avenue, was Bloomfield's first church. Founded in 1872, it was known to area Catholics as the "German Church."

Today, Bloomfield is a predominately Italian community known as Pittsburgh's "Little Italy." The names of old Italian social clubs, such as the Atelea, Castel di Sangro, Rocca Cinque Miglia and the Pesco Costanza continue to be used even though the buildings have been sold. The Bloomfield Italian Independence Club still exists and retains an active membership. Immaculate Conception Church is a spiritual center of the Italian community and remains a prominent presence in the neighborhood.

Liberty Avenue and its connecting side streets retain a bustling retail trade that is visually rich and gastronomically stimulating. Fresh flowers, bakery delicacies, and ethnic cuisine, as well as necessities from shoes to hardware, showcase Bloomfield's vibrant shopping district. ♥

Pastitsio

Greek Layered Pasta Casserole

Meat Sauce:
3 tablespoons butter
2 large onions, finely chopped
2 pounds lean ground meat (beef, chuck or round)
2 (8-ounce) cans tomato sauce
1 teaspoon salt
½ cup red wine
1 stick cinnamon

Pasta:
6 cups water
1 teaspoon salt
1 pound penne pasta
8 tablespoons butter, melted
1½ cups milk
4 eggs, beaten

Cream Sauce:
4 tablespoons butter
¼ cup flour
3 cups milk
½ teaspoon salt
⅛ teaspoon pepper
6 eggs

½ pound grated Kefalotiri or Romano cheese, divided

To prepare meat sauce, melt butter in a 10 to 12-inch skillet. Sauté onion until lightly browned. Add meat and cook until brown, crumbling with fork. Add remaining meat sauce ingredients to skillet; mix well. Cover and simmer for 30 minutes, stirring occasionally. Remove cinnamon stick; let mixture cool. To prepare pasta, place water and salt in a large pot. Bring to a boil. Add the penne and cook until tender, approximately 10 minutes. Drain, rinse and place in a large bowl. Add butter, milk and eggs. Gently toss to coat; set aside. To prepare cream sauce, melt butter over medium heat in a medium saucepan. Stir in flour until smooth. Gradually add milk, stirring, until thickened. Lower heat. Add salt and pepper. Remove from heat. Beat 6 eggs in a large bowl until light and fluffy. Slowly add hot cream sauce to eggs; stir thoroughly. Preheat oven to 350 degrees. Grease a 9x13-inch baking pan. Spread ½ of the penne mixture over bottom of pan. Cover evenly with meat sauce. Sprinkle ⅓ of the cheese over meat sauce. Add remaining ½ of the penne mixture, spreading evenly. Sprinkle another ⅓ of the cheese over top. Pour cream sauce evenly over pan. Top with remaining ⅓ of the cheese. Bake until sauce sets, approximately 45 minutes. Cool slightly before cutting into squares. This dish is very rich and needs to be served with only sharp feta cheese and a salad.

Note: May be frozen after baking.

Yield: 8 to 10 servings

Marcella Karvellis McGuire

Linguine with Fresh Herb and Vodka Sauce

¾ pound linguine
2 tablespoons butter
1 onion, thinly sliced
1 tablespoon chopped fresh thyme
1 tablespoon chopped fresh tarragon
1 tablespoon chopped fresh basil
1 cup whipping cream
½ cup vodka
¾ cup freshly grated Parmesan cheese
Salt and pepper, to taste

Prepare linguine according to package directions. Melt butter in large skillet over medium heat. Sauté onion, until tender, about 10 minutes. Add herbs; sauté 1 minute longer. Add cream and vodka. Simmer until sauce thickens, about 10 minutes. Add linguine and cheese; toss until well-coated. Season with salt and pepper. Serve immediately.

Yield: 4 servings

Maggi Sitko-Sweeney

Chicken Stir Fry with Penne

1 pound penne rigate pasta
1 pound chicken breast, skinned and boned
Salt and pepper, to taste
1 tablespoon vegetable oil
2 cups chopped broccoli
1 red bell pepper, sliced
2 yellow squash, chopped
2 cups sliced mushrooms
½ cup water
2 tablespoons soy sauce
2 tablespoons rice wine vinegar
1 cube chicken bouillon

Cook penne rigate according to package directions. Drain and set aside. Cut chicken breast into strips; season with salt and pepper. In a 10-inch or larger skillet, heat oil. Add chicken; cook until tender. Add vegetables; cook on medium-high heat, stirring, until tender, about 5 minutes. In small bowl, combine water, soy sauce, vinegar and bouillon. Add to skillet; cook, stirring, until bouillon dissolves. Add pasta and mix well. Reduce heat; heat through. Serve immediately.

Yield: 6 servings

Deborah Cameron

Italian Stuffed Shells

1 (12-ounce) package jumbo shells
½ pound Italian sweet sausage
4 cups Basic Tomato Sauce (see Note)
2 (10-ounce) packages frozen chopped spinach, thawed
2 eggs, lightly beaten
1 pound ricotta cheese
½ pound mozzarella cheese, shredded
1 tablespoon minced garlic
2 tablespoons grated Parmesan cheese

Cook shells, according to package directions, to al dente. Drain, rinse with cold water and set aside. Split sausage casing and remove. Crumble meat into skillet; brown over medium heat, stirring frequently. Drain fat. Add tomato sauce. Cover pan; reduce heat to low and simmer about 15 minutes. Place thawed spinach in strainer; press out excess moisture by hand. In a large bowl, combine eggs, spinach, ricotta, mozzarella and garlic; mix thoroughly. Preheat oven to 350 degrees. Spoon ½ cup of the sausage and sauce mixture into bottom of a 3-quart casserole. Stuff each shell with 2 rounded teaspoons of the spinach and cheese mixture. Arrange shells, single layer, in casserole. Pour remaining sauce over shells; sprinkle with Parmesan cheese. Bake for 30 minutes. All you need is a green salad and a loaf of fresh Italian bread!

Note: Both the sausage and sauce mixture and the cheese and spinach mixture can be prepared a day ahead. Refrigerate separately. Recipe for Basic Tomato Sauce can be found in the Beverages, Sauces and Marinades section.

Yield: 6 servings

Pam D'Alessandro

Fettuccine Alfredo

12 tablespoons unsalted butter
½ pound cooked fettuccine
½ pint heavy cream
8 ounces freshly grated Parmigiano cheese
½ teaspoon freshly ground white pepper
½ teaspoon freshly grated nutmeg

Melt butter in large skillet (do not allow butter to boil). Add pasta; toss gently using two forks. Add heavy cream and cheese; stir over very low heat. Continue tossing pasta until sauce is smooth and creamy. Sprinkle with white pepper and nutmeg. Serve immediately.

Yield: 4 servings

Kathy Raffensperger

15 Layer Lasagna

Meatballs:
½ pound ground chuck
½ pound ground pork
2 eggs
1 cup grated Romano cheese
½ cup chopped fresh parsley
2 cloves garlic, minced
1 cup fresh bread crumbs
Salt and pepper, to taste

Ricotta Cheese Mixture:
3 pounds ricotta cheese
3 eggs
1 cup grated Romano cheese
1 cup chopped fresh parsley
Salt and pepper, to taste

Béchamel Sauce:
8 tablespoons butter
½ cup flour
2 cups milk, warmed
¼ teaspoon pepper
½ cup grated Romano cheese
3 egg whites, whipped to form soft peaks

1 pound lasagna noodles
1 quart tomato sauce, divided
1 pound bulk Italian sausage, cooked, drained and crumbled
½ pound mozzarella cheese, shredded
½ cup grated Romano cheese

To prepare meatballs, preheat oven to 350 degrees. Mix together all meatball ingredients in large bowl. Roll into 2-inch balls. Place on ungreased baking sheet; bake until lightly browned, about 5 to 7 minutes (can also fry in skillet, turning to brown all sides). Cool. Slice each meatball in thirds. Set aside. In large bowl, mix together all ricotta cheese mixture ingredients. Set aside. To prepare Béchamel sauce, melt butter in heavy saucepan. Add flour and cook 1 to 2 minutes, stirring until smooth. Stir in milk; add pepper and grated cheese. Remove from heat; allow to cool slightly. Fold in egg whites. Set aside. Cook lasagna noodles according to package directions; drain. Increase oven temperature to 375 degrees. Pour 1 cup of the tomato sauce into bottom of a 10x14-inch baking dish; spread evenly. Place one layer of noodles on top of sauce. Layer as follows, using ½ of each ingredient: meatballs, ricotta cheese mixture, sausage and mozzarella. Drizzle tomato sauce over cheese. Add another layer of noodles. Repeat above layers with remaining ½ of the meatballs, ricotta cheese mixture, sausage and mozzarella. Finish with a layer of noodles; cover with remaining tomato sauce. Sprinkle Romano cheese over top of lasagna; cover and bake for 1 hour. Remove from oven; pour Béchamel sauce over top of lasagna. Bake, uncovered, an additional 15 minutes. Let stand 20 to 30 minutes before cutting. 15 layers of heaven!

Note: If baking dish is overly full, place a baking sheet with sides under lasagna while baking. Extra meatballs may be served on the side or frozen for later use.

Yield: 15 servings

Alberta and Joseph Certo

Lasagna Roll-Ups

12 lasagna noodles
1 pound ground beef
1 large onion, chopped
1 (16-ounce) jar spaghetti sauce
1 (8-ounce) jar sliced mushrooms,
    drained
2 cups ricotta cheese
10 ounces frozen chopped spinach,
    thawed and drained
¼ cup Parmesan or mozzarella
    cheese
1 teaspoon salt
¼ teaspoon pepper
2 cloves garlic, crushed

Preheat oven to 350 degrees. Cook lasagna noodles according to package directions. Drain; set aside. In a large skillet, brown ground beef and onion. Remove from heat; stir in spaghetti sauce and mushrooms. Pour sauce mixture into an 11x13-inch baking pan. In medium bowl, combine ricotta, spinach, Parmesan, salt, pepper and garlic. Spread 3 tablespoons of cheese mixture on each noodle; roll up and cut each noodle in half. Place cut side down in baking dish. Bake for 30 minutes.

Yield: 6 servings

Mary Gehman

Mother's Day Pasta

5 cloves garlic, sliced
3 tablespoons extra virgin olive oil
6-8 shiitake mushrooms, sliced
½ cup sun-dried tomatoes, packed
    in oil, sliced
¼ cup dry vermouth
8 ounces heavy cream
1 ounce Montrechet (goat) cheese,
    cubed
1 pound fettuccine, cooked al
    dente

In heavy skillet, sauté garlic in olive oil until nearly transparent. Add mushrooms and tomatoes; sauté an additional 2 to 3 minutes. Add vermouth; cook over medium heat for 5 minutes. Add cream and cheese; stir continuously until cheese is melted. Pour sauce over fettuccine and toss. Serve immediately.

Yield: 4 to 6 servings

Janet Peterson

Linguine with White Clam Sauce

1 pound linguine
¾ cup extra virgin olive oil
4 cloves garlic, minced
4 (6½-ounce) cans chopped clams, drained, liquid reserved
2 cups bottled clam juice
½ cup finely chopped Italian parsley
1½ teaspoons dried oregano
Freshly ground black pepper, to taste
Grated Parmesan cheese

Cook linguine according to package directions. Heat olive oil in deep heavy saucepan. Add garlic; cook over low heat until golden, about 5 minutes. Combine reserved clam liquid and enough bottled clam juice to make 3 cups. Add to saucepan. Stir. Add parsley, oregano and pepper. Simmer, partially covered, for 10 minutes. (Sauce may be prepared ahead to this point.) Add chopped clams and heat gently (do not overcook or clams will become tough). Place linguine in saucepan; toss with sauce. Serve in individual wide soup bowls and top with Parmesan cheese.

Yield: 6 servings

Pam D'Alessandro

Penne Pasta in Vodka Sauce

1 pound penne pasta
1 medium onion, finely diced
2 ribs celery, finely diced
3 cloves garlic, minced
¼ cup olive oil
½ pound prosciutto, thinly sliced, finely chopped
¾ cup vodka
1 (28-ounce) can crushed tomatoes
¼ teaspoon cayenne pepper
1 tablespoon chopped fresh parsley
1 tablespoon dried basil
¾ teaspoon dried oregano
1 cup half & half
Grated Parmagiano Reggiano or Peccorino Romano cheese

Cook pasta according to package directions. In large skillet, sauté onion, celery and garlic in oil over medium heat until softened. Add prosciutto and vodka; simmer until liquid is almost evaporated. Add tomatoes, cayenne pepper and herbs. Simmer 10 minutes. Stir in half & half; simmer 3 minutes longer. Toss pasta with sauce. Serve with grated cheese.

Note: Wine suggestion: Brunello, a full-bodied, Italian red wine.

Yield: 4 to 6 servings

Camille Bloodworth

Penne with Sun-Dried Tomatoes

8 cups sun-dried tomatoes (not packed in oil)

1½ cups extra virgin olive oil, divided

8 tablespoons chopped garlic

2½ cups chopped fresh basil, divided

1½ teaspoons salt, and to taste

3 teaspoons freshly ground black pepper, and to taste

4 cups pine nuts

5 pounds premium penne pasta

4 pounds feta cheese with peppercorns, crumbled

2 cups fresh, not canned, whole black olives, pitted

Soak tomatoes in hot water for 40 minutes to soften. Drain; cut into ½-inch pieces. Heat 4 tablespoons of the olive oil in large skillet. Sauté garlic over low-medium heat for 3 to 4 minutes, until just golden. (Do not brown.) Add tomatoes, 1¼ cups of the basil and 1¼ cups of the olive oil; heat through. Season with salt and pepper. Transfer skillet ingredients to large bowl; cover and marinate overnight in refrigerator. Preheat oven to 300 degrees. Spread pine nuts on a baking sheet. Toast in oven, 2 to 3 minutes, until golden. Cook pasta, according to package directions, to al dente. Bring tomato mixture to room temperature. Add in the remaining 1¼ cups basil. Drain pasta and place in large bowl or pan. Place tomato mixture in large skillet; briefly warm over low-medium heat. Mix tomato mixture into pasta. Add pine nuts. Add feta cheese and olives just prior to serving; mix well. Season with additional salt and pepper, if desired.

Note: Requires preparation work the night before. Best prepared 1 to 2 days ahead. Recipe keeps 3 to 4 days in the refrigerator. Add feta cheese and olives just prior to serving. Feta cheese with peppercorns is found in the grocery dairy section.

Yield: 16 to 20 servings

Donna Linnelli

Penne and Gruyère Casserole

1 pound penne pasta
4 cups milk
4 tablespoons butter
6 tablespoons flour
Salt and pepper, to taste
1 teaspoon paprika, divided
12 ounces Gruyère cheese, grated

Cook pasta according to package directions. Drain and rinse under cold water; set aside. Preheat oven to 350 degrees. Using heavy saucepan, bring milk to a boil; set aside. In separate pan, melt butter. Add flour and whisk over low heat for 5 minutes. Do not brown. Remove from heat. Add hot milk to flour mixture; whisk until smooth. Stir in salt, pepper and ½ teaspoon of the paprika. Return to heat and allow to thicken. Add to pasta; mix well. Fill a greased 3-quart baking dish with mixture and top with grated cheese. Sprinkle with remaining paprika; bake 20 to 25 minutes. Heat broiler. Broil until top is browned, approximately 3 to 5 minutes.

Yield: 8 servings

Rebecca Lando

Pink Fettuccine Alfredo Hug

1 pound fettuccine
2 tablespoons unsalted butter
2 cloves garlic, crushed
2 cups small broccoli florets
2 cups heavy cream mixed with 1
   tablespoon cornstarch
1 cup drained, sliced stewed
   tomatoes from 1 (8-ounce) can
¼ pound prosciutto, julienned
½ cup freshly grated locatelli
   cheese

Prepare fettuccine according to package directions. In large skillet, melt butter over moderately high heat. Sauté garlic and broccoli, stirring for 2 minutes. Using slotted spoon, transfer mixture to a plate. Add cream to skillet; simmer, stirring, for 3 to 5 minutes until slightly thickened. Stir in tomatoes, prosciutto and broccoli mixture. Cook sauce, stirring, for 2 minutes. Toss sauce with fettuccine and serve sprinkled with locatelli.

Yield: 4 servings

Anna Laufer

Capellini with Fresh Tomato and Basil Sauce

2 pounds plum tomatoes, peeled, seeded and coarsely chopped
1 cup coarsely chopped fresh basil leaves
3 tablespoons white wine vinegar
1 (3¼-ounce) jar capers, drained and rinsed
Salt and freshly ground pepper, to taste
1 pound capellini pasta
¾-1 cup olive oil (preferably extra virgin)

Combine tomatoes and basil. Marinate at room temperature for 1 to 2 hours or refrigerate overnight. Blend vinegar, capers, salt and pepper into tomato mixture. Cook pasta, according to package directions, to al dente. Drain well. Transfer to platter. Add enough oil to coat pasta; toss. Mix in tomato sauce. Let stand 5 minutes before serving. Perfect use for summer tomatoes!

Note: Can also be served at room temperature.

Yield: 6 servings

Marcella Karvellis McGuire

Penne with Tomato-Olive Sauce

1 pound penne pasta
2 tablespoons olive oil
2 tablespoons balsamic vinegar
2 cloves garlic, crushed
⅓ cup chopped fresh basil
½ cup sliced black olives
¼ cup capers, rinsed and drained
¼ teaspoon red pepper flakes
4 large tomatoes, seeded and chopped
4 ounces feta cheese, crumbled

Cook pasta according to package directions. In a small mixing bowl, combine oil, vinegar, garlic, basil, olives, capers and red pepper flakes. Mix well. Add tomatoes and toss. Pour sauce over pasta and sprinkle with feta cheese. Serve at room temperature.

Yield: 4 to 6 servings

Ann Puntel

Creamy Tomato Basil Pasta

1 pound farfalle (bow tie) pasta
8 tablespoons butter
3 large cloves garlic, chopped
1 (½-pint) carton whipping cream
1 (8-ounce) can tomato sauce
1 teaspoon dried or 1½
   tablespoons fresh basil

Cook pasta according to package directions. In a 10-inch skillet, melt butter over medium heat and sauté garlic. (Do not brown.) Add cream, tomato sauce and basil. Stir gently for 3 to 5 minutes. Serve over pasta with green salad, crusty bread and wine.

Note: Best when sauce is spooned over individual pasta servings.

Yield: 4 servings

Sonja Hissom-Braun

Pancit (Pŏn sĭt) Canton

An Asian Noodle Entrée

2 tablespoons vegetable oil
3-4 whole scallions, finely
   chopped
2 cloves garlic, finely chopped
6-12 ounces boneless chicken
   breasts, cut into ½-inch pieces
6-7 carrots, finely chopped
½ medium cabbage, finely
   chopped
2 cups chicken broth
¼ cup soy sauce
1 (8-ounce) package Chinese plain
   noodles (dried)

Heat oil in wok or large heavy skillet. Add scallions and garlic. Stir-fry for 2 minutes. Add chicken; stir-fry for 3 minutes. Add carrots and stir-fry 2 minutes longer. Add cabbage; stir to combine. Add broth and soy sauce; cook for 7 to 8 minutes. Add Chinese noodles and, stirring, cook an additional 3 minutes. Add additional broth or water, if needed, to keep noodles moist. Serve warm or at room temperature. This entrée goes well with stir-fry pea pods or an Asian-style soup.

Note: Stir-fry cooking requires high heat and continuous stirring of wok contents. Chinese noodles can be purchased at Asian food stores or in grocery specialty sections.

Variation: Substitute 6 to 12-ounces pork tenderloin or small shrimp for chicken. Add shrimp when noodles are added to wok.

Yield: 4 to 6 servings

Cynthia Taibbi Kates

Three Cheese Macaroni Casserole

1 (8-ounce) box elbow macaroni
¼ cup grated American cheese
½ cup grated Cheddar cheese
½ cup milk
2 tablespoons butter, melted
¼ pound Brie cheese
2 tablespoons Worcestershire
   sauce
⅛ teaspoon Tabasco sauce
¼ teaspoon salt
⅛ teaspoon pepper
2 tablespoons onion salt
⅛ teaspoon garlic salt
⅛ teaspoon paprika

Cook macaroni according to package directions. Drain and set aside. In a medium bowl, combine American and Cheddar cheeses. Set aside. Preheat oven to 325 degrees. In medium saucepan, over low-medium heat, combine milk, butter and Brie. Cook slowly, stirring, until cheese melts. Add sauces, salt, pepper, onion salt and garlic salt. Pour hot mixture into bowl with cheeses. Mix well. Add cooked macaroni; toss to mix. Pour into a 9x13-inch baking dish. Sprinkle with paprika. Cover and bake for 20 minutes. Uncover and bake an additional 5 to 7 minutes.

Yield: 4 to 6 servings

Kara Ramsay

Grandmom Procario's Ravioli

Filling:
3 pounds ricotta cheese
3 eggs
Salt and pepper, to taste
¼ teaspoon sugar
3 teaspoons chopped fresh parsley
¼ cup grated Parmesan cheese

Dough:
2 cups flour, sifted
6 eggs
1¼ teaspoons salt, divided
½ cup water
3 teaspoons oil, divided

Prepare filling 1 day ahead. Mix ricotta cheese and eggs together in large bowl. Add salt, pepper, sugar, parsley and Parmesan cheese; mix well. Cover and refrigerate overnight. To prepare dough, make a well in middle of flour; add eggs, 1 teaspoon of the salt, water, and 2 teaspoons of the oil. Mix well and roll thin on a floured board. Cut dough into 2-inch squares or larger. Place a spoonful of filling on each square. Fold over; seal edges with fork. Bring an 8-quart pot of water to boil. Add ¼ teaspoon of the salt and 1 teaspoon of the oil. Place ravioli in boiling water. Cook for 12 to 15 minutes after ravioli rise to the top of pot. Drain and serve with your favorite sauce.

Note: Requires advance preparation.

Yield: 6 to 8 servings

Erin Procario

Kneflees

German Egg Noodles

3 eggs
1 teaspoon salt
1 teaspoon pepper
1 cup water
2⅓ cups flour
¼ cup toasted croutons (optional)

In a large mixing bowl, beat eggs, salt and pepper together. Add water and flour; mix to a hearty paste consistency, using spatula to scrape sides of bowl. If dough becomes too thick, add a small amount of water. Prepare a large pot of boiling water. Tilt mixing bowl slightly over pot. Using a knife, slice off tablespoon-size pieces of dough from edge of bowl and drop into boiling water. Boil 8 to 10 noodles at a time for 1 minute or until noodles float to top. Remove with slotted spoon and place into serving dish. Top with croutons. Traditionally served with sauerkraut and spareribs.

Note: Kneflees have the appearance of odd-shaped dumplings.

Yield: 4 servings

Norma Piel and Mary Lou Haramic

Easy Risotto

6 tablespoons unsalted butter
1 small onion, minced
½ cup coarsely chopped green
   pepper
½ cup sliced mushrooms
1 cup uncooked long-grain rice
2½ cups chicken broth
3 tablespoons freshly grated
   Parmesan cheese
¼ teaspoon salt
⅛ teaspoon freshly ground black
   pepper

Preheat oven to 400 degrees. In a heavy skillet, melt butter over medium heat. Sauté onion, green pepper and mushrooms. Add rice; continue cooking, stirring, until rice turns golden in color. Add chicken broth; increase heat to high and bring to a boil. Stir in cheese, salt and pepper. Transfer to a 2½-quart covered casserole; bake for 25 to 30 minutes. Serve immediately. An excellent accompaniment to shish kabobs!

Yield: 4 to 6 servings

Janice Kenney

Pierogie Casserole

1 (16-ounce) box lasagna noodles
8 medium potatoes, peeled and
    cubed
½ teaspoon salt, divided
½ teaspoon pepper, divided
1¼ cups butter or margarine,
    divided
⅓ cup milk
1¼ cups shredded Cheddar
    cheese, divided
4-6 large onions, sliced

Cook lasagna noodles according to package directions. Drain; rinse with cool water. Let dry. Cook potatoes in boiling water until tender. Drain and place in large mixing bowl. Preheat oven to 350 degrees. Add ¼ teaspoon of the salt, ¼ teaspoon of the pepper, ¾ cup of the butter, milk and ½ cup of the cheese to the potatoes. Using an electric mixer, whip potatoes. Melt the remaining ½ cup butter in large skillet. Add onions and the remaining ¼ teaspoons salt and pepper. Sauté onions until tender. Spread onions over bottom of a 9x13-inch baking dish. Add a layer of lasagna noodles. Spread ¼ to ⅓ of the mashed potatoes over noodles. Repeat layers 3 or 4 times. Sprinkle the remaining ¾ cup cheese on top. Cover with aluminum foil and bake for 30 to 40 minutes until bubbly. Cut into squares. Enjoy!

Yield: 8 servings

Joyce Lubinski

Vegetable Rice

2 (2-cup) bags of "boil in the bag"
    rice
2 tablespoons butter
1 large onion, chopped
1 large red pepper, chopped
1 large orange bell pepper,
    chopped
1 large yellow bell pepper,
    chopped
½ teaspoon salt, or to taste
½ teaspoon pepper, or to taste

Prepare rice according to package directions. Set aside. Melt butter in large skillet. Sauté onion and peppers on medium to low heat for 10 to 15 minutes. Season with salt and pepper. Combine rice and vegetables in a bowl. Mix and serve.

Yield: 6 to 8 servings

JoAnn Willey

Quinoa, Black Bean, Red Pepper and Corn Salad

½ cup quinoa
5 tablespoons olive oil, divided
1 cup chicken or vegetable broth
¼ teaspoon ground cumin
¼ teaspoon salt
2 tablespoons fresh lime juice
¼ teaspoon ground black pepper
1 cup (cooked or canned) black beans, drained
1 cup thawed, frozen whole-kernel white corn
1 large tomato, peeled, seeded and diced
1 small sweet red pepper, seeded and chopped
2 green onions, finely chopped (approximately ¼ cup)
3 tablespoons chopped fresh cilantro
2 tablespoons chopped fresh parsley

Rinse quinoa in cold water and drain. In a 1-quart saucepan, heat 1 tablespoon of the olive oil over medium heat. Add quinoa and stir until toasted, about 5 minutes. Stir in broth, cumin and salt. Heat on high until boiling. Reduce heat; cover and simmer until liquid is absorbed, about 15 minutes. Remove from heat; let stand 5 minutes. Fluff with fork; allow to cool to room temperature. In a medium bowl, whisk the remaining 4 tablespoons olive oil, lime juice and black pepper. Add beans, vegetables and herbs. Mix well. Add quinoa. Refrigerate until 30 minutes before serving. Stir well. A great summer salad that can be doubled for a crowd!

Note: Quinoa, a grain pronounced "keen-wah", can be found in specialty markets or natural food stores.

Yield: 8 servings

Barb Pacini

Lemon Rice Pilaf

All natural lemon-flavored non-stick vegetable oil cooking spray
½ cup chopped onion
2 tablespoons orzo
1 cup brown rice
1 (14½-ounce) can fat-free chicken broth
1 teaspoon grated lemon rind

Spray a heavy-bottomed saucepan with cooking spray. Over medium heat, sauté onion until soft, about 2 minutes. Add orzo and rice; cook 2 minutes. Add enough water to the broth to measure 3 cups. Stir into pan; heat to a boil. Reduce heat, cover and simmer 40 to 45 minutes until liquid is absorbed. Spray cooking spray onto mixture for 3 seconds; fluff with fork and garnish with grated lemon rind. A delightful accompaniment to fish, poultry or stir-fry dishes.

Yield: 4 servings

Jessica D'Alesandro

Lebanese Rice

½ cup butter
½ cup pignolia nuts
5 strands cappellini pasta
3 cups uncooked long-grain
   converted rice (do not
   substitute)
3 cups chicken broth
3 cups water
1 teaspoon salt

Melt butter in a 4 or 5-quart Dutch oven. Sauté nuts, stirring, until brown. Break dry strands of cappellini into approximately ½-inch pieces. Add to nuts; continue to brown for another minute, stirring. Add rice; stir an additional minute. Add chicken broth, water and salt to mixture; stir until boiling. Cover; reduce heat. Simmer 20 to 30 minutes or until all liquid is absorbed.

Note: When re-heating rice, add additional chicken broth to keep moist.

Yield: 8 to 12 servings

Joyce Irr

Barley Corn Confetti Salad

1 cup unpearled barley, rinsed
6 cups water
¼ teaspoon sea salt
2 cups cooked corn
½ cup minced scallion
1 red bell pepper, chopped
½ cup minced parsley
⅛ cup extra virgin olive oil
2 tablespoons lemon juice
2 tablespoons Umeboshi (plum)
   vinegar

Place barley and water in a medium saucepan and bring to a boil. Reduce heat; simmer about 1 hour or until barley softens. Drain well and cool. Mix all remaining ingredients in large bowl; toss with barley. Refrigerate for 1 hour and serve. Great salad for picnics!

Note: Unpearled barley can be found in specialty markets or natural food stores.

Yield: 6 servings

Pamela Urbini

Tabbouleh

A Middle Eastern Salad

½ cup bulgur wheat
½ cup water
6 large tomatoes, finely chopped
8 scallions, finely chopped
1 cup finely chopped fresh parsley
½ cup finely chopped fresh mint
2 cloves garlic, minced
2 tablespoons olive oil
Juice of 3 lemons
Salt and pepper, to taste

Place bulgur wheat in a small bowl with the water. Let soak for 20 minutes. In a large bowl, combine tomatoes, scallions, parsley, mint and garlic. Add olive oil; stir gently. Squeeze wheat with hands to remove excess water (wheat will fluff as it is mixed into other ingredients). Add wheat to tomato mixture. Season with lemon juice, salt and pepper. Toss gently and serve.

Variation: Substitute ½ cup lemon juice from concentrate for juice of 3 lemons.

Yield: 6 servings

Michelle Bisceglia

Strip District

The Strip District has had a variety of names in the past — Barnyardstown, O'Harasville, the Northern Liberties and Denny's Bottom. Once a wooded riverbank, then a residential area, this neighborhood is now a wholesale and produce distribution point as well as a manufacturing center.

In 1773, a trader named James O'Hara arrived in Pittsburgh and bought land from Thomas Smallman in the area of today's Strip District. O'Hara named his farm "Springfield Plantation." In 1819, he divided his holdings of over 500 acres between his two daughters, Mary and Elizabeth.

A terminal point for goods that were transported on the Pennsylvania Canal (which connected Pittsburgh and Philadelphia via the Allegheny and Susquehanna Rivers) was built at 11th Street in 1829. Railroads such as the Baltimore & Ohio and the Pennsylvania quickly made the canal obsolete. The Pennsylvania Railroad's roundhouse and some of its repair shops stood on 28th Street.

Industry became increasingly important to the Strip following its annexation to Pittsburgh in 1837. John Schoenbarger McCormick bought the Pittsburgh Blacking Mill and moved it from Downtown to be nearer the foundries and metal casting operations in the area of 25th Street. By 1892, another Strip establishment, the Pittsburgh Gage and Supply Company was the largest industry and supply house east of the Mississippi River. Adam's Market, a small grouping of vendors in the western edge of the Strip, was located in what is now Pittsburgh's major produce center.

The ethnic population of the Strip District has gradually been displaced by the growth of commercial enterprises. Nonetheless, two ethnic churches remain: St. Stanislaus Kostka, a Polish church which merged with St. Patrick's, an Irish church and St. Elizabeth of Hungary, which is Slovak.

As Pittsburgh's waterfronts become more attractive to commercial business, loft-housing development and entertainment ventures, the Strip District continues to insist that its time-honored history be respected and valued. ♥

Creamed Spinach

3 tablespoons unsalted butter,
  divided
3 bunches spinach, washed and
  stemmed
1 small onion, diced
1½ cups heavy cream
1 teaspoon salt
½ teaspoon white pepper
¼ teaspoon grated nutmeg

Melt 1 tablespoon of the butter in a large skillet over medium heat. Add spinach. Cook, tossing gently, until wilted and bright green. Drain and set aside. Melt the remaining 2 tablespoons butter in same skillet. Add onion. Cook until soft; do not brown. Chop spinach; add to onions. Add cream. Over medium heat, bring to a boil and, stirring, cook until mixture thickens slightly, about 5 minutes. Stir in spices; serve immediately.

Yield: 6 servings

Sandra DeBartolo

Asparagus with Sesame and Brown Butter

2 pounds fresh asparagus
4-6 tablespoons butter, to taste
⅛ cup sesame seeds, toasted
1 tablespoon lemon juice
  (optional)
1 lemon, sliced (optional)

Remove tough ends of asparagus by gently bending stalks until they snap. Rinse asparagus; cover with cold water until ready to steam. Drain asparagus. Place in microwaveable baking dish, alternating tips to ends. Add ¼ cup water and cover with plastic wrap. Microwave on high for 7 minutes. Immediately vent. While asparagus is steaming, melt butter over low heat in medium saucepan. Continue heating until butter is evenly browned; swirl pan occasionally to prevent excessive darkening. Remove from heat. Add toasted sesame seeds and lemon juice. Drain asparagus. Place asparagus in butter mixture; coat thoroughly. Transfer to serving dish and garnish with fresh cut lemon.

Yield: 6 servings

Karen Raffensperger

Broccoli Medley

1 head of broccoli
½ pound bacon
½ red onion, chopped
1 cup shredded Cheddar cheese

Dressing:
½ cup mayonnaise
¼ cup sugar
1 tablespoon vinegar

Cut broccoli florets into small pieces. Fry bacon until crisp; drain and crumble. Combine broccoli, bacon, onion and cheese in a bowl. Mix together dressing ingredients. Add to broccoli mixture; toss to coat. Refrigerate 4 hours or overnight. Serve cold.

Yield: 8 servings

Jean Gaffney and Debbie Hlasnik

Lemon and Garlic Broccoli

1½ pounds fresh broccoli florets
2 teaspoons unsalted butter
3 tablespoons lemon juice
1 clove garlic, minced

Steam broccoli until tender, about 4 to 5 minutes. Melt butter in a non-reactive saucepan over medium-low heat. Remove pan from heat; add lemon juice and garlic. Pour over broccoli. Toss and serve.

Yield: 4 servings

Maria DeRenzo

Patty's Baked Green Beans

2 pounds fresh green beans
1 medium onion, thinly sliced
8 tablespoons butter
3 tablespoons Hungarian paprika
1 teaspoon salt (optional)
1 teaspoon freshly ground black
   pepper (optional)

Wash and string the beans. Preheat oven to 350 degrees. In a 2½-quart casserole or baking dish, alternately layer beans and onion. Dot with butter. Sprinkle spices evenly over top. Cover and bake for 1½ hours. Great for a crowd!

Yield: 8 to 10 servings

Patty Just

Swiss Green Bean Salad

1½ pounds fresh, whole green beans

Dressing:
5 tablespoons fresh lemon juice
2 large cloves garlic, crushed
½ cup olive oil
1 tablespoon red wine vinegar
½ teaspoon crushed tarragon
½ teaspoon dried dill weed
½ teaspoon salt, or to taste
Freshly ground black pepper, to taste
2 teaspoons prepared dark or Dijon mustard
½ cup (packed) minced fresh parsley

⅓ pound premium Swiss cheese, cut in thin strips
½ cup chopped ripe olives
½ cup thinly sliced red pepper
½-¾ cup chopped, toasted almonds

Wash and string green beans. Steam beans until just tender. Remove from heat; immediately rinse in cold water. Drain well. In a large bowl, whisk together all ingredients for dressing. Add beans and cheese; toss until dressing is well distributed. Cover tightly and marinate 2 to 3 hours (stirring once an hour) at room temperature. Add olives and sliced pepper. Mix well; re-cover and marinate another 5 hours or overnight in refrigerator. Serve topped with almonds. A great salad to bring to a picnic!

Yield: 4 servings

Pam D'Alessandro

Russian Mushrooms

1 pound of mushrooms
1-1½ teaspoons salt, to taste
½ cup flour
½ cup butter
½-¾ cup sour cream, to taste
½ cup grated Parmesan cheese

Preheat oven to 350 degrees. Clean mushrooms. (Leave stems attached.) Dry and cut each mushroom into 4 or 5 pieces. Sprinkle with salt. Sift flour over mushrooms or place flour and mushrooms in a zip-top plastic bag; shake until coated. Melt butter in a skillet; sauté mushrooms until brown. Place in a baking dish, cover with sour cream and sprinkle with cheese. Bake for 35 to 40 minutes.

Yield: 4 servings

Carolyn Johnson

Corn Pudding

4 eggs
1 tablespoon butter
3 tablespoons flour
1 cup milk
1 teaspoon salt
¼ teaspoon pepper
1 tablespoon sugar
2 tablespoons finely chopped
   green pepper
1 cup canned cream-style corn
1 cup (canned or frozen) whole-
   kernel corn

Preheat oven to 325 degrees. In a large mixing bowl, beat eggs until thick. In a saucepan, melt butter over low heat. Stir in flour. Add milk and cook until slightly thickened. Remove from heat. Stir in salt, pepper and sugar. Slowly combine eggs and milk mixture. Stir in green pepper. Fold in corn. Place in a greased 1½-quart casserole. Bake until set, 50 to 60 minutes.

Yield: 6 to 8 servings

MaryAnne McGuire

Baked Onions with Sun-Dried Tomatoes

1½ pounds fresh, small white
   onions, sliced
3 tablespoons olive oil, divided
1 tablespoon chopped fresh
   rosemary
1 tablespoon chopped fresh sage
¼ cup (oil-packed) sun-dried
   tomatoes
Rosemary sprigs for garnish

Preheat oven to 375 degrees. Place onions in a 9x13-inch baking dish. Drizzle 2 tablespoons of the oil over onions. Sprinkle rosemary and sage evenly over onions. Bake, uncovered, stirring occasionally, until onions are browned and soft, approximately 45 minutes. Drain tomatoes. Remove onions from oven. Stir in sun-dried tomatoes and the remaining 1 tablespoon olive oil. Allow to cool. Serve at room temperature. Garnish with rosemary sprigs.

Note: Recipe can be prepared a day in advance.

Variation: Frozen, bagged onions may be substituted for fresh. Replace fresh herbs with 1½ teaspoons dried herbs. Reserve oil from sun-dried tomatoes and use in place of olive oil.

Yield: 6 servings

MaryLou Wessell

Baked Stuffed Carrots

4 very large carrots
1 medium onion, chopped
½ green or red sweet pepper,
    chopped
3 tablespoons butter, softened,
    divided
Salt and pepper, to taste

Boil carrots whole until mildly cooked, about 30 minutes. Preheat oven to 350 degrees. Cut carrots in half lengthwise. Using a small spoon or melon baller, carefully scoop out carrot centers. Set shells aside. Place scooped-out carrot into a medium mixing bowl and mash. Add onion, pepper and 2 tablespoons of the butter. Season with salt and pepper. Use the remaining 1 tablespoon of butter to grease a 9x9-inch baking dish. Place carrot shells in dish and fill with mashed carrot mixture. Bake for 30 minutes. An elegant side dish for a dinner party!

Note: Recipe can be prepared a day ahead.

Variation: Prepare as above using whole carrots (do not scoop out centers). Place mashed carrot mixture in a 9-inch baking dish or small casserole. Bake for 30 minutes. Less prep time, but just as delicious for a family dinner.

Yield: 8 servings

David Johnson

Pimientos

Spanish Fried Peppers

6 cubanello peppers
½ cup olive oil, divided
¼ cup sea salt

Quarter peppers lengthwise; remove seeds. In a 10-inch skillet, fry ½ of the pepper slices in ¼ cup of the olive oil. Fry the remaining peppers in the remaining oil. Drain on paper towels and sprinkle with sea salt. Delicious!

Yield: 6 servings

Susan Dawson

Baked Red Bell Peppers

3 large red bell peppers
3 plum tomatoes, peeled and
  halved
4 tablespoons olive oil
1 tablespoon balsamic vinegar
2 cloves garlic, crushed
2 tablespoons chopped fresh basil
2 teaspoons grated lemon peel
12 anchovy fillets, packed in oil,
  drained
6 ounces buffalo-mozzarella
  cheese, cut into 6 slices

Preheat oven to 400 degrees. Cut peppers in half lengthwise through the stem; remove seeds. Place, cut-side up, in a roasting pan. Place 1 tomato half in each pepper. Mix oil, vinegar, garlic, basil and lemon peel together. Spoon an equal amount onto each pepper. Bake for 40 minutes. Place 2 anchovy fillets and 1 slice of mozzarella cheese on each pepper. Return pan to oven and bake an additional 15 to 20 minutes. Serve immediately.

Yield: 6 servings

Xiaying Yin and Jingqi Li

Salad Peppers

6-8 red, yellow and green peppers

Brine:
1½ cups white vinegar
½ cup water
2½ tablespoons sugar
1 teaspoon salt

5 bay leaves
5 garlic cloves, sliced

Cut peppers in half and remove seeds. Submerge peppers in boiling water for 30 seconds to soften skins. Cool and cut peppers into ½-inch strips. Mix all brine ingredients in a small saucepan and blend over low-medium heat. Allow brine to cool. Pack peppers in 5 (8-ounce) wide-mouthed jars. Place 1 bay leaf and 1 (sliced) clove of garlic in each jar. Cover with brine. Close jars tightly and refrigerate. Marinate 2 to 3 days before use. A great accompaniment to a sandwich!

Note: Keeps 3 to 4 months in refrigerator.

Yield: 5 (8-ounce) jars

Kay Shaeffer

Stewed Tomatoes

4 tomatoes peeled and quartered
1 onion, finely chopped
2½ tablespoons brown sugar
½ teaspoon salt
⅛ teaspoon pepper
¼ teaspoon dried oregano
¼ teaspoon dried parsley
½ cup Italian bread crumbs

Place all ingredients, except bread crumbs, into a medium saucepan. Cover and cook over low to medium heat for ½ hour, stirring frequently, until tomatoes break down and onions are soft. Remove from heat; stir in bread crumbs.

Yield: 4 to 6 servings

Meghan Raffensperger

Stuffed Eggplant

2 medium eggplants
6 eggs
Salt and pepper, to taste
2 cups flour
1 cup canola or olive oil (to start)

Stuffing:
16 ounces ricotta cheese
¼ pound lean ground beef
⅓ cup grated Romano cheese
1-2 large cloves garlic, minced
2 tablespoons minced fresh
   parsley

1 quart prepared tomato sauce
½ cup shredded mozzarella cheese
1 tablespoon minced fresh parsley

Peel and slice eggplants lengthwise, ¼-inch thick. In a medium bowl, whisk eggs; season with salt and pepper. Place flour in a separate bowl. In a large skillet or electric fry pan, heat oil to 375 degrees or until oil bubbles vigorously when a bread cube is placed in pan. While heating, dredge eggplant slices in flour. Dip into egg mixture; re-coat with flour. Fry slices until golden brown on both sides. Transfer to paper towels to drain and cool. Discard used oil, wipe pan clean and replace with fresh oil as needed throughout frying. Preheat oven to 350 degrees. In a large bowl, mix together stuffing ingredients. Season with salt and pepper. Place a heaping tablespoon of stuffing on the larger half of each eggplant slice. Carefully roll toward smaller end. Pour ½ of the prepared sauce into a baking pan, 9x13-inch or larger. Place rolls side by side atop sauce in baking pan. (Do not stack.) Cover with remaining sauce. Sprinkle evenly with mozzarella. Cover and bake for 1 hour, until eggplant is tender and stuffing firm when pierced with a fork. Garnish with 1 tablespoon parsley.

Yield: 8 to 10 servings

Joanne Redondo

101

Zucchini Italiano

2 medium zucchini
2 teaspoons Italian seasoning
1 teaspoon minced garlic
1 tomato, chopped
½ cup seasoned croutons
½ cup grated mozzarella cheese

Slice or cube zucchini (do not peel). Spray a large skillet with non-stick vegetable oil cooking spray. Sauté zucchini, Italian seasoning and garlic over medium heat until zucchini is tender. Stir in tomato. Top with croutons. Sprinkle on cheese (do not stir). Heat an additional 1 to 2 minutes over low heat. Serve immediately.

Yield: 4 servings

Ellen Gunnell

Spaghetti Squash Casserole

1 (2 to 2½-pound) spaghetti
  squash
¼ pound ground beef
½ cup chopped onion
½ cup chopped green pepper
½ cup sliced fresh mushrooms
1 clove garlic, minced
½ teaspoon dried basil
½ teaspoon dried oregano
¼ teaspoon salt
⅛ teaspoon pepper
1 (14½-ounce) can diced tomatoes,
  drained
¼ cup shredded mozzarella cheese
¼ cup shredded mild Cheddar
  cheese

Preheat oven to 375 degrees. Halve squash lengthwise; remove seeds. Place both pieces, cut-side down, in a 9x13-inch baking pan. Add ½ inch of water. Bake, uncovered, for 30 to 40 minutes or until tender. When cool enough to handle, scoop out squash and separate strands with a fork. Set aside. Reduce oven temperature to 350 degrees. In a large skillet, cook beef, onion and green pepper over medium heat until meat is browned and vegetables are tender. Drain fat. Add mushrooms, garlic, basil, oregano, salt and pepper. Cook and stir for 2 minutes. Add tomatoes, cook and stir for 2 minutes. Add squash, mix well. Cook, uncovered, until liquid evaporates, approximately 10 minutes. Place squash mixture in a 9x13-inch baking pan. Bake, uncovered, for 15 minutes. Remove from oven. Sprinkle with cheeses. Return to oven and bake an additional 5 minutes.

Note: Casserole can be assembled several hours ahead; refrigerate. Bring to room temperature and bake as directed.

Yield: 6 to 8 servings

Barb Pacini

Sabzi Korma

Indian Cauliflower, Eggplant and Potato Curry

2-4 tablespoons vegetable oil
1 medium onion, chopped
3 teaspoons minced garlic
3 tablespoons minced fresh ginger
½ cup chopped fresh cilantro
½ cup sliced almonds
1½ tablespoons ground coriander
1 teaspoon fennel
1 teaspoon cayenne pepper
½ teaspoon tumeric
1½ (16-ounce) cans chopped
   tomatoes
1½ (6-ounce) cans tomato paste
1½ teaspoons paprika
3 cups water
1 head of cauliflower, cut into
   small pieces
1 eggplant, peeled and cut into
   ½-inch cubes
6 medium potatoes, peeled and
   cut into ½-inch cubes
¼ cup sesame seeds

Heat oil in a large skillet or Dutch oven. Brown the onion. Stir in garlic and ginger; cook for 2 minutes. Add cilantro and almonds; cook for 2 minutes. Stir in coriander, fennel, cayenne pepper and tumeric. Sizzle for a few seconds. Add tomatoes, tomato paste and paprika. Lower heat and cook an additional 2 minutes. Add water, cauliflower, eggplant and potatoes. Bring to a boil; decrease heat and simmer for 30 minutes. Let stand for 20 minutes. Add sesame seeds and serve. Great with Basmati rice!

Yield: 6 servings

Babs Carryer

Quesadillas

6 flour tortillas
2 cups shredded Cheddar cheese
1 small tomato, chopped
¼ cup chopped green onion
2 tablespoons diced, canned green
   chilies
1 tablespoon chopped fresh
   cilantro or parsley

Preheat oven to 350 degrees. Top each tortilla with an equal amount of cheese. Top with tomato, onion, chilies and cilantro. Fold tortilla in half; place on baking sheet. Bake for 5 minutes or until cheese is melted.

Yield: 6 servings

Katie Benedict

Onion and Red Pepper Tart

1 (17.3-ounce) box frozen puff
  pastry sheets, well thawed
  (see note)
4 large sweet red peppers, roasted
  (see directions)
4 large onions, peeled and diced
1 cup low-sodium chicken broth
3 tablespoons heavy cream
Salt and pepper, to taste

To prepare pastry for tart, lay out 1 unfolded puff pastry sheet on a lightly floured board or countertop. From the second sheet of puff pastry, cut along a fold line to obtain a pastry strip (⅓ of the pastry sheet). With wet fingertips, press the pastry strip onto one end of the unfolded pastry sheet to form 1 large rectangular sheet. Roll and press with rolling pin until pastry is ⅛-inch thick. Transfer to an ungreased baking sheet and prick dough all over to keep from puffing. Cover with plastic wrap; refrigerate until use. Preheat oven to 400 degrees. To roast peppers, slice into 2 to 3-inch wide strips. Place skin-side up on an ungreased baking sheet and roast until skins are blackened. Remove from oven; turn oven off. Place peppers in a plastic bag; seal and let sit for 15 minutes. Remove peppers from bag and place in a bowl of cold water; peel off skins and blackened edges. Drain well and cut into ½-inch pieces. To prepare tart filling, combine onions and broth in a large saucepan. Over low-medium heat, cook until onions are very soft, approximately 30 to 40 minutes. Stir occasionally. Drain and let cool in a mixing bowl. Add cream; season with salt and pepper. Preheat oven to 350 degrees. Remove pastry from refrigerator. To assemble tart, spread onions evenly over pastry to edges. Spoon on all of the roasted peppers and press down into onions. Season with salt and pepper. Bake tart in lower third of oven until cooked through and lightly browned, approximately 45 minutes.

Note: Wrap unused pastry in plastic wrap or foil and return to freezer. Pastry can be prepared a day ahead of tart preparation. Entire recipe is best when made 1 day in advance of baking. Refrigerate until use.

Yield: 12 to 16 servings

Donna Linnelli

Tomato Phyllo Pizza

7 (12x17-inch) sheets phyllo dough
3 tablespoons butter, melted (for use with phyllo dough)
7 tablespoons grated Parmesan cheese, divided
1 cup grated mozzarella cheese
1 cup thinly sliced onion
5 medium tomatoes, cut into ¼-inch slices
½ teaspoon dried oregano
⅛ teaspoon salt
¼ teaspoon freshly ground black pepper

Preheat oven to 375 degrees. Place phyllo between 2 sheets of waxed paper until ready for use. Brush a 10x15-inch baking sheet with butter. Lay 1 sheet of phyllo on baking sheet and brush lightly with butter, being sure to cover entire sheet, including edges. Sprinkle with 1 tablespoon of the Parmesan cheese. Repeat process with 6 sheets of phyllo. Lay final sheet of phyllo on top and butter (do not sprinkle with Parmesan cheese). Sprinkle mozzarella cheese over top. Spread onions and tomatoes over mozzarella. Sprinkle with oregano, salt, pepper and the remaining 1 tablespoon of Parmesan cheese. Trim excess dough from edges of baking sheet. Bake for 30 to 35 minutes, until edges are golden.

Note: For detailed directions on how to work with phyllo, see recipe for Spanakopita in the Vegetables and Vegetarian Dishes section.

Yield: 8 to 10 servings

Lisa Seguin

Main Dish Broccoli Pie with Ricotta Cheese

1 (10-ounce) package frozen chopped broccoli
1 small onion, chopped
1 tablespoon margarine
½ teaspoon salt
⅛ teaspoon pepper
⅔ cup milk or half & half
1⅓ cups ricotta cheese
⅓ cup grated Parmesan cheese
3 eggs, lightly beaten
1 (9-inch) baked pie shell

Preheat oven to 350 degrees. Cook broccoli according to package directions; drain thoroughly. In a large skillet, sauté onion in margarine until tender. Add broccoli, salt and pepper. In a large mixing bowl, combine milk, ricotta, Parmesan and eggs. Add broccoli mixture to bowl; mix well. Pour into pie shell. Bake for 45 minutes, until set and lightly browned.

Yield: 6 to 8 servings

Millie Linnelli

Spanakopita

Spinach Pie

4 (10-ounce) packages frozen
  chopped spinach, thawed
1 pound butter (do not substitute
  margarine), divided
6 green scallions, finely chopped
  or 1 large onion, grated
¼ cup olive oil
4 eggs, beaten
1½ pounds crumbled Greek feta
  cheese
1 teaspoon salt
½ teaspoon white pepper
½ cup chopped fresh dill
1 (1-pound) box phyllo dough

Place thawed spinach in colander and thoroughly press out all water. Set aside. In a medium skillet, over medium heat, melt 1 tablespoon of the butter. Add scallions; cook for 5 minutes, stirring continuously. Remove from heat; add oil, spinach, eggs, cheese, salt, pepper and dill. Set aside. Melt remaining butter in small pan and set aside. Prepare a 9x13-inch pan by brushing the bottom and sides with a pastry brush dipped into the melted butter. Preheat oven to 350 degrees. Prepare phyllo dough for use. (Read "Note" for instructions on how to work with phyllo dough.) Trim phyllo ½-inch wider than pan. Line prepared pan with half of the phyllo sheets (approximately 12), using the pastry brush to brush melted butter between each sheet. Spread the spinach mixture evenly over top sheet of phyllo. Top with remaining phyllo sheets, brushing each sheet with butter. Brush top sheet with a good coat of butter. Using a sharp knife, score top into square serving-size pieces. Bake for 30 minutes or until a rich, golden brown.

Note: Directions for using phyllo dough: Phyllo comes in 1 pound boxes containing about 22 sheets of (14 to 18-inch) phyllo. An unopened box can be kept frozen for several months. For best results, defrost phyllo in the refrigerator overnight, then at room temperature for about 2 hours before using. Do not open package while defrosting. Phyllo dries out very quickly when opened, so it is best to lay out all ingredients or make filling before opening box. After opening the package, lay out phyllo and cover with plastic wrap or slightly damp towels to keep the moisture in. Leftover phyllo may be refrigerated for up to a week, but cannot be re-frozen. When cutting phyllo, cut through the entire stack of sheets at once, using a sharp knife. If using whole sheets for pans, lift up the entire piece carefully, one at a time. If one happens to rip, smaller pieces can

Spanakopita (continued)

be used in between layers. If possible, use the best sheets for top layers (middle layers do not need to be perfect). The secret to crispy, flaky phyllo is butter. Do not skimp or skip! Begin by coating the bottom and sides of pan to be used with butter. Brush butter, using pastry brush, over the entire phyllo sheet using broad strokes. Be careful not to saturate. Always brush the top layer of phyllo with a good coat of butter. When using pans of phyllo, score top layers with a sharp knife before baking or freezing. A few drops of cold water sprinkled over the top will help prevent phyllo from curling during baking. One of the advantages of phyllo is that it freezes extremely well, either baked or unbaked. To cook frozen phyllo pastries or dishes, place directly, without thawing, into a preheated oven. Previously baked and frozen phyllo dishes can be reheated in a 350 degree oven until hot. Do not be afraid to work with phyllo. It takes a little organization, speed and practice. Give it a try and have fun. It is well worth the effort!

Yield: 12 servings

Marcella Karvellis McGuire

Tortino Al Funghi

Mushroom Tart

½ **pound frozen puff pastry, thawed**
½ **pound sliced portobello mushrooms**
2 **tablespoons unsalted butter**
½ **teaspoon salt, divided**
2 **large eggs**
1¼ **cups whole milk**
⅛ **teaspoon nutmeg**
½ **pound Emmenthaler cheese, cubed**

Preheat oven to 375 degrees. On a lightly floured surface, roll out puff pastry to ¼-inch thickness. Line a lightly buttered and floured 9-inch quiche-type pie pan with pastry. Bake for 5 minutes; set aside. In a medium skillet, sauté mushrooms in butter for 5 minutes or until they release their water. Season with ¼ teaspoon of the salt; set aside. In a medium mixing bowl, beat eggs with milk, nutmeg and the remaining ¼ teaspoon salt until smooth. Distribute cheese evenly in pie shell. Spread mushrooms over cheese. Pour egg mixture over mushrooms and cheese. Bake for 25 minutes or until crust is golden and filling is set.

Note: Best if baked 1 day ahead; serve warm.

Yield: 6 to 8 servings

Lorraine Capozzi

Sushi Nori

Vegetarian Nori Rolls

1½ cups sushi rice
1¾ cups water
¼ cup rice vinegar
2-3 medium carrots, peeled, cut in thin julienne strips
1 medium cucumber, peeled, cut in thin julienne strips
½ avocado, peeled, cut lengthwise in thin julienne strips
8 (8x7-inch) sheets sushi nori roasted seaweed
1-2 tablespoons wasabi paste (Japanese horseradish)

Sauce:
¼ cup tamari or soy sauce
1 tablespoon sesame oil
1 teaspoon minced scallion
½ teaspoon minced fresh garlic

Rinse rice in cold water until clear. Put rice and water into a medium size saucepan and soak for 10 minutes. Cover and bring to a boil, approximately 5 minutes. Reduce heat; simmer until water is absorbed, approximately 5 minutes. Remove from heat and keep covered for 10 to 30 minutes. In a large bowl, toss rice until cool using a wooden paddle, adding vinegar 1 tablespoon at a time. Cover until ready to use. This rice is very sticky and handles best with wet utensils or wet hands. Using a bamboo roller, place 1 sheet of sushi nori roasted seaweed (smooth, shiny side against bamboo) on the roller. Spread ⅛ of the rice in a band across the sheet about ½ inch from the bottom and all the way to the ends. Flatten with wet hand. Place carrots, cucumber and avocado in center of rice and roll tightly with bamboo roller. Repeat for remaining sheets of seaweed. Chill 1 to 8 hours, then slice into 1 to 1½-inch pieces. Place the wasabi in a small flat bowl. To prepare sauce, mix tamari, sesame oil, scallion and garlic in another small flat bowl. The wasabi and the tamari sauce are used for dipping when eating nori rolls.

Note: The ingredients, as well as the bamboo roller, are available at most Asian food stores. For directions on using bamboo roller, refer to the back of a roasted seaweed sushi nori bag.

Variation: Wasabi powder, reconstituted with water according to jar directions, may be substituted for wasabi paste.

Yield: 50 to 60 nori rolls

Anne Franks Gillespie

Dolmathes

Stuffed Grape Leaves

3 medium onions, finely chopped
1 cup olive oil, divided
2 cups uncooked converted rice
¾ cup fresh lemon juice, divided
½ cup chopped fresh parsley
½ cup chopped fresh dill
4 cups water, divided
2 teaspoons salt, divided
2 teaspoons pepper
50 fresh grape leaves or
**   1 (16-ounce) jar**

In a large, heavy skillet, sauté onions in 2 teaspoons of the olive oil until lightly browned. Add rice, ½ cup of the lemon juice, parsley, dill, 1 cup of the water, 1½ teaspoons of the salt and pepper to the onions. Stir, cover, and simmer for a few minutes until liquid is absorbed. Set aside to cool. Thoroughly rinse and drain grape leaves, being careful to remove any excess stem. Place 2 or 3 coarse leaves in the bottom of a 5-quart Dutch oven or deep pot. Arrange leaves to be filled using one large or 2 small leaves together for each "dolma". (Note that the shiny side of the leaf will be on the outside.) Place a rounded teaspoon of filling in the middle of the leaf. To begin rolling, start by folding over the base, fold in the sides and proceed rolling toward the point. Roll semi-tight to allow rice to expand. Place dolmathes in Dutch oven, side by side, then layer upon layer, until all of the filling or the leaves are used. Add the remaining olive oil, 3 cups of water, ½ teaspoon of salt and ¼ cup of lemon juice to pan over top of the dolmathes. Place a heavy plate on top of the dolmathes to weigh them down. Cover pan and simmer for 40 to 45 minutes or until rice is cooked. Drain excess liquid and discard. Dolmathes may be served hot or cold. Arrange on plates or a platter with thin slices of lemon to garnish.

Yield: Approximately 4 dozen

Marcella Karvellis McGuire

109

Caponata

An Italian Antipasto

1 large eggplant, chopped into ½-inch pieces
Olive or vegetable oil for frying
1 large onion, chopped
1 cup diced celery
2-3 medium tomatoes, chopped and drained
¼ cup tomato sauce
½ cup capers, rinsed and drained
⅓ cup green olives, chopped
¼ cup pignolia nuts, chopped
¼ cup wine vinegar
2 tablespoons sugar
½ teaspoon salt
½ teaspoon pepper

In a large skillet, fry eggplant in oil until browned. Remove; set aside to drain. Add more oil to skillet if needed; sauté onions and celery until tender. Add tomatoes, tomato sauce, capers, olives, nuts and eggplant. In a small saucepan, heat vinegar and sugar until dissolved. Add salt and pepper. Pour vinegar mixture onto sautéed vegetables. Simmer, covered, on low heat for approximately 30 to 45 minutes, stirring frequently. Best served as an antipasto on slices of fresh bread or serve chilled as a side dish with meat or poultry.

Note: Will keep in refrigerator for several weeks, if you can keep it around that long!

Variation: Substitute canned diced tomatoes for fresh tomatoes. Drain before use.

Yield: 10 to 12 servings

Jan Stayianos

Potatoes & Legumes

South Side

South Side was once a collection of boroughs that were annexed to the City of Pittsburgh in 1872. They included Birmingham, East Birmingham, South Pittsburgh and Monongahela.

During the late 18th century, the South Side and much of its southern hillside had one owner, John Ormsby. He had been given several thousand acres of this area as payment for his assistance in the building of Fort Pitt. By the late 1700's, he had built an estate on his land and established a ferry service connecting his home with the community of Pittsburgh, across the river.

In 1811, Ormsby's son-in-law, Dr. Nathaniel Bedford, laid out a town on the flats, naming it Birmingham in tribute to his native English city. He named the streets after Ormsby's children —Mary, Jane, Sarah and Sidney—names which South Side streets still bear today.

Birmingham quickly became a sizeable industrial center because of easy river transport and abundant coal supplies. Its infant glass industry grew into the nation's largest, with 76 glass factories in continuous operation. The increase in taxes and the demand for land that accompanied the growth of another Birmingham industry — steel — contributed to the glass industry's post-1860 decline.

In 1850, B.F. Jones invested in a South Side iron works. During the depression of 1873, he formed a partnership with a banker, James Laughlin, and the firm of Jones and Laughlin eventually became the South Side's biggest employer.

Today's South Side reflects its rich ethnic history. Parish churches, now consolidated, such as St. Adalbert's (Polish), St. Casimir's (Lithuanian) and St. Michael's (German) represent the area's varied ethnicity. Serbs, Slovaks, Russians, Ukrainians and Greeks all had their own churches and schools, clubs and halls, and many of these social clubs still retain large memberships.

Restoration efforts along Carson Street and its residential side streets have received national recognition. Tours of the city include the South Side as a showcase of urban preservation and pride. Housed within historic store fronts, restaurants, antique shops, bookstores and art galleries, along with third generation family-owned businesses, create an exciting and attractive streetscape. ♥

Gourmet Shredded Potatoes

12 medium potatoes
1-2 cups shredded Cheddar
  cheese, to taste
1½ tablespoons butter, melted
1½ cups sour cream, room
  temperature
⅓ cup chopped green onion
1 teaspoon salt
¼ teaspoon pepper
1½ tablespoons milk (optional)
4 tablespoons butter
1 cup cooked, crumbled bacon
  (optional)

Place potatoes in a large pot. Cover with water and boil until just fork-tender. Do not over-cook. Cool. Peel and shred coarsely using a grater. Preheat oven to 350 degrees. In large mixing bowl, fold cheese, melted butter, sour cream, onion, salt and pepper into the potatoes. Milk may be added for a creamier texture. Place into a greased 9x13-inch casserole. Dot with the 4 tablespoons butter. Sprinkle with bacon. Cover with foil; bake approximately 40 to 45 minutes or until bubbly and heated through. This recipe is a sure winner, not only with dinner but also with brunch.

Note: Recipe can be made ahead and refrigerated. Take out of refrigerator at least 1 hour before heating.

Yield: 8 to 10 servings

Pam D'Alessandro

Potatoes Alfredo

4-6 large potatoes
½ cup butter
⅔ cup heavy whipping cream
1 cup freshly grated Parmesan
  cheese
¼ teaspoon salt
¼ teaspoon freshly ground black
  pepper
Chopped fresh parsley for garnish

Peel the potatoes. Place in a large pot; cover with cold water. Bring to a boil and cook until fork-tender. Drain and cut potatoes into thick wedges, to total 4 generous cups. In a large saucepan, over medium heat, stir butter and cream together until smooth. Remove from heat; blend in cheese, salt and pepper. Add potatoes. Gently toss to coat. Spoon into a warm serving bowl and sprinkle with parsley.

Yield: 6 servings

Mary Ann Murphy

Crunch Top Potatoes

4 large potatoes, cut into ½-inch
  slices
3 tablespoons butter, melted
1 cup crushed cornflakes
½ cup shredded Cheddar cheese
  (optional)
1 teaspoon paprika
1 teaspoon sugar

Preheat oven to 350 degrees. Coat potatoes with butter in a 1½-quart baking dish. Mix cornflakes, cheese, paprika and sugar together. Sprinkle over potatoes and bake for 30 to 45 minutes, until potatoes are tender. Children really enjoy this dish!

Yield: 4 to 6 servings

Mary Ann Lasky

Cheese Fries

1½ pounds baking potatoes
1 tablespoon grated Parmesan
  cheese
1 tablespoon vegetable oil
¼ teaspoon salt
¼ teaspoon garlic powder
¼ teaspoon paprika
¼ teaspoon pepper

Preheat oven to 450 degrees. Coat a baking sheet with non-stick vegetable oil cooking spray. Peel potatoes and cut into thin strips. In large bowl, combine all other ingredients. Add potatoes and toss to coat. Arrange potatoes in single layer on baking sheet. Bake for 35 minutes or until golden; turn to cook evenly.

Yield: 4 servings

Terry Laskowski

Scalloped Potatoes

5 medium potatoes
2 cups creamy cottage cheese
¼ cup minced green onion
2 teaspoons salt
1 cup sour cream
1 clove garlic, minced (optional)
½ cup shredded Cheddar cheese

Place potatoes, with skins on, in medium pot; cover with water. Boil just until tender when pierced with a fork (do not overcook). Let cool; peel and cut potatoes into 1-inch cubes. Set aside. Preheat oven to 350 degrees. In large bowl, combine cottage cheese, onion, salt, sour cream and garlic. Fold potatoes gently into mixture. Place in a greased 2-quart baking dish. Top with Cheddar cheese. Bake for 40 to 45 minutes. Let stand 10 minutes before serving.

Yield: 6 to 8 servings

Katie Johnson

Hot German Potato Salad

6 large white potatoes, peeled and cut into ½-inch cubes
1 onion, diced
2 teaspoons salt, divided
4 slices bacon, diced
2 tablespoons flour
2 tablespoons sugar
1 teaspoon prepared mustard
¼ teaspoon freshly ground black pepper
⅓ cup cider vinegar
⅔ cup water
½ teaspoon celery seed
1 tablespoon finely chopped fresh parsley

Place potatoes in a large pot. Cover with water. Add onion and 1 teaspoon of the salt. Cover and cook until fork-tender. Drain well. Fry bacon in a 10 to 12-inch skillet. (Do not drain bacon fat.) Add flour to skillet; mix until smooth. Add sugar, mustard, pepper and remaining 1 teaspoon of the salt. Over low heat, mix well. Add vinegar, water and celery seed. Increase to medium heat; cook several minutes until thickened. Place potatoes in skillet; toss with warm mixture to coat. Transfer to serving bowl and sprinkle parsley on top. Serve hot.

Yield: 6 to 8 servings

Kathy Raffensperger

Colcannon

An Irish Potato Dish

2 pounds white potatoes
½ pound green cabbage, quartered
6 slices bacon, cut into 1-inch pieces
6 tablespoons butter
1 teaspoon minced onion
3 tablespoons cream
¼ cup milk
½ teaspoon pepper
½ teaspoon salt

Peel potatoes. Place in a large pot and cover with cold water. Cover and cook for ½ to 1 hour, until soft. Using a slotted spoon, remove potatoes and set aside. Cook cabbage and bacon in reserved water until cabbage softens. Drain and discard bacon. Pass potatoes and cabbage through sieve. In a large saucepan, melt butter. Add onion and sauté until opaque. Add cream, milk and seasonings. Stir over low heat. Add potatoes and cabbage. Heat thoroughly; do not boil. Serve hot.

Yield: 6 servings

Kathy Cauley

Baked Potatoes Stuffed with Spinach and Cheese

4 large russet potatoes
1 (10-ounce) package frozen
   chopped spinach
2 teaspoons olive oil
2 tablespoons finely chopped
   garlic
¼ cup plain non-fat yogurt
¼ cup non-fat milk
Salt and pepper, to taste
2 tablespoons freshly grated
   Parmesan cheese

Preheat oven to 400 degrees. Pierce potatoes in several places with a fork. Bake until potatoes are tender, about 1 hour. Cool potatoes slightly. Reduce oven temperature to 350 degrees. Cook spinach in microwave according to package instructions. Drain well. Cut potatoes in half lengthwise. Using a spoon, scoop out insides of potatoes, leaving ¼-inch thick shell; set shells aside. Place scooped-out potato in bowl and mash slightly. Arrange potato shells on baking sheet. Heat oil in large skillet over medium heat. Add garlic and sauté 30 seconds. Add spinach and sauté 1 to 2 minutes. Remove from heat. Add potato, yogurt and milk; stir until blended. Season with salt and pepper. Spoon into potato shells, dividing mixture equally and mounding slightly. Sprinkle on Parmesan cheese. Bake until tops are golden and potatoes are heated through, about 25 minutes. A great presentation. Delicious, and low fat too!

Note: Potatoes can be prepared and stuffed a day ahead. Cover and refrigerate. Bring to room temperature before baking.

Yield: 8 servings

Pam D'Alessandro

Lemon Horseradish Potatoes

¼ cup olive oil
½ teaspoon salt
⅛ teaspoon pepper
2 tablespoons horseradish
8 small new potatoes
2-3 teaspoons lemon juice, to taste
¼ cup snipped fresh parsley

Preheat oven to 350 degrees. In small bowl, combine olive oil, salt, pepper and horseradish. Set aside. Wash potatoes and peel a strip (approximately ½-inch wide) around each. Place potatoes in a 1½ to 2-quart glass casserole. Pour olive oil mixture on top; stir, being sure to coat potatoes completely. Cover and bake for 50 minutes, stirring every 20 minutes. When cooking is complete, add lemon juice and parsley, stirring gently to coat potatoes. Serve hot or at room temperature.

Yield: 4 servings

Anne Franks Gillespie

Whipped Cream Potatoes

10 large potatoes
1 pint whipping cream
1 pint half & half
8-16 tablespoons butter, divided,
    to taste
Salt and pepper, to taste

Place potatoes, skins on, in a large pot. Cover with water and boil until fork-tender. Preheat oven to 400 degrees. Peel potatoes; shred with a grater. In a small bowl; mix together cream and half & half. Grease a 3-quart casserole. Spread ⅓ of the potatoes over bottom of casserole. Dot with ⅓ of the butter; season with salt and pepper. Pour cream mixture over potatoes, just to cover. Continue layering potatoes, butter, salt and pepper until all potatoes are used. Top with remaining cream mixture. Bake, uncovered, for 35 to 50 minutes.

Note: Potatoes can be prepared up to 4 hours ahead. Refrigerate until use.

Variation: Substitute milk for half & half or cream; increase the amount of salt and pepper used.

Yield: 10 servings

Dorianne DiGregorio

117

Lola's Sweet Potatoes

2 cups cooked, peeled and mashed
   sweet potatoes
½ cup butter, softened
½ cup granulated sugar
½ cup brown sugar
1 cup milk
¼ cup orange juice
1 teaspoon grated orange rind
4 eggs
1 cup chopped pecans
2 cups miniature marshmallows
   (optional)

Preheat oven to 350 degrees. Using an electric mixer, beat together all ingredients, except pecans and marshmallows. Stir in pecans. Spoon potatoes into a greased 2-quart casserole or baking dish. Top with marshmallows. Bake, uncovered, for 30 minutes.

Note: Canned sweet potatoes may be used in place of fresh.

Yield: 8 servings

Mary Jane Driscoll Kelly (In Memory)

Holiday Mashed Potatoes

8-10 medium potatoes, peeled
1 (8-ounce) package cream cheese,
   cut into pieces
4 tablespoons butter or
   margarine, cut into pieces
½ cup sour cream
½ cup milk
2 eggs, lightly beaten
¼ cup finely chopped onion
1 teaspoon salt
Pepper, to taste

Place potatoes in a large pot. Cover with water and boil until fork-tender. Drain. Place potatoes in a large mixing bowl. Using an electric mixer, mash potatoes. Add cream cheese and butter. Beat until well-mixed. Add sour cream. In a separate bowl, mix together milk, eggs, onion, salt and pepper. Add to potatoes. Beat until light and fluffy. Place potatoes in a well-greased 9-inch round casserole. Refrigerate several hours or overnight. Preheat oven to 350 degrees. Cover and bake for 30 minutes. Uncover and bake an additional 15 minutes.

Note: Great recipe to prepare ahead— eliminates last minute mashing of potatoes.

Yield: 8 servings

Jean Gaffney and Mary Jo Matthews

Bubbles and Squeak

Colcannon or Cally

2 cups shredded cabbage
1 small onion, finely chopped
3 tablespoons bacon drippings
2 cups mashed potatoes
Salt and pepper, to taste

Steam cabbage for 15 minutes. In large skillet, sauté onion in bacon drippings until soft. Add cabbage to skillet; stir for 2 minutes over low-medium heat. Fold in mashed potatoes. Press mixture down in skillet; cook 5 minutes or until brown. Turn and brown on other side. Season with salt and pepper. In Ireland, this traditional dish is served for Halloween. The sounds that the "Bubbles and Squeak" makes as it cooks are the witches escaping.

Yield: 4 servings

Mary Jane Driscoll Kelly (In Memory)

Thanksgiving Sweet Potato Soufflé

6 cups cooked, peeled and mashed sweet potatoes (about 4 large sweet potatoes, baked)
4 eggs, beaten
2 teaspoons vanilla extract
⅔ cup flour
2 cups milk
1½ cups chopped pecans
1½ cups flaked coconut
½ cup brown sugar

Preheat oven to 350 degrees. Using an electric mixer, beat together potatoes, eggs, vanilla, flour and milk. Place mixture in a greased 9x13-inch baking dish. In a separate bowl, combine pecans, coconut and brown sugar. Sprinkle over potatoes. Bake, uncovered, for 45 minutes.

Yield: 6 servings

Charlotte Broome

Three Bean Casserole

8 slices bacon
2 large onions, sliced
1½ teaspoons garlic powder
1 teaspoon dry mustard
½ cup brown sugar
¼ cup cider vinegar
1 (16-ounce) can dark red kidney
   beans, drained
1 (16-ounce) can New England
   baked beans, undrained
1 (16-ounce) can green lima beans,
   drained

In a large skillet, fry bacon until crisp. Drain on paper towels. Crumble bacon; set aside. Discard bacon fat. Place onion, garlic powder, mustard, brown sugar and vinegar in skillet; cover and cook for 20 minutes over medium heat. Preheat oven to 350 degrees. Combine beans in a 3-quart casserole. Stir in bacon and onion mixture. Bake, covered, for 45 minutes.

Yield: 10 servings

Anne Kuligowski

Baked Beans Canadienne

1 pound navy pea beans
1 medium onion, finely chopped
¼ cup brown sugar
1 teaspoon dry mustard
½ cup molasses
3 tablespoons ketchup
½ pound salt pork, thinly sliced

Rinse and drain beans. Place beans in a 4 to 8-quart pot. Cover with cold water to 4 inches above the level of the beans. Do one of the following: soak beans for 12 hours and, using the same water, boil for 10 minutes *or* soak beans for 6 hours and, using the same water, boil for 45 minutes. Drain beans; reserve water. In a large bowl, mix together onion, brown sugar, mustard, molasses and ketchup. Add beans; toss to coat. In a 3-quart casserole, or preferably a large clay bean pot, layer bean mixture alternately with slices of salt pork. Add enough bean water to cover. Bake, covered, at 200 degrees for 7 to 8 hours. Add water, as needed, to keep beans covered throughout cooking.

Yield: Serves a crowd!

Mathilda Roberge

Cannellini Fresca

4 cups dried cannellini beans
16 cups water
10 teaspoons vegetarian bouillon
   powder
8 sprigs fresh sage, with leaves
10 cloves garlic, crushed
1¾ cups extra-virgin olive oil,
   divided, to taste
2 teaspoons salt, and to taste
Freshly ground black pepper, to
   taste
8 fresh sage leaves, minced
10 tablespoons minced scallions or
   green onion

Rinse and pick through the beans; discard any that float or are discolored. Place beans in a 6 to 8-quart pot. Cover with water. Soak for 6 hours. Drain beans and return to pot. Add water, bouillon, sage sprigs, garlic, ¼ cup of the olive oil, salt and pepper. Bring to a boil. Lower heat, cover and simmer for 1 to 1½ hours, until beans are tender. (Do not overcook.) Let beans cool. Using a slotted spoon, transfer beans to a large bowl; reserve broth. Add 1 cup of bean broth, minced sage leaves, scallions and ½ cup of the olive oil. Toss well to coat. Season with salt and pepper; refrigerate. Before serving, allow beans to return to room temperature; drizzle with additional ½ to 1 cup of the olive oil.

Note: Recipe is best made a day ahead. Do not use canned beans. Great Northern White beans may be substituted for cannellini beans.

Yield: 16 servings

Carole Natali

Black Bean Salsa

Beans and Vegetables:
1 (15-ounce) can black beans, drained and rinsed
½ cup chopped, seeded Roma tomatoes
1 cup (cooked or canned) white shoepeg corn, drained
¼ cup sliced green onions

Dressing:
⅓ cup canola oil
2 tablespoons lemon juice
2 tablespoons red wine vinegar
1 tablespoon minced fresh or 1 teaspoon dried thyme
¼ teaspoon ground black pepper
1 tablespoon Dijon mustard
1 teaspoon minced jalapeño peppers

In a large bowl, alternately layer ½ of the beans and vegetables. Repeat layering one more time. In a separate bowl, combine all dressing ingredients; mix thoroughly. Pour dressing over top. Gently stir. Cover and refrigerate overnight, stirring occasionally. Serve as a side dish with fish or poultry.

Note: Must be made ahead.

Yield: 4 servings

Susan Dawson

North Side

*T*he North Side, a city in its own right until its annexation to the City of Pittsburgh in 1907, was formerly known as Allegheny. The name is derived from "Allegewi," an Indian tribe who settled along the banks of the Allegheny River.

The first known settler of this area was Andrew Long who settled at the base of Monument Hill in 1740. By 1800, Allegheny had a population of 275, most of whom were farmers, and by 1826, Allegheny's population had reached 1000.

Allegheny was incorporated as a city in 1840. Its citizens worked as bow string makers, wagoners, porter bottlers, chair makers and weavers. Others cut nails, manufactured swords, made soap, brushes, shoes, saddles, harnesses and sails. By the late 19th century, Allegheny was very prosperous with established steel mills and textile, glass and cotton factories.

As Allegheny grew economically, it sought political expansion and annexed several surrounding communities, including Troy Hill, the East Street Valley, Spring Garden, Manchester and Woods Run. By 1900, Allegheny's population was 53,000. Alleghenians were an ethnic mix of early English settlers, followed by Scotch-Irish, Scots and Irish. Germans came in large numbers as did Croatians, Czechs, Slovaks, Carpatho-Russians, Ukrainians and Greeks. All were drawn to the city's promise of employment.

Reflecting the variety of work activity that went on there, Alleghenians achieved great prominence in numerous fields. Andrew Carnegie, H.J. Heinz, Samuel Pierpont Langley and Stephen Collins Foster all worked there. Two apostles of the avant-garde, Gertrude Stein and Martha Graham were born in Allegheny.

In 1903, Exposition Park, at School Street and Shore Avenue, was the site of the first baseball World Series with Pittsburgh losing to Boston. Ironically, Three Rivers Stadium was built very close to this location. New baseball and football stadiums ensure that the North Side remains the "home of the Pirates and the Steelers." ♥

Spinach Stuffed Turkey Loaf

Meat mixture:
1½ pounds ground turkey breast
½ cup Italian bread crumbs
½ cup milk or ½ cup tomato juice
2 tablespoons chopped onion
½ teaspoon garlic powder
½ teaspoon black pepper
1 egg

Filling:
1 (10-ounce) package frozen
    chopped spinach, thawed and
    drained
1 cup shredded Cheddar cheese
¼ cup grated Parmesan cheese

Topping:
½ cup ketchup
1 tablespoon brown sugar
1 teaspoon prepared mustard

Preheat oven to 350 degrees. In large bowl, combine all meat mixture ingredients; mix well. Place on waxed paper and pat into a 9x12-inch rectangle. Combine all filling ingredients; mix well. Spread filling evenly over meat. Roll up from 9-inch side. Press ends and sides closed to seal filling inside meat roll. Place seam-side down in a loaf pan or on a baking sheet with sides. Bake for 1 hour. Combine all topping ingredients. Spoon topping over loaf and bake an additional 30 to 35 minutes.

Yield: 6 to 8 servings

Cynthia A. McKenna

Easy Chicken Nuggets

1 pound boneless chicken breast
¼ cup "quick" oats
¼ cup cornflake crumbs
¼ cup Italian bread crumbs
¼ cup grated Parmesan cheese
1 cup milk
¼ cup melted butter or margarine

Preheat oven to 350 degrees. Trim chicken and cut into 1-inch cubes. Mix oats, cornflake crumbs, bread crumbs and Parmesan cheese in a (1-gallon) zip-top plastic bag. Moisten chicken pieces in milk; place in bag and shake to coat. Arrange chicken pieces on baking sheet and drizzle with melted butter. Bake for 15 to 20 minutes.

Yield: 4 to 6 servings

Lisa Anselmo

Bayou Turkey Burger

1 pound ground turkey
2 scallions with 3-inches of green, thinly sliced
1 red bell pepper, finely chopped
1 teaspoon finely minced garlic
2 tablespoons chopped cilantro leaves
¾ teaspoon dried thyme
½ teaspoon ground cumin
½ teaspoon paprika
¼ teaspoon red pepper flakes
¼ teaspoon seasoned salt
⅛ teaspoon black pepper
4 hamburger buns, toasted
Mayonnaise
1 small ripe avocado, sliced

Prepare a barbecue grill or preheat broiler. (Oil grill rack, if barbecuing.) Place turkey, scallions, bell pepper, garlic, cilantro, thyme, cumin, paprika, red pepper flakes, seasoned salt and pepper in large bowl; mix together well. Form mixture into 4 burger patties. Grill or broil 3 inches from heat source until cooked through, about 5 to 6 minutes on each side. Serve immediately on toasted buns. Serve with mayonnaise and top each burger with avocado.

Yield: 4 servings

Clara Lee

Another One Dish Chicken

1½ pounds boneless chicken
1 pound fettuccine
12 tablespoons butter
12 tablespoons flour
2 cups chicken broth
2 cups milk
⅛ teaspoon salt
⅛ teaspoon pepper
⅛ teaspoon paprika
⅛ teaspoon poultry seasoning
⅛ teaspoon seasoned salt
⅛ teaspoon garlic salt
¼ cup grated Parmesan cheese, divided
½ cup seasoned bread crumbs

Place chicken in large cooking pot. Cover with water. Boil for ½ hour, until chicken is fully cooked. Reserve stock. Cut chicken into 1-inch cubes and set aside. Cook fettuccine according to package directions; drain and set aside. Preheat oven to 350 degrees. Melt butter in large saucepan over low heat. Slowly stir in flour until smooth. Add 2 cups reserved stock, chicken broth and milk. Cook, stirring, until smooth and thickened. Stir in seasonings. In a 3-quart casserole, layer ½ of the fettuccine, ½ of the sauce, ½ of the chicken and ½ of the Parmesan cheese. Repeat layering. Top with bread crumbs. Bake ½ hour, until bubbly. Kids love this dish!

Note: Can be made ahead.

Yield: 8 servings

Lisa Anselmo

Walnut Fried Chicken Drumettes

24 chicken drumettes
2 cups buttermilk
1 cup flour
2 cups chopped walnuts
1½ teaspoons salt
¼ teaspoon cayenne pepper
½ teaspoon freshly ground black
    pepper
½ teaspoon paprika
Vegetable oil for frying
2 cups Roquefort Yogurt Dressing
    (see Note)

Wash chicken and place in large bowl. Cover with buttermilk and allow to soak for 1 hour in refrigerator. Combine flour, nuts, salt, cayenne, pepper and paprika. Using a blender or food processor, process until nut mixture is finely ground. Coat chicken with nut mixture; place on rack to air dry for 15 minutes. Preheat oven to 350 degrees. Heat 1 inch of oil in a 10 to 12-inch skillet. Fry chicken for 3 to 5 minutes, until crisped and brown on all sides. Transfer to a rack placed atop a baking sheet. Bake for approximately 15 minutes until meat pulls easily off the bone. Serve hot, at room temperature or chilled. Serve with Roquefort Yogurt Dressing and fresh cut celery sticks.

Note: Recipe for Roquefort Yogurt Dressing can be found in the Beverages, Sauces and Marinades section.

Yield: Serves 4 to 6

Tony DiLembo

Fireman's Chicken BBQ

1 whole chicken, cut into pieces
1 cup olive oil
1 cup white vinegar
¼-½ cup seasoned salt, to taste

Place chicken in large baking dish. In medium bowl, mix oil, vinegar and salt. Pour over chicken while stirring to keep salt evenly distributed. Marinate for at least ½ hour. Prepare outdoor grill. Cook chicken over hot coals, turning frequently. Brush with marinade occasionally while grilling. Discard marinade after use.

Yield: 3 to 4 servings

Karen Storb

Chicken and Sour Cream Enchiladas

8 tablespoons butter, divided
1½ large onions, sliced, divided
1½ pounds chicken breast,
  skinned and boned
4 cloves garlic, crushed
½ teaspoon salt
½ teaspoon white pepper
1 cup sour cream
8 (8 to 10-inch) flour tortillas
½ pound Monterey Jack cheese,
  grated
1 (16-ounce) jar mild picante
  sauce

Using an electric skillet set at 200 degrees, melt 4 tablespoons of the butter. Sauté ⅔ of the onion until soft. Place chicken breasts in skillet. Place remaining onion on top. Sprinkle garlic, salt and pepper over chicken. Place remaining 4 tablespoons of the butter evenly on top of chicken breasts. Cover and cook 30 minutes. Do not uncover skillet. Let cool 45 minutes to 1 hour. Preheat oven to 350 degrees. In large bowl, tear up cooked chicken. Add onions and ½ of the liquid from cooking; mix well. Stir in sour cream until chicken is well-coated. Place equal amounts of mixture just off center on each tortilla and roll tightly. Place, seam-side down, in a shallow, well-greased 9x13-inch baking pan. (Enchiladas should be side by side.) Top with Monterey Jack and pour picante sauce in lines across top of enchiladas. Cover with aluminum foil and bake for 35 to 40 minutes.

Variation: Substitute hot for mild picante sauce.

Yield: 4 to 6 servings

Martha Elder

Chicken in Orange Sauce

4-6 chicken breasts
½ teaspoon salt
8 tablespoons butter
2 tablespoons flour
2 tablespoons sugar
¼ teaspoon dry mustard
¼ teaspoon cinnamon
⅛ teaspoon ginger
1½ cups orange juice
3 cups hot steamed rice

Season chicken breasts with salt. In a large skillet, melt butter and brown chicken. Remove chicken; set aside. Add flour, sugar, mustard, cinnamon and ginger to skillet, stirring to make a smooth paste. Gradually stir in orange juice. Cook, stirring, until mixture thickens and comes to a boil. Reduce heat. Add chicken breasts, cover, and simmer until chicken is tender, about 20 to 25 minutes. Serve with rice.

Yield: 4 to 6 servings

Anne McCafferty

Grilled Pesto-Prosciutto Chicken with Basil Cream

Chicken:

**8 chicken breast halves, skinned
  and boned**
**8 (1-ounce) slices prosciutto or
  ham**
½ cup pesto
¼ cup olive oil
2 cloves garlic, minced
¼ teaspoon pepper

Basil Cream:

⅓ cup dry white wine
3 shallots, chopped
1½ cups whipping cream
¼ cup minced fresh basil
1 cup chopped canned tomatoes

To prepare chicken, place each chicken breast half between 2 sheets of plastic wrap. Using a smooth meat mallet or rolling pin, flatten chicken to ¼-inch thickness. Place 1 slice of prosciutto and 1 tablespoon pesto in center of each chicken breast. Roll up crosswise and secure with a toothpick. Cover chicken and chill (overnight, if desired). Prepare outdoor grill. Let chicken stand at room temperature 15 minutes before grilling. Combine olive oil, garlic and pepper in small bowl. Grill chicken over medium coals, 15 to 20 minutes, or until cooked through. While chicken is grilling, turn and brush occasionally with olive oil mixture. To prepare basil cream, combine wine and shallots in medium saucepan. Bring to a boil and cook about 2 minutes, or until liquid is reduced to about ¼ cup. Add whipping cream, return to a boil, stirring continuously. Cook 8 to 10 minutes or until reduced to 1 cup. Continue stirring; add basil and tomato. Cook just until heated. Arrange chicken rolls on a platter; drizzle lines of the basil cream across top. Serve remaining sauce on the side.

Yield: 6 to 8 servings

Mary Roberge

Chicken Breasts with Asparagus and Artichokes

6 whole chicken breasts, boned and skinned
6 large or 12 small fresh asparagus spears
6 (1½-ounce) slices mozzarella cheese, cut in half, divided
6 large fresh mushrooms, sliced
1 (14-ounce) can artichoke hearts, drained and chopped
1 tablespoon diced pimento or roasted red pepper
½ teaspoon salt
¼ teaspoon pepper
1 cup all-purpose flour
2 eggs, beaten
1 cup fine dry bread crumbs
3 tablespoons butter or margarine
3 tablespoons vegetable oil

Preheat oven to 350 degrees. Pound chicken breasts to ¼-inch thickness. Snap off tough ends of asparagus. Arrange 1 large or 2 small pieces of asparagus, 1 cheese slice and the slices of 1 mushroom on half of each chicken breast. Top with artichoke hearts and pimentos. Season with salt and pepper. Fold other half of each breast over vegetables. Secure with wooden picks. Dredge chicken in flour, dip in beaten egg and coat with bread crumbs. Combine butter and oil in a large skillet; melt over medium heat. Add chicken and cook 7 minutes on each side or until browned. Remove chicken from skillet; drain on paper towels. Place chicken on baking sheet. Top with remaining cheese slices. Bake 15 minutes or until cheese melts and chicken is done.

Note: See recipe for Grilled Pesto-Prosciutto Chicken for directions on how to pound chicken.

Yield: 6 servings

Shawn Gatto

Lemon Chicken with Thyme

3 tablespoons flour
½ teaspoon salt
¼ teaspoon pepper
4 (4-ounce) skinless, boneless
    chicken breasts
2 tablespoons olive oil, divided
1 tablespoon butter or margarine
1 medium onion, coarsely chopped
1 cup chicken broth
3 tablespoons lemon juice
½ teaspoon thyme
Lemon wedges (optional)
2 tablespoons chopped fresh
    parsley (optional)

In a plastic or paper bag, combine flour, salt and pepper. Shake to mix. Add chicken breasts and shake to lightly coat. Remove chicken and reserve excess flour. In large skillet, heat 1 tablespoon of the olive oil over medium heat. Add chicken and brown on one side, about 5 minutes. Add the remaining 1 tablespoon olive oil to skillet. Turn chicken and brown well on second side, about 5 minutes longer. Transfer chicken to a plate and set aside. Add butter to skillet. Add onion and cook, stirring, until tender, about 2 to 3 minutes. Add the reserved flour, stirring until smooth, about 1 minute. Add broth, lemon juice and thyme. Bring mixture to a boil, stirring continuously. Return chicken to skillet. Reduce heat to medium-low. Cover and simmer until chicken is cooked through, about 20 minutes. Serve with lemon wedges and sprinkle with parsley.

Variation: After chicken is returned to skillet, add capers (rinsed and drained) or fresh sliced mushrooms.

Yield: 4 servings

Marcella Karvellis McGuire

Chicken Florentine

6 (8-ounce) chicken breast halves
1 cup seasoned bread crumbs
2 tablespoons olive oil
2 tablespoons butter
2 cups marinara sauce (see Note)
½ cup dry red wine
1½ cups chicken stock, boiling hot
1 cup uncooked long grain rice
1 (2½-ounce) can sliced black olives
2 (10-ounce) packages frozen chopped spinach, thawed and pressed dry
1 cup ricotta cheese
2 eggs, beaten
Salt, to taste
¼ cup grated Parmesan cheese

Preheat oven to 350 degrees. Coat chicken breasts with bread crumbs. Heat oil and butter in a 12-inch skillet. Add chicken breasts; sauté until brown. Remove from pan and set aside. In a bowl, combine marinara sauce and wine. Place 1 cup of the sauce in skillet. Add chicken stock, rice and olives. Stir, over low heat, scraping bottom of skillet, for 1 minute. Transfer mixture to a lightly oiled 3-quart casserole or paella pan. Arrange chicken on top of rice. Cover and bake for 20 minutes. Turn chicken, re-cover and bake for an additional 25 minutes. While chicken is baking, combine spinach, ricotta, eggs and salt. Spoon spinach mixture around edge of baking dish. Pour remaining sauce over chicken. Sprinkle with Parmesan cheese. Bake, uncovered, until spinach mixture is heated, 10 to 15 minutes.

Note: Use your own marinara sauce recipe or refer to "Italian Gourmet" Marinara Sauce in the Beverages, Sauces and Marinades section.

Yield: 6 servings   *Carol McCloud*

Chicken with Basil Cream Sauce

4 chicken breast halves, skinned and boned
¼ cup milk
¼ cup seasoned bread crumbs
3 tablespoons butter
½ teaspoon (1 cube) chicken bouillon
½ cup water
1 cup heavy cream
½ cup packed, thinly sliced fresh basil leaves
¼ cup grated Parmesan cheese

Dip chicken into milk; coat with bread crumbs. Heat butter in large skillet. Cook chicken breasts until golden brown on both sides. Remove and keep warm. Stir bouillon and water into the same skillet. Over medium-high heat, bring to a boil, stirring to loosen brown bits. Stir in cream. Over high heat, return to a boil. Cook, stirring frequently, for 1 minute. Reduce heat to medium; add basil and cheese. Pour sauce over chicken and serve.

Yield: 4 servings   *Karen DiFiore*

Chicken Cacciatore

3 pounds chicken pieces, skinned
¼ cup olive oil
1 (35-ounce) can Italian peeled
    tomatoes, juice reserved
½ cup chopped onion
½ cup dry wine (red or white)
1 cup red, green or yellow
    peppers, thinly sliced
1 bay leaf
2 tablespoons chopped fresh basil
Salt and pepper, to taste
1 cup mushrooms, quartered
2 tablespoons corn starch mixed
    with 1 tablespoon cold water
Freshly grated Parmesan cheese

In Dutch oven or large deep skillet, sauté chicken in olive oil until golden brown. Chop the tomatoes and add to pan along with ½ cup of the reserved juice. Add onion, wine, peppers, bay leaf, basil, salt and pepper. Cover and simmer for 45 minutes. If needed, add additional juice. Add mushrooms and simmer for an additional 15 minutes. Transfer chicken to serving bowl; remove bay leaf. Add corn starch to sauce; stir until thickened. Pour sauce over chicken. Serve over pasta or noodles with Parmesan cheese. Very tasty and easy to prepare for a family dinner!

Yield: 6 to 8 servings

Marcia Walsh

Chicken Cordon Bleu

3 whole chicken breasts, split,
    skinned and boned
6 (1-ounce) slices Swiss cheese
6 (1-ounce) slices cooked ham
6 tablespoons butter
½ pound fresh mushrooms, sliced
1 medium onion, sliced
3 tablespoons flour
2 cups milk
⅓ cup brandy

Pound chicken breasts to ¼-inch thickness. Lay 1 slice of cheese and 1 slice of ham atop each chicken breast. Roll up and secure with toothpicks or skewers. In large skillet, melt butter. Brown chicken rolls; remove from pan and set aside. Add mushrooms and onions to skillet; sauté until tender. Blend in flour. Gradually add milk and brandy, stirring continuously until thick. Return chicken to skillet and simmer approximately 20 minutes or until tender. Serve with rice or noodles.

Note: See recipe for Grilled Pesto-Prosciutto Chicken for directions on how to pound chicken.

Yield: 6 servings

Mary Claire Kasunic

Sautéed Chicken Breasts in Mushroom Cream Sauce

4 chicken breast halves
¼ teaspoon salt
¼ teaspoon pepper
1 tablespoon corn oil
3 tablespoons butter, divided
1 small onion, chopped
¼ cup chopped fresh parsley
1 (13¾-ounce) can chicken broth
12 button mushrooms, sliced
½ cup sour cream

Season chicken breasts with salt and pepper. In Dutch oven or large deep skillet, heat oil and 1 tablespoon of the butter. Sauté onion until translucent, 5 to 8 minutes. Add parsley and stir for 1 minute. Add chicken to skillet; brown on both sides. Add broth. Cover skillet and simmer until chicken is cooked through, about 40 minutes. Add mushrooms, re-cover and cook until mushrooms are tender, about 8 minutes. Remove chicken to a plate and cover with foil to keep warm. Increase heat. Boil until liquid is reduced to about ¾ cup. Stir in sour cream and remaining 2 tablespoons of the butter. Return to a boil and stir until thickened. Return chicken to skillet; re-heat. Serve chicken and sauce over egg noodles or pasta.

Yield: 4 servings

Jan Grice

Baked Rainbow Trout

2 (7 to 8-ounce) rainbow trout
**   fillets, butterflied**
½ teaspoon seasoned salt
½ teaspoon pepper
½ teaspoon celery salt
1 teaspoon dried basil
1 teaspoon dried oregano
1 tablespoon fresh lemon juice
3 tablespoons butter, melted

Preheat oven to 350 degrees. Arrange fish in a greased 9x13-inch baking dish, skin-side down. In small bowl, mix dry seasonings together. Sprinkle over top of fish. Drizzle on lemon juice, then butter. Bake for 20 minutes or until fish flakes easily.

Note: Trout can also be grilled.

Variation: Any type of trout may be substituted.

Yield: 2 servings

Mary Anne McGuire

Fried Mealed Catfish

2-3 cups vegetable shortening
1 cup corn meal
½ cup all-purpose flour
2 teaspoons salt
1 teaspoon pepper
½ teaspoon onion salt
1 pound of boneless catfish fillets
Lemon wedges (optional)

Heat shortening to 365 degrees in deep fryer or deep, heavy saucepan. Combine corn meal, flour, salt, pepper and onion salt in a paper or plastic bag. Put 3 to 4 pieces of fish in bag at a time. Shake until well coated. Fry fish until brown and tender. Garnish with lemon wedges.

Yield: 2 servings

Sharon Lyles

Crab Cakes with Pink Grapefruit Sauce

Sauce:
1½ cups strained pink grapefruit juice
¾ cup dry white wine
6 large shallots, sliced
15 whole white peppercorns
1 cup plus 2 tablespoons chilled unsalted butter, cut into pieces

Crab cakes:
¾ pound crabmeat, picked through
¼ cup minced celery
¼ cup minced red onion
3 tablespoons mayonnaise
1 egg, slightly beaten
2 tablespoons diced, canned mild green chilies
1 teaspoon Worcestershire sauce
2¼ cups fresh bread crumbs, divided
2 tablespoons unsalted butter

To prepare sauce, combine all ingredients except chilled butter in large, heavy saucepan. Boil until liquid is reduced to 3 tablespoons, about 20 minutes. Strain; return to saucepan and set aside. To prepare crab cakes, combine crabmeat, celery, onion, mayonnaise, egg, chilies, Worcestershire and ¼ cup of the bread crumbs in a bowl. Divide mixture into 8 mounds. Flatten into ¾-inch thick patties. Coat crab cakes in remaining 2 cups crumbs, covering completely. Preheat oven to 180 degrees. Melt butter in large, heavy skillet over medium-high heat. Add crab cakes in batches and cook until golden brown, about 4 minutes per side. Transfer to baking sheet; keep warm in oven. Bring sauce to a simmer. Reduce heat to low. Gradually add chilled butter, whisking until melted. Transfer crab cakes to plates. Spoon sauce around crab cakes and serve.

Note: Sauce can be prepared a day ahead. Cover and refrigerate. Crab cakes can be prepared 2 hours ahead. Cover and refrigerate.

Yield: 8 servings

Sandra DeBartolo

Herb Roasted Orange Salmon

2 tablespoons olive oil
¼ cup fresh orange juice
Zest of 1 orange
2 teaspoons minced garlic
2 teaspoons dried tarragon
¼ teaspoon salt
¼ teaspoon pepper
4 (8-ounce) salmon fillets
2 teaspoons freshly chopped
    chives

In large bowl, whisk together olive oil, orange juice, zest, garlic, tarragon, salt and pepper. Add salmon. Marinate for 1 hour at room temperature. Preheat oven to 475 degrees. Place salmon skin-side down in glass baking dish. Pour marinade on top. Bake 7 to 10 minutes, until salmon flakes easily. Remove from oven. Sprinkle with fresh chives and serve.

Yield: 4 servings

Maria Sisco

Stone Harbor Crab Brunch

2 eggs, beaten
2 cups milk
2 cups seasoned croutons
½ pound Cheddar cheese, grated
1 tablespoon minced onion
1 tablespoon minced parsley
Salt and pepper, to taste
1 pound lump crabmeat, picked
    through
¼ cup grated Parmesan cheese

Preheat oven to 325 degrees. In large bowl, combine all ingredients except Parmesan cheese. Pour into a greased shallow 2-quart casserole. Sprinkle on Parmesan cheese. Bake, uncovered, for 1 hour or until knife inserted in center comes out clean.

Note: Recipe can be made ahead; refrigerate.

Yield: 6 servings

Virginia Gatto

Shrimp Scampi

4 tablespoons butter
4-5 cloves garlic, chopped
1½ pounds large shrimp or 1
    pound jumbo shrimp, peeled
    and deveined
1 tablespoon chopped fresh parsley
⅛ teaspoon salt
⅛ teaspoon pepper
¼ cup white cooking wine

Melt butter in large skillet over low heat. Add garlic; sauté until golden. Add shrimp; sauté 5 to 10 minutes or until no longer opaque. Sprinkle with parsley, salt and pepper. Add wine; cook on high for approximately 3 minutes. Shake pan and turn shrimp while cooking. Serve over rice. A quick and delicious seafood entrée.

Yield: 4 servings

136

Joanne Willey

Lemon Grilled Shrimp

24 large shrimp, peeled and deveined, with tails left on

Marinade:
½ cup lemon juice
½ cup vegetable oil
1 tablespoon finely chopped fresh parsley
2 cloves garlic, minced
2 teaspoons grated lemon rind
2 teaspoons dry mustard
¼ teaspoon cayenne pepper
Pinch of black pepper

Place shrimp in a plastic zip-top bag and set in a bowl. Combine all marinade ingredients and stir well. Pour marinade into bag; close tightly and squeeze gently to coat shrimp. Refrigerate for 30 minutes. Remove shrimp from bag, reserving marinade. Thread shrimp onto skewers. Oil grill rack and prepare outdoor grill. Cook shrimp over medium heat, brushing often with marinade, until pink and firm to the touch, approximately 2 minutes on each side. Discard marinade after use.

Note: Shrimp and marinade can be prepared up to 4 hours in advance of grilling.

Yield: 6 to 8 servings

Anne Price

Seafood Casserole

1 pound jumbo lump crabmeat, picked through
1½ pounds medium raw shrimp, cleaned
1 pound sea sticks, cut into 1-inch pieces
1½ cups finely chopped celery
½ cup finely chopped onion
1 cup chopped green pepper
1 cup chopped red pepper
1 cup Hellmann's mayonnaise
1 tablespoon Worcestershire sauce
½ teaspoon salt
½ teaspoon paprika

Preheat oven to 400 degrees. Place seafood in large bowl. Place chopped vegetables on paper towels and pat dry; toss with seafood. Mix mayonnaise, Worcestershire and salt in small bowl. Stir into seafood mixture. Place in a 2-quart baking dish and sprinkle with paprika. Bake for 25 minutes.

Yield: 6 to 8 servings

Georgina Senger

Perfect Lobster Tail

2 (8 to 10-ounce) lobster tails
4 tablespoons unsalted butter,
    melted, divided
Paprika for sprinkling
½ cup clarified butter (see Note)
1 lemon, seeded and cut into
    wedges

Preheat oven to 450 degrees. Using kitchen shears, cut down the middle of the lobster shells, leaving tail flippers intact. Cut through underside membranes where they meet shell on both sides, from top of tail to flippers. Pull off membranes and discard. Gently pry tail meat from shells, keeping it attached at the flipper ends. Pull tails gently through shell cuts and lay tailmeat atop the outside of the shells. Place shells, with lobster meat on top, in a baking dish. Brush meat with melted butter. Bake for 8 to 10 minutes, brushing with additional melted butter after 4 minutes. Remove from oven and sprinkle with paprika. Serve with clarified butter and lemon wedges. A beautiful presentation and simply succulent.

Note: Recipe for Clarified Butter can be found in the Beverages, Sauces and Marinades section.

Yield: 2 servings

Julia Raffensperger

Poor Man's Lobster

2 cups water
1 tablespoon vinegar
1 teaspoon salt
1 teaspoon Old Bay seasoning
1 pound frozen haddock, cut in
    large pieces

In a medium saucepan, combine water, vinegar, salt and Old Bay seasoning. Bring to a boil. Add frozen fish. Simmer 15 to 20 minutes. Drain. Serve with melted butter.

Yield: 2 servings

Jeanine Sismour

Coquilles St. Jacques

Scallop Mixture:
1 pound bay scallops
1 tablespoon butter
2 tablespoons minced onion
1 tablespoon lemon juice
¾ teaspoon salt
⅛ teaspoon paprika
¾ cup dry white wine
¼ pound mushrooms, cleaned, trimmed and coarsely chopped

Sauce:
⅓ cup butter
¼ cup all-purpose flour
1 cup whipping cream
2 teaspoons finely chopped fresh parsley

Topping:
1 tablespoon butter
⅓ cup dry bread crumbs

Rinse scallops and drain. In medium saucepan, melt 1 tablespoon butter and sauté onion until tender. Add scallops, lemon juice, salt, paprika and wine. Simmer, uncovered, for 10 minutes. Add mushrooms and simmer 2 minutes longer. Drain liquid from scallop mixture and reserve. Set scallops aside. Preheat oven to broil. To prepare sauce, melt ⅓ cup butter in medium saucepan over low heat. Blend in flour, stirring, until mixture is smooth and bubbly. Remove from heat. Stir in reserved liquid and whipping cream. Return to heat; bring to a boil stirring continuously. Boil, stirring, for 1 minute. Remove from heat. Stir in parsley. Remove ½ cup of sauce from pan and set aside. Add scallop and mushroom mixture to remaining sauce. Heat through, stirring frequently. Immediately spoon scallop mixture into 6 individual baking shells or ramekins. Place 1 tablespoon of the reserved sauce on top of each portion. For topping, melt 1 tablespoon butter in small skillet. Add bread crumbs and stir until brown. Place shells or ramekins on a baking sheet and broil 5 to 8 minutes, until bubbly and brown. Before serving, top each dish with bread crumbs.

Yield: 6 servings

Nancy Dixon

139

Manhattan-Style Seafood Stew

5 slices bacon, chopped
1 large onion, chopped
5 large shallots or green onions, chopped
3 (28-ounce) cans Italian plum tomatoes, drained
3 (8-ounce) bottles clam juice
¾ cup dry white wine
3 bay leaves
¼ teaspoon crushed red pepper flakes
1 pound small white potatoes, peeled, quartered lengthwise and thinly sliced
Salt and pepper, to taste
24 clams (about 3½ pounds), well scrubbed
½ pound sea scallops, halved crosswise
½ pound uncooked medium shrimp, peeled and deveined, tails left on
30 fresh basil leaves, thinly sliced, divided
1 tablespoon julienned lemon peel

Cook bacon in large heavy pot over medium heat until fat renders, about 5 minutes. Add onion and shallots; sauté until tender, about 8 minutes. Chop tomatoes in a blender or food processor. Add tomatoes, clam juice, wine, bay leaves and red pepper to pot. Simmer 20 minutes, stirring occasionally. Add potatoes; simmer until tender, about 20 minutes. Season with salt and pepper. Add clams; cover and simmer until clams begin to open, about 5 minutes. Add scallops and shrimp; cover and simmer until scallops and shrimp are cooked through, about 3 minutes. (Discard any clams that do not open.) Remove and discard bay leaves. Mix in ½ of the basil. Transfer stew to a soup tureen or large serving bowl. Sprinkle with remaining basil and lemon peel.

Note: Stew can be prepared one day ahead. (Do not add seafood.) Return to a simmer and add seafood as directed.

Yield: 4 to 6 servings

Sandra DeBartolo

The Hill

$\mathscr{T}$he Hill began as a residential community in the 1840's when Thomas Mellon bought farmland on the slopes nearest Downtown. He subdivided the parcels into city-size plots and sold them at a profit. Seen as a place to move up and away from the grimy urban center, Pittsburgh's first planned residential neighborhood was

comprised of well-off professionals and their families. Historically, the Hill had been the first stop for European and Chinese immigrants, as well as African-Americans, newly arrived in the city. From the 1870's through World War I and thereafter, African-Americans from the south were encouraged by labor recruiters to move to Pittsburgh. Many of these workers re-located to the Hill.

By the 1930's, the Hill was a bustling community of African-Americans, Jews and Italians. Wylie and Bedford Avenues and Logan Street were lined with "mom and pop" stores like Gropper's Grocery, Benkovitz Fish Market, Forbes Coffee Shop, Kalson's Delicatessen, Shapiro's Market, Gorton's Cod Fish and the Live Chicken Store.

Through the years, the energy and variety of people in the Hill attracted the attention of those outside the neighborhood as well. Writer Willa Cather found it a place she wanted to write about; Stephen Foster attended a black church in the Hill as a child; August Wilson captured its pulse for the theater; and legend has it that the popular television show "Hill Street Blues" was modeled after life in Pittsburgh's Hill District.

From the 1930's through the 1950's, the Hill was well known on the national jazz circuit, with places like the Crawford Grill and the Hurricane Lounge as regular stops for big name entertainers. Musicians like Ramsey Lewis, Oscar Peterson, Cannonball Adderly and others entertained in the Hill, and Adolph Menjou, Lena Horne, Art Blakey and Oscar Levant got their start here.

In the early 1990's, Crawford Square, the largest residential development undertaken in Pittsburgh in the last 30 years, broke ground in the Hill. Crawford Square is viewed by city officials and Hill residents as a vibrant enclave of hundreds of people that has sparked not only private sector housing development, but retail development as well. The development's tree-lined streets and pastel townhouses with neat lawns, have attracted a diverse community of buyers and renters. ♥

Three Generations Pork Roast with Sauce

6 cloves garlic, minced
½ teaspoon chopped fresh parsley
½ teaspoon salt
½ teaspoon pepper
1 (2 to 3-pound) pork roast

Sauce:
1 (28-ounce) can crushed tomatoes
4 (6-ounce) cans tomato paste
2 teaspoons chopped fresh basil
1½ teaspoons chopped fresh parsley
3 tablespoons sugar

Preheat oven to 400 degrees. Mix garlic, ½ teaspoon parsley, salt and pepper in a small bowl. Cut ½-inch slits, ½ to 1-inch deep, over top of roast (8 to 10 slits in all). Press garlic mixture into slits, rubbing any excess over the top of roast. Place pork roast into a large roaster or Dutch oven (roast should not touch the sides of pan). Roast for 1 hour. Decrease oven temperature to 325 degrees. Mix all sauce ingredients in a large bowl; add enough water for a thin consistency. Pour sauce over roast, cover and continue roasting 2 to 3 hours, until pork is fork-tender. Add water as necessary to maintain a thin sauce consistency. Slice pork; serve with sauce over a favorite pasta.

Variation: Add ½ pound of pepperoni, cut into chunks, when adding sauce to roast.

Yield: 8 to 10 servings

Fay Benedict

Barbecued Country Ribs

3 pounds country-style pork ribs
2 tablespoons butter
1 medium Vidalia onion, chopped
1½ cups ketchup
2 teaspoons salt
½ teaspoon Tabasco sauce
½ teaspoon chili powder
2 teaspoons prepared mustard
6 tablespoons light brown sugar
½-1 teaspoon garlic powder, to taste
3 cups water

Preheat oven to 450 degrees. Place ribs in a 3-quart, or larger, baking dish; do not cover. Brown meat in oven for 40 minutes, turning once. In a medium saucepan, melt butter and sauté onion until translucent. Add all remaining ingredients to saucepan, stirring until smoothly mixed. Remove meat from oven; drain fat. Reduce oven temperature to 325 degrees. Pour sauce over ribs. Bake ribs for 1 additional hour. Remove meat from bone before serving.

Yield: 6 servings

Sister Patricia Laffey

143

Pizza Casserole

1 pound bulk sausage
6 ounces cooked noodles
1 (14½-ounce) can stewed
   tomatoes
½ green pepper, diced
5 ounces grated sharp Cheddar
   cheese
1 teaspoon Italian seasoning
1 teaspoon onion powder
¼ teaspoon garlic powder
¼ cup grated Parmesan cheese

Preheat oven to 400 degrees. In a large skillet, crumble, brown and drain sausage. Add noodles, tomatoes, pepper, Cheddar cheese, Italian seasoning, onion and garlic powders. Mix well. Place in a greased 2-quart casserole; top with Parmesan cheese. Bake for 25 minutes or until lightly browned on top.

Note: Can be prepared ahead of time.

Variation: For a moister casserole, use 1½ cans of stewed tomatoes and 2 teaspoons of Italian seasoning.

Yield: 4 servings

Kelly Pollock

Beer Mustard Bratwurst

Marinade:
1 cup beer
¼ cup Dijon mustard
3 tablespoons light molasses
2 teaspoons white wine
   Worcestershire sauce
½ teaspoon ground nutmeg
¼ teaspoon ground cloves

2-3 pounds bratwurst

To prepare marinade, in a small bowl, mix together beer, mustard, molasses, white wine Worcestershire and spices. Place meat and marinade in a zip-top plastic bag; seal tightly. Marinate in refrigerator 8 to 24 hours. Prepare outdoor grill. Grill meat, brushing occasionally with the marinade. Discard left over marinade. Terrific summer recipe!

Variation: Marinade can also be used to flavor pork chops.

Yield: 8 to 12 servings

Anne Price

Uncle Ron's Sportin' Ribs

Braising Liquid and Ribs:
4 quarts beef stock or canned beef broth
1 cup red wine vinegar
½ cup honey
1 cup tomato paste
1 teaspoon cayenne pepper
1½ tablespoons ground cumin
1½ tablespoons garlic powder
1 tablespoon ground ginger
1 tablespoon paprika
1 tablespoon salt

4 (1¼ to 1½-pound) slabs baby back ribs, cut in half

Spice mixture:
¼ cup Worcestershire sauce
¼ cup red wine vinegar
¼ cup garlic salt
½ cup paprika
¼ cup dry mustard
1 tablespoon ground white pepper
1 (12-ounce) can of beer

Barbecue Sauce:
2 cups prepared barbecue sauce
1 cup cola

Combine all braising liquid ingredients in an 8-quart (or larger) pot, stirring well over medium heat. Add ribs to braising liquid; simmer for exactly 1 hour and 45 minutes (do not overcook or meat will fall off of the bones). Remove ribs and place each ½-slab on separate sheets of aluminum foil; set aside. Combine all spice mixture ingredients in a medium bowl, adding beer slowly as the final ingredient. Evenly coat each rib slab with the spice mixture. Wrap each slab in the aluminum foil and refrigerate until ready to cook. In a medium bowl, mix barbecue sauce and cola together. Preheat oven to 400 degrees; heat outdoor grill. Prior to baking, wipe spice mixture off of ribs. Arrange ribs on foil-lined baking sheets. Coat ribs with barbecue sauce; bake in oven for 10 minutes; transfer to grill and barbecue just long enough to char.

Note: Ribs will keep in refrigerator, wrapped in foil and coated in spice mixture, for up to 4 days. Great recipe to make ahead!

Yield: 6 to 8 servings

Ron Hillenburg

Pennsylvania-Dutch Baked Spareribs

4-5 pounds (2 strips) spareribs
Salt and pepper, to taste
1 medium onion, chopped
¼ cup butter or margarine
1½ cups pared, chopped apple
2 cups soft bread cubes
1 teaspoon salt
1 teaspoon celery salt
¼ teaspoon caraway seeds
¼ teaspoon marjoram
⅛ teaspoon pepper
¾ cup apple juice, divided

Season both rib strips with salt and pepper. Preheat oven to 375 degrees. In a large skillet, sauté onion in butter. Mix in apple, bread cubes and seasonings. Add ¼ cup of the apple juice to moisten the bread. Place 1 strip of ribs on a rack in a roasting pan. Arrange bread mixture over ribs. Cover with second strip of ribs; fasten together with toothpicks or skewers. Cover and bake for 1 hour. Add the remaining apple juice to roasting pan; mix with drippings. Baste ribs well; re-cover and bake for an additional 30 minutes (continue to baste frequently throughout remaining cooking time). Reduce oven temperature to 300 degrees. Bake an additional 15 minutes. Place on a platter and remove skewers before carving into 6 pieces. An impressive looking dish!

Yield: 6 servings

Mrs. D. Schrock

Italian Sausage and Spinach Pie

1 pound bulk Italian sausage
1 medium onion, chopped
6 eggs, divided
2 (10-ounce) packages frozen chopped spinach, thawed and well-drained
16 ounces shredded mozzarella cheese
1 cup ricotta cheese
½ teaspoon garlic powder
¼ teaspoon pepper
2 (10-inch) pie crusts
1 tablespoon water

Preheat oven to 375 degrees. In a skillet, brown sausage and onion together until sausage is cooked and onion is tender; drain. Separate 1 egg; set aside yolk. In a mixing bowl, beat remaining egg white and 5 whole eggs. Stir in sausage and onion, spinach, mozzarella, ricotta, garlic powder and pepper. Line a 10-inch pie plate with 1 pie crust; add filling. Top with second crust; seal and flute edges. Cut slits in top crust. Combine water with reserved egg yolk; brush over top crust. Bake for 50 minutes or until golden brown. Let stand 10 minutes before serving.

Yield: 8 servings

Nancy Michel

Southern Pork Barbecue

1 (5-pound) pork roast
4 tablespoons butter
1 cup diced celery
2 medium onions, chopped
3 tablespoons Worcestershire
  sauce
1 cup lemon juice
4 tablespoons vinegar
4 tablespoons brown sugar
2 cups ketchup
1 cup beef broth
1-2 teaspoons salt
½ teaspoon pepper

Place meat in a large pot; add enough water to cover. Bring to a boil; reduce heat and simmer for 4 hours. Remove meat from pot; discard liquid. Shred meat into small pieces; set aside. Heat butter in a Dutch oven over medium-high heat. Sauté celery and onion for approximately 5 minutes; add remaining ingredients. Bring to a boil; reduce heat and simmer for 15 minutes. Add shredded meat and heat through. Serve on your favorite sandwich rolls. A great recipe for parties!

Note: Best made a day ahead and reheated before serving.

Variation: Substitute beef roast for pork.

Yield: 20 servings

Shawn Gatto

Veal Picatta

1½ pounds veal scallops
¾ cup flour
½ cup butter
½ cup chicken broth
1 cup dry white wine
½ teaspoon salt
Freshly ground black pepper, to
  taste
1 lemon, thinly sliced

Dredge veal in flour; shake off excess. In a large skillet, melt butter over medium heat. Sauté veal quickly to brown; remove and keep warm. Pour chicken broth into skillet. Stir well to loosen any brown residue from bottom of pan and incorporate into broth. Add wine and salt. Cook for 1 minute. Return veal to skillet; cook 2 to 3 minutes until bubbly. Season with pepper. Arrange veal on a platter and pour wine mixture over top. Garnish with lemon slices.

Variation: Season the flour, before dredging, with seasonings of choice.

Yield: 6 servings

Virginia Gatto

Ossobuco

6 veal shanks, 2-inches thick
½ cup all-purpose flour
⅓ cup olive oil
1 medium onion, finely chopped
2 cloves garlic, finely chopped
1 carrot, finely chopped
1 rib celery, finely chopped
¾ cup dry white wine
1 (28-ounce) can crushed Italian-style tomatoes
3 tablespoons chopped fresh parsley, divided
Salt and freshly ground black pepper, to taste

Dredge veal shanks in flour. Heat oil in a large heavy Dutch oven. Add veal; brown on all sides over medium heat. Remove veal from Dutch oven. Add onion, garlic, carrot and celery; sauté until lightly browned. Return veal to Dutch oven. Stir in wine. When wine is reduced by half, add tomatoes. Cover Dutch oven; reduce heat. Simmer 1½ hours or until meat falls away from the bone. Add 2 tablespoons of the parsley. Season with salt and pepper. Arrange meat and sauce on a warm platter. Garnish with the remaining parsley. Serve immediately.

Yield: 6 servings

Pam D'Alessandro

Veal Scallopini

1½ pounds veal steak, ½-inch thick
1 teaspoon salt
1 teaspoon paprika
½ cup olive oil
¼ cup lemon juice
1 clove garlic, split
1 teaspoon nutmeg
½ teaspoon sugar
¼ cup vegetable oil
¼ cup flour
1 medium onion, thinly sliced
1 green pepper, cut into strips
1 (10-ounce) can chicken broth
1 teaspoon butter
¼ pound mushrooms, sliced
6 pimento olives, sliced

Cut veal into six serving pieces and set aside. To prepare sauce, combine salt, paprika, olive oil, lemon juice, garlic, nutmeg and sugar; mix thoroughly. Place veal in a shallow baking dish and cover with mixture. Let marinate for 20 minutes; remove garlic. Heat vegetable oil in a large skillet. Reserving the marinade, dredge veal in flour and brown in oil. Add onion and green pepper; sauté until tender. Combine chicken broth with reserved marinade; pour over the veal and vegetables. Cover and simmer until meat is tender, about 30 minutes. In a separate pan, melt butter; sauté mushrooms until tender. Add mushrooms and olives to skillet and stir. Serve over noodles.

Yield: 6 servings

Margaret Campbell

48

Oriental Beef

1½-2 pounds (2-inch thick) boneless chuck
1 tablespoon peanut oil
1 cup cocktail vegetable juice
2 tablespoons dry sherry
2 tablespoons soy sauce
3 tablespoons sesame oil
2 tablespoons toasted sesame seeds
1 medium clove garlic, minced
1 cup sliced fresh mushrooms (approximately ¼ pound)
1 medium green pepper, cut in strips
1 small onion, thinly sliced

Cut meat into 3x½-inch strips. In a large skillet, brown meat in peanut oil. In a bowl, blend all remaining ingredients. Arrange meat in a 3-quart glass container. Pour blended mixture over meat and marinate in the refrigerator for at least 6 hours. Serve meat chilled or at room temperature with a small amount of the marinade. Serve with salad greens and crisp Chinese noodles.

Yield: 6 to 8 servings

Karen Raffensperger

Kao Soi

A Thai Entrée

1 pound ground beef or turkey
2 medium white onions, diced
2 medium tomatoes, diced
1 (14-ounce) can coconut milk
1 tablespoon curry paste
2 tablespoons fish sauce
1 tablespoon sugar
4 (4-ounce) packages Chinese noodles (discard seasoning packet)
1-2 tablespoons vegetable or canola oil

In a large skillet, brown meat. Drain if necessary. Add onions; cook for 2 minutes. Add tomatoes, coconut milk, curry paste, fish sauce and sugar. Cook until slightly thickened, approximately 5 to 10 minutes. Cook noodles according to package directions; drain and toss with oil. Add noodles to meat mixture. Serve in individual bowls topped with your choice of garnish.

Yield: 4 servings

Jit Bunyaratapan

Garnish Options:
1 lime, cut into wedges
1 hard boiled egg, cut into wedges
Ground red pepper, to taste
Bean sprouts

Moussaka

Greek Eggplant and Meat Casserole

Eggplant, Meat and Cheese Layers:

3 eggplants, peeled and sliced into ½-inch rounds
2 teaspoons salt, divided
2 onions, chopped
5 tablespoons butter
2 pounds ground beef or chuck
⅛ teaspoon pepper
½ teaspoon cinnamon
½ teaspoon oregano
2 (8-ounce) cans tomato sauce
½ cup red wine
¼ cup olive oil
1 cup grated Kefalotiri or Romano cheese, divided

Cream Sauce:

¼ cup butter
¼ cup flour
3 cups milk
½ teaspoon salt
⅛ teaspoon pepper
6 eggs

To prepare the eggplant and meat layers, sprinkle eggplant rounds with 1 teaspoon of the salt. Place on paper towels to remove excess moisture; set aside. In a 10 to 12-inch heavy skillet, sauté onion in butter over medium heat until brown. Add meat, the remaining 1 teaspoon of salt, pepper, cinnamon and oregano; stir, crumbling meat with a fork. When meat is evenly browned, add tomato sauce and wine. Stir well; simmer on low heat until liquid is absorbed. Remove from heat. Preheat broiler. Brush both sides of eggplant rounds with oil; place on baking sheets and broil until lightly brown. Turn and lightly brown the other side. Lower oven temperature to 350 degrees. To assemble Moussaka, arrange a layer of eggplant in a greased 9x13-inch baking pan; top with ½ of the meat mixture and ⅓ cup of the cheese. Repeat. Finish with one additional layer of eggplant and the remaining ⅓ cup of cheese. To prepare cream sauce, in a medium saucepan, melt butter over medium heat. Blend in flour until smooth. Gradually add milk, stirring, until thickened. Add salt and pepper. Remove from heat. In a large bowl, beat eggs until light and foamy. Very slowly stir hot cream sauce into eggs (to prevent curdling of eggs). Pour cream sauce over the top layer of eggplant, covering entire pan. Bake for 40 minutes. Cool slightly before cutting into squares.

Note: Moussaka can be frozen and reheated.

Variation: Substitute potato or zucchini for eggplant. To prepare, slice, brush lightly with oil, and broil. A favorite variation uses potato for the bottom layer, meat for the center layer and eggplant for the top layer.

Yield: 8 to 10 servings

Marcella Karvellis McGuire

Chili

1 tablespoon olive oil
2 cloves garlic, chopped
1 green bell pepper, seeded and
   chopped
1 hot banana pepper, seeded and
   chopped
1½ pounds beef sirloin, cut into
   1-inch pieces
1 pound lean ground beef
2 (28-ounce) cans whole tomatoes
1 (15½-ounce) can light kidney
   beans, undrained
1 (15½-ounce) can dark kidney
   beans, undrained
1 (15½-ounce) can black beans,
   undrained
4 teaspoons chili powder
4-5 shakes of Tabasco sauce
¼ teaspoon crushed red pepper
2 teaspoons cumin
Salt and pepper, to taste

Heat the olive oil in a Dutch oven or large pot. Add garlic; sauté until tender. Add both peppers; sauté until tender. Push pepper and garlic to side of pot; add sirloin and brown. Add ground beef and brown. Add tomatoes, crushing them against the side of the pot using a wooden spoon. Cook, uncovered, on medium-low heat for approximately 1 hour or until liquid has reduced. Add beans, with their liquids, and all seasonings. Bring to a boil; reduce heat and simmer, uncovered, for 2 to 3 additional hours. Serve with grated Cheddar cheese, pepperoncini or sour cream.

Yield: 6 servings

Jan Grice

Sweet Sauerbraten Round

2 teaspoons vegetable oil
1 (4-pound) eye of round beef
   roast, fat trimmed
2 medium onions, quartered
2 cloves garlic, minced
1 teaspoon allspice
1 teaspoon black pepper
1 cup apple cider
2 tablespoons light molasses
2 tablespoons cornstarch blended
   with 2 tablespoons cold water

Heat oil in a non-stick frying pan over medium heat. Brown beef on all sides. In a large crock pot or slow cooker, combine onions, garlic, allspice and pepper. Place beef in crock pot. Mix apple cider and molasses together; pour over beef. Cover and cook on low for 10 hours. Remove meat to a warm platter. Skim fat from liquid and discard. In a small saucepan, add liquid mixture and cornstarch. Cover and heat on medium-high for 15 minutes, stirring twice. Slice beef against the grain; spoon sauce over meat. For a traditional German meal, serve with potato pancakes and braised red cabbage.

Yield: 8 servings

Lynne Ada Roberge

151

Beef Stroganoff

2 tablespoons vegetable oil
2 pounds chuck roast, cut in
   1-inch cubes
1 large onion, sliced
1 (6-ounce) can tomato paste
2 tablespoons flour
4 beef bouillon cubes, dissolved in
   2 cups water
½ teaspoon salt
¼ teaspoon pepper
2 bay leaves
2 tablespoons Worcestershire
   sauce
1 pound mushrooms, sliced
18 white pearl onions
1 cup sour cream

Heat oil in a large, deep-sided skillet or Dutch oven. Add meat to skillet and brown evenly. Remove meat; set aside. Sauté the onion. While stirring, add tomato paste and flour; cook until thickened. Slowly add the bouillon, stirring until it boils. Season meat with salt and pepper; return to sauce. Add bay leaves and Worcestershire; simmer for 1 hour. Add mushrooms and pearl onions; simmer for 1 additional hour or until meat is fork-tender. Just before serving, remove bay leaves; stir in sour cream. Serve over rice or noodles.

Variation: Substitute canned or frozen pearl onions.

Yield: 6 to 8 servings

Marion Peterson

Junk in the Oven

1½ pounds ground beef
3 (10½-ounce) cans condensed
   tomato soup
6 tablespoons water
¼ teaspoon salt
¼ teaspoon pepper
3 onions, thinly sliced
3 carrots, thinly sliced
3 ribs celery, thinly sliced
3 large potatoes, peeled,
   uncooked, thinly sliced

Preheat oven to 400 degrees. In a large skillet, brown the ground beef; drain fat. In a mixing bowl, combine tomato soup, water, salt and pepper. In a 2-quart casserole, layer in the following order: ⅓ of the meat, onions, carrots, celery, potatoes and soup mixture. Repeat twice, ending with the soup mixture. Cover and bake for ½ hour. Reduce heat to 375 degrees; bake for 1 additional hour. A hearty and easy to prepare casserole that can feed a crowd!

Note: Casserole can be frozen before baking. Bring to room temperature and bake as directed.

Yield: 6 to 8 servings

Dorothy Van Wassen

Tourtiere

French-Canadian Meat Pie

½ pound ground veal
1 pound ground pork
⅔ cup chopped onion
1 teaspoon salt
¼ teaspoon pepper
¼ teaspoon ground cloves
¼ teaspoon cinnamon
½ cup water
2 (9-inch) pastry pie crusts,
  unbaked

In a large skillet, mix veal, pork, onion and spices together; add water. Cook slowly on low heat, stirring frequently, until meat loses its redness. Simmer for 1 hour until water is almost absorbed. Preheat oven to 350 degrees. Place 1 pie crust into a 9-inch pie pan. Pour meat mixture into pie shell. Cover with second crust; pinch edges together. Place 8 (¼-inch) slits, in a decorative fashion, in top crust. Bake for 45 minutes or until crust has started to brown. This traditional dish was prepared by my mother for Jour de Nöel (Christmas Day).

Note: Baked pie can be frozen for up to 2 months. Bake, unthawed, at 350 degrees for 1 hour or until piping hot.

Yield: 6 to 8 servings

Raymond Roberge

French Beef Stew

1 cup tomato juice
¼ cup tapioca
2 pounds beef chuck, cut into
  1½-inch cubes
2 medium onions, cut into eighths
3 ribs celery, diced
4 medium carrots, cut into ½-inch
  pieces
1 tablespoon sugar
1 teaspoon salt
¼ teaspoon pepper
1 tablespoon dried basil
3 medium potatoes, peeled and cut
  into wedges

Preheat oven to 300 degrees. Mix all ingredients together except for potatoes. Place in a 2½-quart casserole. Cover and bake for 2 hours. Add potatoes. Bake for 1 additional hour. Serve with crusty French bread.

Yield: 4 to 6 servings

Lorraine Raffensperger

Beef Brisket

4 pounds beef brisket
6 cloves garlic, crushed
Salt and pepper, to taste
1 teaspoon paprika, or to taste
2 tablespoons vegetable oil
2 large onions, chopped
6 carrots, chopped
4-5 ribs celery with leaves,
    chopped
1 cup water, tomato juice or
    tomato sauce
1 envelope dried onion soup mix

Preheat oven to 325 degrees. Rub meat on all sides with garlic. Season with salt, pepper and paprika. Heat oil in a heavy-bottomed casserole or Dutch oven; brown meat on all sides. Add onions, carrots and celery. Mix together water and soup mix; pour over meat and vegetables. Cover and roast for 3 hours. Remove cover; roast for an additional ½ hour. Skim off fat before serving.

Note: Best prepared 1 day in advance; skimming the fat off after the meat has cooled, prior to reheating.

Yield: 6 to 8 servings

Pam Weiss

Grilled Delmonico Roast à la Raff

1 (4-pound) rolled boneless rib
    Delmonico roast
2 tablespoons olive oil
1 tablespoon kosher salt
2 tablespoons freshly ground
    black pepper

Bring meat to room temperature. In a small bowl, mix olive oil, salt and pepper to create a paste; coat all sides of roast, pressing into crevices. Prepare an outdoor grill. Place meat directly on grill, allow to flame. Rotate meat for about 10 to 20 minutes until all sides are evenly charred; remove from grill. Place in a metal pan; cover lightly with aluminum foil. Place pan on grill and close grill lid. Using a meat thermometer, heat to desired internal temperature. Allow roast to stand 5 to 10 minutes before carving. We love it very rare, at about 130 to 140 degrees.

Note: Allow ½ pound of meat per person.

Variation: Roast can be finished in a standard oven at 350 degrees after initial blackening on grill.

Yield: 8 servings

John Raffensperger

154

Italian Stuffed Flank Steak

8 ounces fresh spinach, trimmed
½ cup dried fresh bread crumbs
½ cup freshly grated Parmesan
  cheese
¼ cup plus 1 tablespoon olive oil,
  divided
2 cloves garlic
3 roasted red bell peppers (see
  Note)
1 (1½-pound) flank steak,
  butterflied
Salt and freshly ground black
  pepper, to taste
4 ounces thinly sliced prosciutto
1 fresh hot cherry pepper cored,
  seeded and minced (optional)

Preheat oven to 350 degrees. Place spinach in a saucepan with just the water that clings to leaves from rinsing. Cover and cook over medium heat until wilted, about 5 minutes. Drain in colander; press out excess moisture using the back of a spoon. Combine spinach, bread crumbs, Parmesan, ¼ cup of the olive oil and garlic in a food processor; purée until thick and smooth. Transfer to a medium bowl. Peel, core and seed roasted peppers; cut into ½-inch strips. Open steak and season with salt and pepper. Arrange prosciutto in 1 layer over steak. Top with a layer of roasted peppers. Spread spinach mixture over top and sprinkle with minced cherry pepper. Starting with a long side, roll steak up jelly-roll style. Tie with string at 2-inch intervals; brush with remaining 1 tablespoon of the olive oil. Season with additional salt and pepper. Place steak in a shallow baking dish or pan. Bake for 40 minutes for medium rare. Cool slightly or to room temperature before slicing and serving. A great dish for any occasion!

Note: For directions on how to roast peppers see recipe for Onion and Red Pepper Tart in the Vegetables and Vegetarian Dishes section.

Variation: Use sun-dried tomatoes in place of prosciutto.

Yield: 4 to 6 servings

Pam D'Alessandro

Mexican Grilled Steak

2 (1 to 1½-pound) flank steaks
Juice of 2 limes
4 cloves garlic, crushed
⅓ cup snipped fresh or
    2 tablespoons dried oregano
2 tablespoons olive oil
2 teaspoons salt
½ teaspoon pepper

Place steaks in a shallow glass baking dish. Mix remaining ingredients together and pour over beef. Cover and marinate in refrigerator at least 8 hours, turning occasionally. (Use within 24 hours.) Grill over medium coals, turning once until desired doneness, 10 to 15 minutes. Cut beef into thin slices across the grain at a slanted angle. Discard marinade. Serve with tortillas and guacamole.

Yield: 8 servings

Marge Muldoon

Teriyaki Beefsteak

Teriyaki Sauce:
2 tablespoons soy sauce
2 tablespoons brown sugar
2 tablespoons rice or white wine
1 teaspoon grated ginger

4 (¼ to ½-pound) boneless rib
    steaks
Salt and pepper, to taste
1 green onion, chopped (optional)

In a small bowl, combine all sauce ingredients; set aside. Season steaks with salt and pepper. In a 12-inch heavy skillet, cook steaks over medium-high heat to desired doneness. Just prior to end of cooking time, drain fat and add sauce to skillet. Lower heat and sauté 1 additional minute. Serve steaks garnished with onion.

Yield: 4 servings

Yun Tahara

Rack of Lamb with Wine Sauce

2 (1½-pound) racks of lamb, trimmed
¼ cup Dijon mustard
¾ cup (packed) fresh French bread crumbs
¾ cup grated Asiago cheese
6 tablespoons chopped fresh mint, or to taste
4 cloves garlic, minced
3 tablespoons butter, softened

Wine Sauce:
2 cups beef stock
2 cups chicken stock
⅔ cup dry red wine
⅓ cup minced shallots
2 teaspoons minced fresh tarragon
1 tablespoon all-purpose flour
2 tablespoons butter, melted

Preheat oven to 450 degrees. Place lamb on a baking sheet with sides. Spread mustard over lamb. Place bread crumbs, cheese, mint, garlic and 3 tablespoons butter in bowl of a food processor; process to paste consistency. Press mixture over lamb to completely coat. Place lamb in oven for 15 minutes. Decrease oven temperature to 325 degrees. Roast to desired internal temperature, about 30 to 45 minutes. To prepare sauce, place beef and chicken stocks, wine, shallots and tarragon in a heavy saucepan. Boil over medium high heat until reduced to 1½ cups, about 40 minutes. Mix the flour with the butter, until smooth; whisk into sauce. Simmer until slightly thickened, about 3 minutes. Strain sauce; keep warm. Cut lamb between ribs into chops. Serve with sauce.

Yield: 4 to 6 servings

Antonia DeNardo Piccoli

Lamb Shanks Leider

2 small lamb shanks
  (approximately ¾ pound each)
2-3 carrots, sliced
2 large onions, sliced
1 cup chili sauce

Preheat oven to 350 degrees. Place lamb shanks side by side in the center of a large sheet of heavy duty aluminum foil. Layer carrots and onions on top of lamb. Pour chili sauce over top. Seal foil tightly. Place foil packet into a pan with sides (in case leakage occurs). Bake for 1½ hours. Reduce oven temperature to 325 degrees; bake an additional 1 hour. Remove from oven; let rest for 10 minutes before opening foil.

Yield: 2 servings

Dorothy Van Wassen

Grilled Lamb Chops

12 lamb chops
Salt and pepper, to taste
¾ cup olive oil
4 tablespoons balsamic vinegar, to taste
2-3 sprigs fresh mint, chopped

Arrange a single layer of lamb chops in a 3-quart baking dish; lightly salt both sides. In a small bowl, combine olive oil, vinegar, mint, salt and pepper. Whisk to blend; pour over lamb chops. Marinate for 10 to 15 minutes at room temperature. Prepare outdoor grill. Discard marinade. Grill chops to desired doneness.

Yield: 6 servings

Maria DePasquale

Squirrel Hill

*O*nce a wilderness whose abundance of grey squirrels conferred its name, Squirrel Hill was a favorite hunting ground of Native Americans and is, today, one of Pittsburgh's most heavily populated neighborhoods.

In 1764, Mary Girty Turner settled in the wilderness. "Old Widow Girty" originally had lived in Kittanning where she had two husbands killed by Native Americans, and a son, Simon, kidnapped. The Girty family, especially the infamous Simon, were notorious for collaborating with the British and Native Americans against Western Pennsylvania patriots during the Revolutionary War.

Squirrel Hill remained rural for a long time, with farmland stretching south of Forbes Avenue up to the 1930's. Poles and German Jews operated dairy farms in the area. As late as 1865, the only thoroughfare was Shady Avenue. A perennial reminder of the area's rural nature was established in 1889 when Mary Croghan Schenley gave the city 308 acres along Squirrel Hill's western boundary to be preserved as green space — Schenley Park.

Formerly a part of Peebles Township, Squirrel Hill was annexed to the city in 1868. In 1893 an electric street car line opened, running up Forbes Avenue from Schenley Park and down Murray Avenue to Homestead. Despite the development of the electric street car line, Murray Avenue continued to be a dirt road until 1920.

Henry Clay Frick made yet another gift of greenery to the city in 1919. One hundred and fifty acres along the neighborhood's eastern edge became Frick Park, and reinforced Squirrel Hill's rustic nature. The population soon swelled as many Eastern European Jews moved here from the Hill District. The neighborhood quickly became the center of Jewish culture in Pittsburgh, and Murray Avenue became its commercial center. Cafés, kosher food shops, delicatessens, bookstores, ethnic restaurants, designer boutiques and other distinctive businesses give this popular neighborhood a unique metropolitan mix. ♥

Apple Crisp

6 cups peeled, thinly sliced apples
⅓ cup sugar
1 teaspoon cinnamon
½ teaspoon salt
2 tablespoons butter, melted

Topping:
¾ cup sugar
½ cup all-purpose flour
⅓ cup butter, chilled

Preheat oven to 375 degrees. Mix apples, sugar, cinnamon, salt and butter together in a large bowl. Place in a greased 8-inch square baking dish or 10-inch quiche dish. Set aside. To prepare topping, combine sugar and flour. Cut in butter until crumbly; sprinkle over apples. Bake for 45 minutes or until apples are tender. Delicious served warm with vanilla ice cream or whipped cream.

Yield: 6 servings

Vinny Nally

Blueberry-Raspberry Kuchen

A German Dessert

Crust:
1½ cups flour
⅓ cup sugar
¾ teaspoon baking powder
7 tablespoons unsalted butter, cut into ½-inch chunks
1 egg

Filling:
1 tablespoon flour
⅓ cup raspberry preserves
3 cups fresh or frozen blueberries, unthawed

Preheat oven to 350 degrees. To prepare crust, place flour, sugar and baking powder into a food processor. Process 1 second to combine. Add butter; process for 3 to 4 seconds, until crumbly. Scrape sides and bottom of bowl. Break egg over mixture. Pulse processor until soft dough forms. (Dough should be very loose and dry.) Coat a 9½-inch springform pan with non-stick vegetable oil cooking spray. Press dough evenly over bottom and 1½ inches up side of pan. Refrigerate dough while preparing filling. To prepare filling, mix flour and preserves in a medium bowl; fold in berries. Spread evenly over crust. Bake 50 to 70 minutes or until crust is lightly browned. Remove from oven; place pan on wire rack; remove sides. Cool 1 hour before serving.

Yield: 8 servings

Anna Laufer

161

Lemon Shortbread

Crust:
½ cup butter, softened
¼ cup confectioners' sugar
1 cup flour

Filling:
2 eggs
1 cup sugar
1 tablespoon flour
1 tablespoon grated lemon rind
3 tablespoons lemon juice

Preheat oven to 350 degrees. To prepare crust, mix butter, sugar and flour together. Spread in an 8-inch square glass baking dish. Bake until slightly browned, about 15 minutes. To prepare filling, beat eggs in a small bowl. Mix in sugar, flour, lemon rind and lemon juice. Pour over crust. Bake for 20 minutes. When cool, cut into squares and sprinkle with additional confectioners' sugar.

Note: Recipe can be doubled and baked in a 9x13-inch glass pan. Freezes well.

Yield: 16 servings

Donna Linnelli

Peach Berry Cobbler

Cobbler:
⅓ cup packed light brown sugar
1 tablespoon corn starch
½ cup water
1 tablespoon butter
1 tablespoon lemon juice
2 cups sliced fresh peaches
1 cup fresh blueberries

Topping:
1 cup flour
½ cup plus 2 tablespoons sugar, divided
1½ teaspoons baking powder
½ teaspoon salt
¼ cup butter
½ cup milk
1 teaspoon nutmeg or cinnamon

Preheat oven to 350 degrees. In a medium saucepan, combine brown sugar and cornstarch. Stir in water. Cook, stirring continuously, until thickened and bubbly. Add butter and lemon juice. Stir in peaches and blueberries. Heat thoroughly; keep warm. To prepare topping, combine flour, ½ cup of the sugar, baking powder and salt. Using a pastry blender, cut in butter. Add milk all at once; stir just to moisten. Pour fruit mixture into a greased 8x1½-inch round baking dish. Spoon topping over fruit. Mix the remaining 2 tablespoons sugar with nutmeg. Sprinkle over topping. Bake for 30 to 35 minutes. Serve warm with vanilla ice cream. Great dessert for a summer cookout!

Yield: 6 servings

Shawn Gatto

Old Time Vanilla Ice Cream

4 egg yolks, slightly beaten
2 cups sugar
¼ cup cornstarch
2 quarts whole milk, divided
4 egg whites
¼ teaspoon salt
3 tablespoons vanilla
2 cups half & half

Place egg yolks in a heavy 3 to 4-quart saucepan. Slowly add sugar, cornstarch and 1 quart of the milk. Cook on medium heat until thickened. Remove from heat when liquid begins to boil. Beat egg whites until stiff and gently fold into mixture. Add salt, vanilla and half & half. Add the remaining 1 quart milk. Pour into ice creamer. Cool in freezer for ½ hour. Crank 30 minutes until stiff. Serve with fresh cut strawberries.

Yield: 3 quarts

Kristen Raffensperger

The Most Decadent Brownie

1 cup all-purpose flour
½ teaspoon salt
¾ cup unsweetened cocoa powder
1 pound unsalted butter, softened
3 cups sugar
3 eggs
2 tablespoons vanilla extract
1½ cups chopped pecans

Preheat oven to 350 degrees. Line a 10x16x1-inch baking sheet with heavy-duty aluminum foil, cut 4 inches larger than pan. Fold edges of foil to form a 2-inch rim on all sides. Sift flour, salt and cocoa together. In a large mixing bowl, cream butter and sugar until light and fluffy. With mixer on low speed, add eggs one at a time. Add vanilla. Turn off mixer. Add flour mixture all at once; blend by hand with spatula until all ingredients are just combined (batter should be thick). Stir in pecans. Transfer batter to prepared pan. Using a spatula dipped in hot water, spread batter evenly to sides of pan. Bake for 25 to 28 minutes. Check the center of brownies for firmness. When just barely set, remove from oven. Allow to cool at room temperature. Refrigerate until firm. Invert onto a cutting surface; peel off foil and cut into squares. Serve brownies chilled from refrigerator.

Note: Brownies may be frozen for several months.

Yield: 2 to 3 dozen

Patti Hanley

Pat's Brownies

4 (1-ounce) blocks unsweetened
  chocolate
⅔ cup shortening
2 cups sugar
4 eggs
1 teaspoon vanilla extract
1¼ cups flour
1 teaspoon baking powder
1 teaspoon salt
1 cup chopped nuts (optional)

Preheat oven to 350 degrees. Grease a 9x13x2-inch pan. Melt chocolate and shortening in a medium saucepan over low heat. Remove from heat. In a large mixing bowl, combine sugar, eggs and vanilla. Mix well. Stir in chocolate mixture. Add flour, baking powder, salt and nuts; mix well. Spread evenly in pan. Bake for 30 minutes or until brownies pull away from pan.

Yield: 1½ dozen

Pat Miller

Raspberry Truffle Brownies

¾ cup unsalted butter
4 ounces unsweetened chocolate
3 large eggs
2 cups sugar
⅓ cup raspberry jam
3 tablespoons black raspberry
  liqueur
1 cup all-purpose flour
¼ teaspoon salt
1 cup semi-sweet chocolate chips
Powdered sugar

Preheat oven to 350 degrees. Spray a 9-inch springform pan with non-stick vegetable oil cooking spray. Melt butter and chocolate in a large saucepan over low heat, stirring until smooth. Remove from heat. Whisk in eggs, sugar, jam and liqueur. Stir in flour and salt. Fold in chocolate chips. Transfer batter to prepared pan. Bake until toothpick inserted into center comes out with moist crumbs attached, about 45 minutes. Cool in pan on wire rack. Run knife around edges of pan; remove sides. Dust with powdered sugar before serving. A recipe for chocolate lovers! Deliciously rich and easy to make.

Note: Brownies can be prepared 2 days ahead. Wrap tightly with plastic wrap and store at room temperature.

Yield: 8 to 10 servings

Pam D'Alessandro

Easter Eggs

Filling:
2 cups confectioners' sugar
4 tablespoons butter, softened
½ teaspoon vanilla
¼ cup sweetened condensed milk
⅓ cup creamy-style peanut butter

Coating:
1 (7-ounce) chocolate bar (light or dark)
2 cups chocolate chips
½ bar of paraffin, shaved
Few drops vegetable oil (optional)

To prepare filling, cream together sugar and butter in a medium bowl. Add vanilla. Slowly blend in condensed milk and peanut butter. Mold filling into egg shapes, 2½x1x1-inch; set aside on waxed paper. To prepare coating, place chocolate bar, chocolate chips and paraffin in a double-boiler. Melt over low-medium heat. (If mixture seems too thick, add a few drops of vegetable oil.) Remove from heat. Working one egg at a time, cradle egg with fork and dip into chocolate mixture to coat. Place eggs on a baking sheet; refrigerate overnight.

Variation: Substitute 3½-ounces of coconut for peanut butter.

Yield: 2 dozen

Linda Hillenburg

Buckeyes

1 (1-pound) box confectioners' sugar
1 (1-pound) jar creamy-style peanut butter
10½ tablespoons butter, softened
1 (12-ounce) package chocolate chips

In a large bowl, blend together sugar, peanut butter and butter. Roll into 1-inch balls and chill. Melt chocolate chips in a double boiler over low-medium heat. Using a toothpick, dip ½ of each ball into the melted chocolate. Place chocolate-side up on waxed paper to cool. Refrigerate to harden.

Note: Do not use a low-fat peanut butter. Do not substitute margarine for butter. Freezes well.

Variation: Add 3 cups crispy rice cereal to peanut butter mixture to give the buckeyes a crunch! Add ⅓ bar of paraffin wax to chocolate chips. Melt completely before dipping. (This keeps chocolate coating a bit smoother.)

Yield: Approximately 8 dozen

Judy Rodgers

Cocoa Pepper Cookies

3 cups all-purpose flour
1 cup sugar
½ cup unsweetened cocoa powder
3 teaspoons baking powder
1 teaspoon ground cinnamon
1 teaspoon freshly ground black pepper
½ teaspoon ground cloves
¼ teaspoon salt
½ cup unsalted butter, chilled and sliced
1 extra large egg
½ cup milk
1 teaspoon vanilla extract

Glaze:
1 cup confectioners' sugar
¼ teaspoon ground cinnamon
¼ teaspoon vanilla extract
1 tablespoon milk

Preheat oven to 350 degrees. Place all dry ingredients for cookie dough in a large bowl. Mix well with a wire whisk. Cut butter slices into dry ingredients, using a pastry cutter or two knives, until it resembles very coarse crumbs. Beat together egg, milk and vanilla; add to flour mixture to form a soft dough. Knead until dry ingredients are just moistened. Handle lightly. (Dough should be veined with butter.) Roll out sections of dough into snake-like pieces, ¾-inch in diameter. (Refrigerate unused dough until ready to use.) Cut into 1-inch slices and place on a cookie sheet. Bake for 8 to 10 minutes, until set. Do not over-bake. Cool on rack. Mix all glaze ingredients together, using enough milk for a drizzling consistency. Dip tops of cookies in glaze. Store in sealed container; refrigerate.

Yield: 5 dozen

Grandma Til

Anna's Lace Cookies

½ cup dark corn syrup
½ cup butter, softened
1 cup sweetened coconut flakes
¼ teaspoon salt
1 cup flour
⅔ cup sugar

Heat corn syrup in a medium saucepan to boiling. Add butter and coconut; stir until butter is melted. Remove from heat; cool slightly. Sift salt, flour and sugar together in a large bowl. Add wet mixture to dry ingredients. Chill overnight. Preheat oven to 325 degrees. Drop by ½ teaspoonfuls onto a foil-lined or non-stick baking sheet. Bake for 10 minutes. Allow cookies to cool slightly, but not harden, before removing from sheet.

Yield: 5 dozen

Anna and Harry Weaver (In Memory)

Irene's Chrusuki

A Polish Dessert

1⅞ cups flour
¼ teaspoon salt
5 egg yolks
3 tablespoons sugar
5 tablespoons sour cream
1 tablespoon brandy
¼ teaspoon grated lemon rind
½ teaspoon vanilla extract
½ teaspoon almond extract
Oil for frying
Powdered sugar

Sift flour and salt together; set aside. In a large mixing bowl, stir egg yolks and sugar until smooth. Add sour cream, brandy, lemon rind, vanilla and almond extracts; mix well. Combine wet and dry ingredients. Knead lightly on a floured board until smooth and of a rolling consistency. Chill dough for 1 hour. Roll ⅛-inch thin. Cut dough into 1x8-inch strips. (Continue with rolling and cutting until all dough is used.) Cut a gash in center of strip. Pull one end of strip through center gash. Heat ½ to 1 inch of oil in a cast iron skillet or deep fryer. Fry Chrusuki until golden brown, approximately 1 to 2 minutes; drain on paper towels. Sprinkle with powdered sugar. A Polish dessert meant to feed a crowd!

Yield: Approximately 10 to 12 dozen

Judy Rodgers

Orange Walnut Biscotti

½ cup butter, softened
2 eggs
¾ cup sugar
2 cups flour
½ teaspoon baking powder
½ teaspoon baking soda
⅛ teaspoon salt
2 tablespoons orange zest
1 teaspoon vanilla
1 cup walnuts, chopped and
   lightly toasted

In a large mixing bowl, beat butter, eggs and sugar together until light and fluffy. Add flour, baking powder, baking soda and salt; mix until blended. Mix in orange zest, vanilla and walnuts. Cover bowl; refrigerate for 1 hour. Preheat oven to 350 degrees. Butter and flour a cookie sheet or line with parchment paper. Divide dough in half. Make 2 logs 1½-inches in diameter. Place logs on prepared cookie sheet, a few inches apart. Bake for 30 minutes. Cool 10 minutes. Cut logs into ¾-inch slices; lay on cut sides and bake for an additional 10 minutes. Remove from oven and cool. Store in an airtight container.

Yield: 2½ dozen

Mary Bernacki

Pumpkin Cookies

Cookies:
2 cups flour
1 teaspoon baking powder
1 teaspoon baking soda
1 teaspoon cinnamon
1 cup sugar
1 cup butter or margarine,
  softened
1 egg
1 cup pumpkin, unspiced
½ cup chopped walnuts
½ cup raisins
1 teaspoon vanilla extract

Icing:
3 tablespoons butter
4 tablespoons milk
½ cup light brown sugar
1 cup powdered sugar
1 teaspoon vanilla extract

Preheat oven to 350 degrees. In a small bowl, combine flour, baking powder, baking soda and cinnamon; set aside. In a large mixing bowl, cream sugar, butter, egg and pumpkin together. Add dry ingredients. Stir in nuts, raisins and vanilla. Drop by teaspoonfuls onto ungreased cookie sheets. Bake for 20 minutes. To prepare icing, in small saucepan, combine butter, milk and brown sugar. Boil for 2 minutes, stirring often; cool. Add powdered sugar and vanilla. Spread icing on cooled cookies.

Note: Cookies freeze well.

Yield: 4 dozen

Pam Buongiorno

Pumpkin Cheesecake Bars

1 (16-ounce) package pound cake
  mix
3 eggs, divided
2 tablespoons margarine or
  butter, melted
4 teaspoons pumpkin pie spice,
  divided
1 (8-ounce) package cream cheese,
  softened
1 (14-ounce) can sweetened
  condensed milk
1 (16-ounce) can pumpkin
½ teaspoon salt
1 cup chopped nuts

Preheat oven to 350 degrees. In a large mixing bowl, with electric mixer on low speed, combine cake mix, 1 of the eggs, margarine and 2 teaspoons of the pumpkin pie spice until crumbly. Press mixture onto bottom of a 10x15-inch baking pan. In a large mixing bowl, beat cream cheese until fluffy. Gradually beat in condensed milk, pumpkin, the remaining 2 eggs and 2 teaspoons pumpkin pie spice and salt. Mix well. Pour batter over crust. Sprinkle with nuts. Bake for 30 to 35 minutes or until set. Cool. Cut into bars; store covered in refrigerator. A great recipe to make ahead and freeze!

Yield: 3 to 4 dozen

Donna Linnelli

Tudells

An Italian Cookie

Cookies:
1 dozen eggs
2 cups sugar
⅛ teaspoon salt
2 tablespoons vanilla extract
1 tablespoon lemon extract
1 pound margarine, melted and cooled
6 tablespoons baking powder
8-9 cups flour

Icing:
1 pound confectioners' sugar
1 cup margarine, melted
2 tablespoons lemon extract
2-3 tablespoons milk

Preheat oven to 350 degrees. In a large mixing bowl, mix all cookie ingredients together with an electric mixer. Let dough rest for 15 minutes. Roll into 1-inch balls. Place on ungreased cookie sheets. Bake for 9 to 10 minutes or until set in the middle. Combine all icing ingredients, adding just enough milk for a smooth consistency. When cool, ice the tops of each tudell.

Note: Because of the amount of baking powder, batter rises considerably. It is easier to mix half of the batter at a time. Tudells keep well; layer with waxed paper, store in an air-tight container in a cool place.

Yield: 10 dozen

Pam D'Alessandro

Claires

1¼ cups flour
1 teaspoon baking powder
¼ teaspoon salt
½ cup margarine, softened
1 cup sugar
1 egg
1 teaspoon vanilla
½ cup finely chopped nuts
2 teaspoons cinnamon
1 tablespoon sugar

In a small bowl, sift together flour, baking powder and salt; set aside. In a large mixing bowl, cream margarine and sugar. Blend in egg and vanilla. Add flour mixture; mix well. Chill dough for 1 hour. Preheat oven to 375 degrees. Combine nuts, cinnamon and sugar in a small bowl. Shape teaspoons of dough into balls; roll in nut mixture. Place on greased cookie sheets and bake for 15 minutes. Remove immediately from baking sheets and cool. If you like snickerdoodles, this recipe is for you!

Note: For a moister, softer cookie, use table-spoon-sized dough balls.

Yield: 3 dozen

Marcia Walsh

Italian Biscotti

2 cups sugar
2 cups coarsely chopped walnuts
1 cup butter, melted
¼ cup anise extract (pure)
2 tablespoons water
2 teaspoons vanilla
6 eggs, room temperature
5½ cups all-purpose flour
1 tablespoon baking powder

Mix sugar, nuts, butter, anise, water and vanilla in a large bowl. Beat in eggs one at a time. Combine flour and baking powder; stir into mixture. Cover with plastic wrap; refrigerate for 3 hours. Preheat oven to 375 degrees. Grease 2 baking sheets. Divide dough into 4 equal portions; shape each into a long loaf, ½-inch high and 3-inches wide. Place on prepared baking sheets, spacing 4 inches apart. Bake until firm to the touch, approximately 20 minutes. Let cool for 30 minutes. Cut loaves on the diagonal into ½ to ¾-inch thick slices. Arrange slices, cut side down, on baking sheets. Bake until light brown, about 7 minutes on each side. Cool completely on racks. Store biscotti in an airtight container. Dunk into your favorite hot or cold beverage for a real treat!

Variation: For almond flavored biscotti, omit anise extract and use 1 tablespoon vanilla extract and 2 tablespoons almond-flavored extract. For chocolate lovers, omit anise extract and use 2 tablespoons vanilla extract and ½ cup mini chocolate chips.

Yield: 4½ dozen

Joanne Redondo

Chocolate Swirls

1½ cups butter, softened
1 teaspoon salt
2 teaspoons vanilla extract
1½ cups brown sugar
4 cups flour
Few drops of milk
12 ounces semi-sweet chocolate
   morsels
14 ounces sweetened condensed
   milk
2 tablespoons vegetable oil
1 cup chopped walnuts or pecans
Powdered sugar

In a small bowl, cream together butter, salt and vanilla. In a large mixing bowl, combine brown sugar and flour. Cut butter mixture into flour mixture using a pastry cutter. Add milk by drops until consistency of dough is adequate for rolling. Divide dough into 6 equal parts and chill for ½ to 1 hour before rolling. Using a double boiler, heat chocolate morsels, condensed milk and oil until chocolate melts and mixture is smooth. Preheat oven to 350 degrees. Roll each dough portion into a 10x6-inch rectangle on lightly-floured waxed paper. Spread chocolate mixture evenly over each rectangle; sprinkle nuts evenly over top. Using waxed paper, fold lengthwise edges over to form a log shape. (Overlap 1 to 2 inches at top.) Using waxed paper, flip seam-side down onto a cookie sheet. Bake for 20 to 25 minutes. Cool slightly and sprinkle tops with powdered sugar. Slice each log into 15 (½-inch) slices and serve.

Note: Freezes well; slice before freezing.

Yield: 7½ dozen

Elaine DiLembo

Pizzelles

A Traditional Recipe

12 eggs
3½ cups sugar
2 cups margarine, melted and
    cooled
1 teaspoon anise oil
1 teaspoon vanilla extract
1 tablespoon lemon extract
½ teaspoon salt
14¼ cups flour

Preheat electric pizzelle iron for at least 15 minutes. Grease upper and lower grid surfaces using vegetable shortening or cooking spray. In a large mixing bowl, beat eggs. Add sugar and beat well. Add margarine, anise oil, vanilla and lemon extracts; mix well. Add salt and enough of the flour to form a dough that is not sticky. Make 1-inch dough balls; Drop onto center of preheated grid. Close the lid and clip handles of iron together. Cook until steaming stops, about 30 seconds. Remove with a fork; cool on wire racks or towels.

Note: Discard first 2 pizzelles.

Variation: Omit anise oil and increase vanilla extract to 2 teaspoons.

Yield: 11 to 12 dozen

Lee Argentine

Rum Pizzelles

8 eggs
½ cup vegetable oil
1 tablespoon vanilla
3 ounces rum
1 teaspoon baking powder
1½ cups sugar
½ teaspoon salt
2½ cups flour

Preheat electric pizzelle iron for at least 15 minutes. Grease upper and lower grid surfaces using vegetable shortening or cooking spray. In a large mixing bowl, beat eggs with oil. Add vanilla and rum. Add baking powder, sugar and salt. Gradually add flour. Cook on pizzelle iron following the same instructions used in the "Traditional Pizzelle" recipe. A very light pizzelle!

Yield: 8 dozen

Deborah Hellett

Bread Pudding with Whiskey Sauce

Pudding:
1 loaf very dry bread
4 cups milk
4 eggs, beaten
2 cups sugar
2 tablespoons vanilla extract
1 cup raisins
2 apples, peeled, cored and cubed
1 (8-ounce) can crushed pineapple,
   drained
¼ cup butter

Sauce:
½ cup butter, melted
1 cup sugar
1 egg, beaten
1-2 ounces whiskey, to taste

Preheat oven to 350 degrees. To prepare the pudding, tear or cut bread into small cubes; place in a large bowl. Add milk; mix well. Add eggs, sugar, vanilla, raisins, apples and pineapple to bread mixture; mix well. Melt butter in a 9x13-inch baking pan. Spread bread mixture evenly in pan. Bake for 1 hour. To prepare sauce, blend butter and sugar in a double boiler over low-medium heat. Remove from heat. Add egg, stirring rapidly to prevent curdling. Allow to cool. Add whiskey. Serve sauce warm over pudding.

Note: To dry-out fresh bread, bake in a 200 degree oven for 1 hour, turning slices once. Bread pudding and sauce store well in refrigerator.

Yield: 15 to 20 servings

Georgia Moncada

Strufoli or Fried Bows

6 eggs
¾ cup vegetable oil
½ cup milk
1 teaspoon anise extract
4 teaspoons baking powder
1 cup sugar
3-3½ cups flour
Vegetable oil for frying
Powdered sugar
1 cup honey

In a large mixing bowl, beat together eggs, oil, milk and anise extract. Add baking powder, sugar and enough flour to form a pliable dough. Heat 2 inches of oil to 375 degrees in a deep 12-inch skillet. While oil is heating, roll dough by tablespoonfuls into 6-inch long ropes on a lightly-floured surface. To make Strufoli, cut each rope into ¼-inch pieces. In 3 or more batches, fry dough in hot oil, about one minute, until puffed and golden. Using a slotted spoon, remove fried dough to paper towels; drain. (Allow oil to return to 375 degrees between batches.) To make Fried Bows, roll tablespoonfuls of dough, very thin, on a floured surface. Cut dough into 1½ to 2-inch squares. Slit dough horizontally in the middle of each square. Turn down top-side of square and gently pull through slit. Heat oil as you would to cook Strufoli. Using tongs, dip Bows, one by one, into hot oil until puffed and golden. Remove Bows to paper towels; drain. When cool, sprinkle Strufoli or Bows with powdered sugar or dip in honey. To prepare honey for dipping, in a 3-quart saucepan, over medium to high heat, bring honey to a boil. Remove from heat. Stir in fried dough balls (Strufoli) to coat thoroughly; let excess honey drip off into pan. Spoon honey coated balls onto a platter lightly sprayed with non-stick cooking spray. To coat Bows, use tongs to dip them in honey. Let excess honey drip off before placing on a platter coated with non-stick cooking spray.

Variation: To make Christmas Strufoli, omit anise extract and substitute 1 tablespoon grated orange peel, 2 teaspoons grated lemon peel and 1 teaspoon vanilla extract. After Strufoli (dough balls) have been dipped in honey, stack balls, pyramid-style, to form a "Christmas tree" shape. Decorate with nonpareils and candied peel.

Yield: An Italian dessert meant to feed a crowd.

Carolyn Capozzi and Donna Linnelli

Our Favorite Tiramisu

8 ounces semi-sweet chocolate
1 cup sugar
4 egg yolks
1½ teaspoons vanilla
1 (8-ounce) package cream cheese,
cut into pieces, softened
1¾ cups chilled whipping cream
1 tablespoon instant espresso
powder, diluted in 1¼ cups hot
water, cooled
1 (12-ounce) prepared pound
cake, cut into 3½x1x½-inch
strips

Finely chop chocolate in food processor; set aside. Mix sugar and egg yolks in food processor for 30 seconds. Add vanilla; process until pale yellow, about 1 minute. Add cheese in batches and process until smooth. Transfer to medium bowl; cover and chill 1 hour. Beat whipping cream until stiff. Fold into chilled cream cheese mixture. Cover and refrigerate until well chilled, about 1 hour. (Can be prepared 2 days ahead.) Pour espresso into large shallow dish; dip in cake strips, turning to lightly coat all sides. Arrange cake pieces on bottom of a 2½-quart shallow baking dish in a single layer; smooth edges with fingers to mold together. Sprinkle on ½ of the chocolate; top with cream cheese mixture. Sprinkle on remaining chocolate. Cover and refrigerate at least 2 hours. Tiramisu means "pick-me-up" in Italian. This dessert does just that!

Note: Recipe contains raw eggs. Tiramisu can be prepared one day ahead.

Variation: Substitute 2 packages of frozen lady fingers for pound cake. Partially thaw before use. To serve Tiramisu in individual (large) goblet glasses, arrange cake pieces along sides of glass; sprinkle on ½ of the chocolate, add cheese mixture and top with remaining chocolate. An elegant presentation.

Yield: 8 servings

Pam D'Alessandro

Velvety Chocolate Sauce

2 ounces baking chocolate, cut into small pieces
1 cup half & half, heated
2 cups confectioners' sugar, sifted
1 tablespoon butter
1-2 teaspoons vanilla, to taste

In a 1-quart saucepan or double boiler, melt chocolate. Alternately add small amounts of half & half and sugar; beat well after each addition. Cook over medium heat, stirring, until thick. Lower heat and simmer 5 minutes, stirring continuously to prevent scorching. Remove from heat; add butter. Let cool slightly; stir in vanilla. If sauce is too thick, add 1 to 2 tablespoons of hot water. Serve hot or cold. Delicious over pound cake!

Yield: About 2 cups

Betty Ferons

West End

$\mathcal{T}$he West End began as the "Warden and Alexander Temperanceville Village" of St. Clair Township, Allegheny County. This 96-acre plan of lots was laid out in 1839. The tract of land was purchased from the Daniel Elliott family which had

owned several hundred acres of land south of the rivers in 1785 and had operated a saw mill at the mouth of a creek. Saw Mill Run, Saw Mill Creek and Elliott, which adjoins the West End, are all historically significant names in this community.

The site of this tract of land was a natural one for development. Industrial development had already begun on the south side of the Ohio River and included a glassworks (1796), a salt well and the Pittsburgh Iron Works (1833). From 1839 until annexation to the city in 1873, development progressed rapidly in "Temperanceville." The area was home to the Sheffield Iron Works (1848), the Eagle Ironworks (1850), a glass factory and even oil refineries. Illuminating gas and salt were also produced in the town.

Following a building boom of residential and residential/commercial units in the 1890's, many improvements were made in the West End. The second branch of the Carnegie Library system opened here in 1899. The main streets were paved with cobblestones, new water mains were installed and the city purchased land for West End Park.

By 1900, the population was 3,725, almost a thousand more people than in 1800. West End was a thriving commercial and transportation center interspersed with industrial plants. Mirroring the industrial potential of Pittsburgh as a whole, the community was also influenced by immigrants who poured into the region for jobs in the mills and factories. In 1939, sixty percent of the population was either foreign or had non-native parents. Many were of Polish descent and most of the other immigrants had their origins in Germany, the Austro-Hungarian Empire, Great Britain, Russia or Lithuania.

Spectacular scenery of the magnificent valley below and a breathtaking view of the Downtown skyline can be seen from almost any point in the lofty West End. With its historic gazebo and flower-strewn lawns, West End Park and the West End Overlook continue to attract thousands of visitors each year. The West End remains a neighborhood where civic involvement to renovate homes, businesses and storefronts is of great importance. ♥

Kentucky Pound Cake

1 cup unsalted butter, softened
3 cups granulated sugar
1 teaspoon vanilla extract
1 teaspoon almond extract
6 large eggs
3 cups cake flour
½ pint whipping cream

Do not preheat oven. Generously grease a 10-inch Bundt or tube pan with butter. In a large mixing bowl, cream butter and sugar together. Add vanilla and almond extracts. Add eggs, one at a time, beating well after each addition. Alternately add flour and whipping cream in small amounts, beating well after each addition. Set oven temperature to 300 degrees. Pour batter into pan. Bake for 1 hour and 40 minutes. Let cake cool before removing from pan.

Note: Cake must be put into a cold oven.

Yield: 12 to 16 servings

Mary Lou Wessell

Old Fashioned Banana Cupcakes

2 cups sifted flour
1 teaspoon baking powder
1 teaspoon baking soda
1½ cups sugar
½ cup shortening
2 eggs
1 cup mashed bananas (about 4 whole)
½ cup milk
1 teaspoon vanilla extract

Preheat oven to 375 degrees. Combine flour, baking powder and baking soda; set aside. In a large mixing bowl, cream together the sugar and shortening. Add eggs and banana; mix well. Alternately add dry ingredients and milk to mixture. Add vanilla. Fill 24 paper-lined cupcake tins ½ full with batter. Bake for 10 to 15 minutes. These cupcakes are so moist they do not need icing!

Yield: 24 cupcakes

Georgia Moncada

Perfect Chocolate Cake

2 cups flour
1 teaspoon baking powder
2 teaspoons baking soda
¾ cup cocoa powder
2 cups sugar
2 eggs
½ cup canola or vegetable oil
1 cup milk
1 cup boiling water

Preheat oven to 350 degrees. In a small bowl, combine flour, baking powder, baking soda and cocoa powder; set aside. Using an electric mixer, blend sugar, eggs, oil and milk together. Gradually add dry ingredients. Add boiling water and beat an additional 3 minutes. Pour batter into a greased 9x13-inch baking pan or 2 (8-inch) round cake pans. Bake for 35 to 45 minutes. Recipe testers report that this is a cake to rival your mother-in-law's!

Yield: 12 servings

Anne McCafferty

Cinnamon Apple Cake

1¾ cups sugar, divided
½ cup margarine, softened
1 teaspoon vanilla extract
6 ounces (block-style) fat-free
   cream cheese, softened
   (about ¾ cup)
2 large eggs
1½ cups all-purpose flour
1½ teaspoons baking powder
¼ teaspoon salt
2 teaspoons ground cinnamon
3 cups chopped and peeled Rome
   apples (about 2 large)

Preheat oven to 350 degrees. Coat an 8-inch springform pan with non-stick vegetable oil cooking spray. Using an electric mixer, beat 1½ cups of the sugar, margarine, vanilla and cream cheese at medium speed until well-blended, about 4 minutes. Add eggs, one at a time, beating well after each addition. In a separate bowl, combine flour, baking powder and salt. Add flour mixture to cream cheese mixture, beating at low speed until well-blended. Combine remaining ¼ cup of the sugar with the cinnamon. Combine 2 tablespoons of the cinnamon mixture with the apples. Stir apples into the batter. Pour batter into prepared pan; sprinkle remaining cinnamon mixture on top. Bake for 1 hour and 15 minutes or until cake easily pulls away from sides of pan. Cool completely on a wire rack. Serve this very moist cake for any occasion.

Note: To bake in a 9-inch square baking pan or 9-inch springform pan, reduce cooking time by 5 minutes.

Yield: 12 servings

Pam D'Alessandro

Carrot Cake

Cake:
1 cup butter, softened
2 cups sugar
4 eggs
2 cups flour
2 teaspoons baking soda
2 teaspoons cinnamon
1 teaspoon salt
1½ teaspoons vanilla extract
3 cups grated carrots
1 cup chopped walnuts
1 cup golden raisins

Frosting:
3 ounces cream cheese, softened
4 tablespoons butter, softened
1 cup powdered sugar
1 teaspoon vanilla extract

Preheat oven to 325 degrees. Grease a 9x13-inch pan with non-stick vegetable oil cooking spray. In a large mixing bowl, cream butter with sugar until light and fluffy. Add eggs, one at a time, mixing well. In a separate bowl, sift flour, baking soda, cinnamon and salt together; add to mixture. Add vanilla, carrots, walnuts and raisins; mix well. Pour batter into prepared pan. Bake for 55 minutes. To prepare frosting, combine cream cheese, butter and powdered sugar; beat until fluffy. Add vanilla. Spread icing on cooled cake.

Note: Use a food processor to grate the carrots in a jiffy.

Yield: 12 servings

Georgina Senger

Sour Cream Coffee Cake

2 cups flour
1 teaspoon baking powder
¼ teaspoon salt
1 cup butter, softened
2 cups plus 4 teaspoons sugar, divided
2 eggs
1 cup sour cream
½ teaspoon vanilla extract
1 cup chopped pecans
1 teaspoon cinnamon

Preheat oven to 350 degrees. Sift flour with baking powder and salt; set aside. In a large mixing bowl, cream the butter. Add 2 cups sugar gradually; beat until light and fluffy. Beat in eggs, one at a time. Fold in sour cream. Add vanilla. Fold in flour mixture. In a separate bowl, combine remaining 4 teaspoons of the sugar, pecans and cinnamon. Place ⅓ of the batter in a well-greased and floured 8 or 9-inch Bundt pan. Sprinkle ½ of the pecan mixture over batter; add remaining batter. Sprinkle remaining pecan mixture over top. Bake for 1 hour. This recipe is from the *New York Times,* January 19, 1968.

Yield: 8 to 10 servings

Betty Ferons

Grandma's Coffee Cake

2 cups sugar
3 cups flour
¾ cup butter or margarine,
   softened
¾ cup raisins
½ cup chopped nuts
1 teaspoon cloves
½ teaspoon allspice
½ teaspoon cinnamon
½ teaspoon salt
2 teaspoons baking soda
2 cups buttermilk

Preheat oven to 350 degrees. In a large mixing bowl, combine sugar, flour and butter to a crumb consistency. Set aside ¾ cup of the crumbs for top of cake. To remaining crumb mixture, add raisins, nuts, cloves, allspice, cinnamon and salt; mix well. Combine baking soda and buttermilk; using an electric mixer, beat into dry ingredients. Pour batter into a greased 9x13-inch baking pan and top with the remaining ¾ cup of crumbs. Bake for 35 to 40 minutes.

Variation: May substitute 2 cups milk, mixed with 2 teaspoons vinegar, in place of the buttermilk.

Yield: 12 servings

Pamela Giardina

Pumpkin Log

Cake:
⅔ cup canned solid pack pumpkin
1 teaspoon baking soda
2 teaspoons cinnamon
½ teaspoon nutmeg
1 teaspoon ginger
½ teaspoon salt
3 eggs, slightly beaten
1 cup sugar
¾ cup flour
Powdered sugar

Filling:
1 (8-ounce) package cream cheese,
   softened
1½ teaspoons vanilla extract
1 cup powdered sugar
2 teaspoons butter, softened

Preheat oven to 350 degrees. Grease a 12x18-inch jelly roll pan or sided baking sheet. Line with waxed paper and grease. In a large mixing bowl, combine pumpkin, baking soda, spices, salt, eggs and sugar; mix well. Add flour; mix well. Spread onto prepared pan and bake for 15 minutes. To prepare filling, in a medium bowl, blend together all filling ingredients until smooth and creamy. Remove cake from oven; flip onto waxed paper dusted with powdered sugar. Peel off hot waxed paper. Spread filling over cake and roll immediately, starting at a short end. Cool; slice to serve. A great dessert for the holidays!

Yield: 12 servings

Mary Ann Lasky

Chocolate Chip Pumpkin Cheesecake

2 cups vanilla wafer crumbs
(about 60 wafers)
½ cup cocoa powder
½ cup powdered sugar
½ cup butter, melted
3 (8-ounce) packages cream
cheese, softened
1 cup granulated sugar
3 tablespoons flour
1 teaspoon pumpkin pie spice
1 cup canned pumpkin
4 eggs
1½ cups semi-sweet chocolate
mini-chips

Preheat oven to 350 degrees. In a medium bowl, stir together crumbs, cocoa and powdered sugar. Stir in melted butter. Press mixture into a 9-inch springform pan, covering bottom and ½ inch up the sides. Bake for 10 minutes. Remove from oven; allow to cool slightly. Increase oven temperature to 400 degrees. In a large mixing bowl, beat together cream cheese, sugar, flour and pumpkin pie spice. Add pumpkin and eggs; beat until well-blended. Stir in chocolate chips. Pour batter into the crust-lined pan. Bake for 10 minutes. Reduce oven temperature to 250 degrees; continue baking for 60 to 65 minutes. Place on a wire rack to cool. Run a knife along inside edge of springform pan to loosen cake before releasing sides. Refrigerate before serving.

Yield: 12 servings

Cindy McKenna

Overnight Coffee Cake

⅔ cup margarine, softened
1 cup granulated sugar
½ cup packed brown sugar
2 eggs
2 cups flour, divided
1 teaspoon baking powder
1 teaspoon baking soda
1 teaspoon ground cinnamon
¼ teaspoon salt
1 cup buttermilk, divided

Topping:
½ cup packed brown sugar
¾ cup chopped pecans or walnuts
½ teaspoon ground cinnamon
¼ teaspoon ground nutmeg

In a large mixing bowl, cream margarine and sugars together. Add eggs, one at a time, mixing after each addition. Add 1 cup of the flour, baking powder, baking soda, cinnamon and salt. Add ½ cup of the buttermilk; mix well. Add remaining flour and buttermilk; mix well. Spread batter into a greased 9x13-inch pan. To prepare topping, mix all ingredients in a small bowl. Sprinkle over batter. Cover pan; refrigerate for 8 hours or overnight. In the morning, preheat oven to 350 degrees. Bake for 30 to 35 minutes. Cut into squares and serve warm. Store leftovers in a covered container. A very moist cake with a crunchy topping!

Yield: 8 servings

Pam D'Alessandro

Chocolate Cheesecake with Hot Fudge Sauce

Crust:
2 cups crushed saltine crackers
1 cup finely chopped walnuts
⅔ cup butter or margarine, melted
⅓ cup sugar

Filling:
12 (1-ounce) squares semi-sweet chocolate
1½ cups butter or margarine
2 (8-ounce) packages cream cheese, softened
1½ cups sugar
6 large eggs

Sauce:
1 (12-ounce) package semi-sweet chocolate morsels
1 cup half & half
1 tablespoon butter or margarine
1 teaspoon vanilla extract

Preheat oven to 350 degrees. To prepare the crust, combine crackers, walnuts, butter and sugar; mix well. Firmly press onto bottom and 2½ inches up the sides of a lightly greased 9-inch springform pan. Bake for 8 minutes. Cool pan on a wire rack. Reduce oven temperature to 300 degrees. To prepare filling, combine chocolate squares and butter in a heavy saucepan. Cook over medium-low heat until mixture is melted and smooth, stirring frequently. Remove from heat; let cool. With an electric mixer, beat cream cheese at medium speed until light and creamy. Add 1½ cups sugar; beat well. Add eggs, one at a time, beating after each addition. Stir in the cooled chocolate mixture. Pour filling into prepared crust. Bake for 1 hour and 20 to 30 minutes or until almost set. Turn oven off. Let cheesecake cool in oven for 1 hour; then cool to room temperature on wire rack. Remove sides of pan. To prepare the sauce, combine chocolate morsels and half & half in a heavy saucepan. Cook over medium heat until chocolate melts and mixture is smooth, stirring frequently. Remove from heat; stir in butter and vanilla. Serve sauce warm, drizzled over cheesecake.

Note: Cheesecake can be served at room temperature or chilled.

Yield: 12 servings; 2 cups sauce

Donna Linnelli

Scripture Cake

3½ cups sifted all-purpose flour
  (1 Kings 4:22)
3 teaspoons baking powder
  (Galatians 5:9)
¼ teaspoon salt (Leviticus 2:13)
1½ teaspoons ground cinnamon
  (1 Kings 10:10)
½ teaspoon nutmeg (1 Kings 10:10)
¼ teaspoon cloves (1 Kings 10:10)
½ teaspoon allspice (1 Kings 10:2)
1 cup butter, softened (Judges 5:25)
2 cups light brown sugar
  (Jeremiah 6:20)
2 tablespoons honey (Exodus 16:30)
6 eggs (Luke 11:12)
8 ounces chopped dates
  (Deuteronomy 34:3)
2 cups dark raisins (1 Samuel 30:12)
1 cup chopped walnuts (Solomon
  6:11)
1 cup milk (Judges 5:25)

Preheat oven to 325 degrees. Grease and flour a large tube pan. In a bowl, sift together flour, baking powder, salt, cinnamon, nutmeg, cloves and allspice. In a large mixing bowl, blend together butter, brown sugar, honey and eggs. Beat until light and fluffy. Dredge dates, raisins and walnuts in ¼ cup of the flour mixture; set aside. Alternately add the remaining flour mixture and the milk to the butter mixture; beat until smooth. Add dates, raisins and walnuts. Spoon batter into prepared pan. Bake for 1½ hours or until a cake tester inserted in the center of the cake comes out clean. Cool for 10 to 15 minutes before removing from pan.

Note: Cover and refrigerate after serving.

Yield: 8 to 10 servings

Shelley B. Hall

Pineapple Cake

Cake:
2½ cups flour
1½ teaspoons baking soda
1½ cups sugar
2 eggs
1 teaspoon vanilla extract
1 (20-ounce) can crushed
  pineapple, with juice
1 cup chopped walnuts

Topping:
2 cups confectioners' sugar
Water

Preheat oven to 350 degrees. Combine flour and baking soda in a small bowl; set aside. In a large bowl, blend sugar, eggs and vanilla. Stir in pineapple, with juice, and walnuts. Add flour mixture. Pour into a 10x16x1-inch baking sheet. Bake for 20 minutes. To prepare the topping, add just enough water to the confectioners' sugar to obtain a consistency for drizzling. Drizzle topping over hot cake. A tremendous low-fat treat!

Note: This can be a "one-bowl" cake, mixed by hand; quick and easy!

Yield: 12 servings

Dorianne DiGregorio

185

Strawberry Charlotte

Cake:
4 egg yolks
¾ cup sugar
1 teaspoon vanilla extract
¾ cup sifted cake flour
¾ teaspoon baking powder
½ teaspoon salt
4 egg whites, room temperature
Powdered sugar

Syrup:
⅓ cup sugar
¼ cup plus 2 tablespoons water
2-3 tablespoons orange liqueur

Almond Cream:
1 cup unsalted butter, room
  temperature
1 cup super-fine sugar
⅓-½ cup orange liqueur
¼ teaspoon almond extract
1⅓ cups ground almonds, lightly
  toasted
2 cups whipping cream

4-6 cups fresh strawberries, hulled
1 cup whipping cream, whipped

Preheat oven to 375 degrees. Line a 10x15-inch jellyroll pan with parchment or waxed paper; grease paper. In a large mixing bowl, beat egg yolks. Gradually add sugar, beating until creamy. Blend in vanilla. In a separate bowl, resift cake flour with baking powder and salt. Gradually add flour mixture to egg yolks, beating until smooth. In a large bowl, whip egg whites until stiff, but not dry. Fold egg whites into batter. Pour batter onto prepared pan, spreading evenly. Bake until toothpick inserted in center of cake comes out clean, about 12 minutes. Lightly sprinkle powered sugar over a kitchen towel large enough to cover cake. Arrange towel, sugared-side down, over cake. Holding towel taut at ends of pan, invert cake onto towel. Immediately peel off paper. Trim any rough edges. Roll cake up lengthwise in towel. Cool on a rack. To prepare syrup, combine sugar and water in a small saucepan. Stirring continuously, bring to a boil over high heat. Let cool. Blend in orange liqueur. To prepare almond cream, place butter and sugar in a large mixing bowl; cream together until pale and fluffy. Beat in orange liqueur and almond extract. Stir in almonds. Whip cream lightly; fold into butter mixture. To assemble Charlotte, line bottom of a 9x3-inch springform pan or a 2-quart soufflé dish with waxed paper. Lightly grease sides of pan. Unroll sponge cake and cut long pieces to fit sides of pan; set aside remaining cake. Brush 1 side of the cut cake pieces with syrup. Line sides of pan with cut cake pieces, syrup-side in. Set aside 16 uniform strawberries for garnish. Spoon ⅓ of the almond cream into pan, directly on top of the waxed paper. Arrange a layer of strawberries, stem-end down, over cream. Repeat layering, ending with cream. Trim excess cake off the sides at top of cake. Arrange reserved cake over top

Strawberry Charlotte (continued)

(this will become the bottom of finished Charlotte), covering completely. Cover with waxed paper. Set plate on top and weigh with heavy object. Refrigerate at least 8 hours. To serve, invert Charlotte onto a serving platter; peel off waxed paper. Brush remaining strawberries with syrup; arrange on top of Charlotte, around outside rim. Spoon whipped cream into pastry bag fitted with a star tip. Pipe stars around base and between berries. Worth every minute and every calorie!

Note: Requires at least 8 hours of refrigeration.

Variation: Try almond liqueur in place of orange liqueur.

Yield: 12 servings

Terry Laskowski

Cheesecake

Crust:
1¼ cups graham cracker crumbs
3 tablespoons sugar
**⅓ cup butter or margarine,
    melted**

Filling:
1 pound ricotta cheese
16 ounces sour cream
**2 (8-ounce) packages cream
    cheese, softened**
1½ cups sugar
3 eggs
3 tablespoons cornstarch
3 tablespoons flour
1 tablespoon vanilla extract
Juice of 1 lemon
8 tablespoons butter, softened

Preheat oven to 350 degrees. To prepare crust, combine crumbs and sugar in a medium bowl. Stir in butter; blend thoroughly. Press mixture firmly into bottom and completely up the sides of a 9-inch springform pan. Bake for 8 minutes. Let cool on a wire rack. Turn oven off. To prepare filling, blend together ricotta cheese, sour cream, cream cheese, sugar and eggs in a large mixing bowl. Adding 1 ingredient at a time, mix cornstarch, flour, vanilla and lemon juice into batter. Spoon butter into batter; stir to blend. Pour batter into prepared crust and place in cold oven. Bake at 300 degrees for 1 hour and 10 minutes. Turn oven off. Leave cake in oven for 1 additional hour. Chill for 4 hours before serving. Serve with fresh strawberries.

Note: This cheesecake is best when made the day before.

Yield: 12 servings

Pam D'Alessandro

187

Sour Cream Apple Pie

Filling:
6 medium-sized cooking apples
2 tablespoons flour
¾ cup sugar
⅛ teaspoon salt
1 egg, beaten
1 cup sour cream
1 teaspoon vanilla extract
⅛ teaspoon nutmeg
1 9-inch pie crust shell, unbaked

Topping:
⅓ cup sugar
⅓ cup flour
4 tablespoons butter
1 teaspoon cinnamon

Preheat oven to 400 degrees. Peel and core apples; slice ½-inch thick. In a large mixing bowl, sift together flour, sugar and salt. Add the egg, sour cream, vanilla and nutmeg; mix thoroughly. Fold in apple slices. Spoon filling into pie shell. Bake for 15 minutes. Reduce heat to 350 degrees; bake an additional 30 minutes. While pie is baking, make topping. In a small bowl, work together sugar, flour, butter and cinnamon until crumbly. After the 30 minutes of baking, remove pie from oven. Sprinkle on topping. Increase oven temperature to 400 degrees; bake an additional 10 minutes.

Yield: 6 to 8 servings

Georgia Moncada

Fresh Fruit Pie

Filling:
½ cup sugar
3 tablespoons corn starch
1½ cups orange juice
¼ cup lemon juice
1 teaspoon grated lemon rind
6 cups assorted fresh fruit, cut into 1-inch chunks, drained

Cookie Crust:
¼ cup butter or margarine, softened
¼ cup sugar
1 egg yolk
1 cup flour

To prepare filling, mix sugar and cornstarch in a saucepan. Gradually stir in orange juice over medium-low heat until smooth. Stirring continuously, bring to a boil over medium heat; boil 1 minute. Remove saucepan from heat; stir in lemon juice and lemon rind. Cool completely. Fold in fresh fruit. To prepare cookie crust, preheat oven to 400 degrees. Beat together butter, sugar and egg yolk. Using a pastry blender, mix in flour until crumbly. Press firmly into a 9-inch pie pan. Bake for 8 minutes, until edge is browned. Cool on a wire rack. Pour filling into crust. Chill for 4 hours.

Note: Cookie crust recipe can be doubled to make a thicker crust; flute at top. Recommended fruits: peaches, grapes, strawberries, blueberries, oranges, cherries, cantaloupe, honeydew and Mandarin oranges. Raspberries can be used as garnish.

Yield: 8 servings

Joanne Redondo

Cream Puff Cake

Crust:
1 cup water
½ cup butter
1 cup flour
4 eggs

Filling:
1 (8-ounce) package cream cheese, softened
4 cups milk, divided
3 (3⅜-ounce) packages vanilla instant pudding

1 (12-ounce) container frozen whipped topping (optional)
1 cup chocolate syrup (optional)

Preheat oven to 400 degrees. To prepare crust, combine water and butter in a saucepan over medium heat; bring to a boil. Reduce heat to low. Using a wooden spoon, and stirring vigorously, add flour gradually to saucepan. Continue stirring until mixture forms a ball and leaves sides of pan. Remove from heat; add eggs one at a time, beating after each addition. Spread mixture evenly onto bottom and up the sides of a 9x13-inch pan. Bake for 35 minutes. Let cool completely. (Do not break bubbles that may rise in crust during baking.) To prepare filling, beat cream cheese and 1 cup of the milk together in a large bowl using an electric mixer. (This will avoid mixture getting lumpy when it is added to the pudding.) Add pudding and the remaining 3 cups of milk. Continue beating until well-blended. Pour into cooled crust. Top with frozen whipped topping and drizzle with chocolate syrup.

Yield: 12 to 15 servings

Nancy Michel

Peaches-n-Cream Pie

¾ cup flour
½ teaspoon salt
1 teaspoon baking powder
3 tablespoons butter, softened
1 egg
1 (3¼-ounce) package regular
   vanilla pudding (not instant)
½ cup milk
1 (15-ounce) can sliced peaches,
   drained, 2 tablespoons of juice
   reserved
1 (8-ounce) package cream cheese,
   softened
½ cup sugar

Topping:
1 tablespoon sugar
½ teaspoon cinnamon

Preheat oven to 350 degrees. Grease a 9-inch pie plate. In a small bowl, combine flour, salt, and baking powder; set aside. Using an electric mixer, beat butter, egg, pudding and milk together in a large mixing bowl. Add flour mixture and beat 2 minutes at medium speed. Pour mixture into pie plate. Place peach slices and reserved juice over top of mixture. Combine cream cheese and sugar; blend well. Spoon over peaches to within 1 inch of the edge of the pie. For topping, mix sugar and cinnamon together; sprinkle on top of pie. Bake for 30 to 35 minutes, until edges of "cake-like" crust are golden brown and filling is soft.

Note: Pie is best if made at least 12 hours prior to serving; refrigerate. Chill leftovers immediately.

Variation: To substitute fresh peaches, use 2½ to 3 cups of sliced peaches; sprinkle on 1 tablespoon of sugar. Let stand for ½ hour, stirring occasionally. Reserve juice.

Yield: 6 to 8 servings

Kathy Leh

Helen's Chocolate Bavarian Pie

Crumb Crust:
1¼ cups chocolate wafer crumbs
⅓ cup butter or margarine,
melted

Filling:
3 egg yolks, slightly beaten
½ cup sugar
¼ teaspoon salt
1 cup milk, scalded
1 tablespoon unflavored gelatin
¼ cup cold water
1 teaspoon vanilla extract
3 egg whites, stiffly beaten
1 cup heavy cream, whipped

Topping:
¼ cup chocolate wafer crumbs

To prepare crust, combine the 1¼ cups wafer crumbs with melted butter. Press firmly into a 9 or 10-inch pie pan; chill until set. To prepare the filling, combine egg yolks, sugar and salt in the top of a double boiler. Slowly add the hot milk. Cook, stirring, until mixture coats spoon. Soften gelatin in cold water; add to mixture, stirring until gelatin dissolves. Cool in refrigerator until partially set. Add vanilla. Fold in egg whites and whipped cream. Pour filling into prepared crust. Sprinkle with ¼ cup wafer crumbs. Chill thoroughly.

Note: May substitute pasteurized powdered egg whites.

Yield: 6 to 8 servings

Mary Gehman

Best Pecan Pie

1¼ cups white corn syrup
1 cup granulated sugar
½ cup butter, cold
1 teaspoon vanilla extract
1½ cups pecan pieces
4 eggs, beaten well
1 (10-inch) unbaked pie shell

Preheat oven to 350 degrees. In a large saucepan, bring syrup and sugar to a boil; boil for 3 minutes. Remove from heat; add butter, stirring until melted. Add vanilla and pecans. Add eggs, whisking vigorously to prevent curdling. Pour mixture into pie shell and bake for 35 to 45 minutes. Remove from oven when just set; do not overbake. (Shake gently to check that pie is set.) Serve with whipped cream or vanilla ice cream.

Note: To fill 2 standard (9-inch) pie shells, use 1½ times this recipe.

Yield: 8 servings

Charlotte Broome

Miracle Custard Pie

2 cups milk
4 eggs
½ cup sugar
½ cup all-purpose flour
¼ cup butter or margarine,
    softened
1 teaspoon vanilla
¼ teaspoon salt
1 cup flaked coconut
Dash of nutmeg (optional)

Preheat oven to 350 degrees. In a blender, combine milk, eggs, sugar, flour, butter, vanilla and salt. Cover and blend 10 seconds or until well-mixed. (Do not over blend.) Stir in coconut. Pour into a greased 9-inch pie plate. Sprinkle on nutmeg. Bake for 40 minutes or until a knife inserted in the center of the pie comes out clean. Cool. Serve chilled.

Note: Pie forms layers as it bakes, creating its own crust.

Yield: 6 to 8 servings

Millie Linnelli

Mount Washington began as a major land purchase in 1794. Dr. Abraham Kirkpatrick, a veteran of the Revolutionary War, bought the land from William Penn's heirs.

Residential development did not begin in earnest until the mid-19th century when Kirkpatrick's three daughters inherited the Mount. The names of several streets — Shiloh, Merrimac, and Kearsage — commemorate the battles of the Civil War then raging.

The English, Scotch-Irish and Welsh, Mt. Washington's first settlers, labored as iron and glass workers in the mills along the southern banks of the Ohio and Monongahela Rivers. Difficult and dangerous footpaths provided the only access to their new homes. Wooden steps eventually replaced the paths, but still required strenuous exertion to scale the 500 foot hill.

Germans moved into the neighborhood in the 1860's and 70's. Their technical and engineering skills led to the construction of four inclines which solved the long-standing problem of transportation. Two of these inclines, the Monongahela and the Duquesne, remain in operation today.

The 1880's saw many Irish metal rolling contractors moving up from the South Side mills. They built St. Mary's of the Mount Catholic Church, a Grandview Avenue landmark.

A fond attachment to Mount Washington has always been prevalent among its residents. A 1930's survey showed that they had the highest percentage of homeowners in the city, with many families living their entire lives in the houses in which they were born. The majority of these houses were both designed and built by their owners.

Mount Washington's striking view of Pittsburgh's post-Renaissance downtown led to the development of many sophisticated restaurants and apartment buildings in the neighborhood. National attention was focused on Mount Washington in 1994 when President Bill Clinton and British Prime Minister John Major dined together at one of Mount Washington's cliffside restaurants — the Tin Angel. ♥

Elizabeth M. Sullivan, Proprietor
Elizabeth Damron, Chef
Opened for business in 1996.

Located in a beautifully restored 1884 Victorian home, the Appletree B&B boasts exceptional architectural detail including the decorative moldings and 12-foot high ceilings that grace the common areas. After strolling through picturesque Shadyside, guests can relax in the B&B's delightful garden.

Appletree Breakfast Bake

2 sheets frozen puff pastry
1 (½-pound) lean ham steak, diced
1 jumbo baking potato, diced
3 tablespoons vegetable oil
Salt, pepper and paprika, to taste
1½ cups shredded Cheddar cheese
12 eggs
1¼ cups milk
2 large tomatoes, thinly sliced
1 cup shredded aged Swiss cheese

Thaw puff pastry according to package directions. Preheat oven to 400 degrees. Position 1½ puff pastry sheets end to end on a rolling surface, overlapping ends slightly; press lightly to seal. Roll pastry with a rolling pin until large enough to line a 3-quart rectangular baking dish. Trim pastry; flute edges. Set aside. In a non-stick skillet, sauté ham for 3 to 5 minutes to reduce moisture content. Spoon ham evenly into pastry-lined baking dish. Using same skillet, combine potato and oil. Cook over medium-high heat until potatoes are tender. Season with salt, pepper and paprika. Spoon potato mixture evenly over ham layer; sprinkle with Cheddar cheese. In a large bowl, whisk eggs and milk together. Pour egg mixture into baking dish. Bake for 25 to 30 minutes, or until eggs are set. Remove from oven; arrange tomato slices around edge of puff pastry. Sprinkle Swiss cheese over tomatoes. Preheat broiler; place baking dish 6-inches from heat and broil for 2 minutes, or until cheese melts. Remove from oven. Allow to cool for 5 minutes before cutting into squares.

Yield: 8 servings

(In Memory)

Muzz Meyers, Owner
Paul Krause, Chef
Open for business from February, 1980 to December, 1997.

A favorite Shadyside restaurant, jazz club and gathering place for eighteen years, the Balcony was known for both its food and atmosphere. The name lives on with the Balcony Big Band, a local jazz group that performed a regular weekly gig at the restaurant.

Balcony Seafood Quiche

1 (10-inch) frozen or homemade pie crust shell, uncooked

Filling:
2 eggs
1 cup milk
2 tablespoons flour
3 scallions, finely chopped
½ cup mayonnaise
9 ounces jumbo lump crabmeat, picked through
9 ounces Jarlsberg cheese, shredded

If using a frozen pie shell, defrost according to package instructions. Preheat oven to 350 degrees. If using a homemade crust, place in pie pan; flute edges. Mix all filling ingredients together thoroughly in a large bowl. Fill pie shell with mixture. Bake for 55 to 65 minutes; rotate pie halfway through cooking time. Quiche is cooked completely when a knife inserted into the middle comes out clean.

Yield: 4 to 6 servings

Toni Pais, Owner and Chef
Carl Lashley, Chef
Opened for business in 1992.

A fine dining establishment featuring a fusion of European cuisines, Baum Vivant specializes in Portuguese fare. This intimate restaurant has received *Pittsburgh Magazine's* Restaurant of the Year Award annually for the last three years.

Crème Carmel

Caramelized Sugar:
1 cup sugar
½ cup water

Custard:
1 cup milk
1 cup heavy cream
Peel from a small orange
¼ cup Porto wine
8 egg yolks
1 egg
½ cup sugar

To prepare caramelized sugar, place sugar and water in a 10-inch sauté pan and bring to a boil over medium-high heat. Allow mixture to boil, without stirring, until it turns a medium-brown color. Working very quickly, cover the bottoms of 6 ramekins with a ⅛-inch layer of the caramelized sugar (sugar will harden after pouring, but will liquefy as custard bakes); set aside. Preheat oven to 325 degrees. To prepare custard, in a medium heavy saucepan, combine milk, cream, orange peel and wine. Bring to boil over medium heat. Remove from heat. Skim off any foam from top of milk mixture. Remove and discard orange peel. In a large bowl, beat egg yolks, egg and sugar until a creamy lemon color. Pour the hot milk mixture slowly into the egg mixture; mix well. Fill prepared ramekins evenly with custard. Place ramekins in a pan filled with 1-inch of hot water. Place in oven; bake for 2 hours. Remove ramekins and let cool in refrigerator. To serve, run a knife along the sides of each ramekin to loosen custard; invert onto small serving plates. Caramel will pool around the custard.

Yield: 6 servings

Michael DiFiore, Owner
Joe Watkins, Chef
Opened for business in April, 1996.

Adding to the Pittsburgh music and dining scene, Buffalo Blues has established itself as a favorite spot for listening to the "Blues" and sampling great food. The menu includes award-winning wings and many BBQ selections.

Jambalaya

Sauce:
3 (8-ounce) cans tomato sauce
3 (8-ounce) cans stewed tomatoes
2 cups chicken stock
½ cup chopped green onions
½ tablespoon minced garlic
½ cup chopped green pepper
¾ cup chopped celery
4 tablespoons butter
¼ teaspoon dried thyme
1 teaspoon black pepper
1 teaspoon white pepper
1 teaspoon dried oregano
½ teaspoon cayenne pepper, or to taste
1 teaspoon salt
2 bay leaves

Meat:
1 pound boneless chicken breast, diced
½ pound Andouille sausage, cubed or sliced
2-4 tablespoons olive oil
½ pound small to medium shrimp, peeled and deveined

Cajun Rice:
6 tablespoons butter

1 quart chicken stock
2 tablespoons minced garlic
1½ cups diced green pepper
1½ cups diced celery
1½ cups diced onion
3 bay leaves
½ tablespoon dried oregano
½ tablespoon dried thyme
1 tablespoon ground cumin
1 tablespoon dry mustard
¾ teaspoon paprika
1 teaspoon black pepper
1 teaspoon salt
½ teaspoon cayenne pepper
2 cups heavy cream
6 cups cooked white rice

Combine all sauce ingredients in a 4-quart saucepan. Simmer for 20 minutes. In a large skillet, sauté chicken and sausage in olive oil until cooked, approximately 5 to 10 minutes. Add shrimp; cook an additional 3 minutes. Add meat and shrimp to sauce; stir to combine. In a 12 to 14-inch sauté pan, combine all of the Cajun rice ingredients except the cream and rice; simmer for 10 minutes, until slightly thickened. Remove from heat; stir in heavy cream. Mix with cooked rice. Serve Jambalaya on the side of or over the Cajun rice.

Yield: 8 servings

Sean Davies, Owner
Darrell Barnes, Chef
Opened for business in March, 1998.

Nestled in Pittsburgh's historic Highland Park neighborhood, Café Baci is an intimate dining spot featuring contemporary European-inspired cuisine. Beautiful large-scale murals both inside and out add elegance to the dining experience.

Oriental Duck

Marinade:
½ **cup low-salt soy sauce**
1 tablespoon grated fresh ginger
½ **tablespoon chopped fresh**
   oregano
½ **tablespoon chopped shallots**
½ **tablespoon coarsely chopped**
   garlic

4 (6-ounce) boneless duck breast
   halves, skin on

Vegetables:
1-2 tablespoons olive oil
6 ounces bok choy, sliced
½ **red pepper, seeded and sliced**
4 ounces white mushrooms, sliced
3 ounces shiitake mushrooms,
   sliced

Combine all marinade ingredients in a 9x13-inch baking dish. Place duck breasts in marinade; cover and refrigerate for 2 to 3 hours, turning once. Discard marinade. Lightly oil and heat sauté pan. Brown duck, skin-side down, on medium-high heat for 2 to 3 minutes. Lower heat. Turn and cook an additional 5 to 10 minutes, until cooked through. In a separate pan, heat the olive oil. Add the vegetables; sauté 3 to 4 minutes or until desired tenderness. Slice duck breasts and serve with vegetables. Excellent with rice or couscous.

Yield: 4 servings

The Café at Club One
East Liberty

Jim Rosenbloom, Owner
Rachel DeCarlo, Chef
Opened for business in 1979.

Club One is a full-service health club attracting clients from Pittsburgh and the surrounding suburbs. After a healthy workout, members can enjoy friendly conversation and nutritious refreshments in the café and lounge area.

Club One Steak and Cheese

1 Spanish onion, thinly sliced
1 red pepper, cut in ½-inch strips
1 green pepper, cut in ½-inch
  strips
2 tablespoons olive oil
1-2 cloves garlic, minced
½ teaspoon ground black pepper,
  or to taste
½ teaspoon onion powder
  (optional)
1 teaspoon beef base
¼ cup steak sauce
12 ounces thinly sliced lean roast
  beef
4 (1-ounce) slices low-fat
  mozzarella cheese
4 (6-inch) hoagie rolls

Sauté onion and peppers in olive oil until tender. Add the seasonings and beef base. Add steak sauce; stir to mix. Adjust seasonings. Add roast beef; cook until heated through, about 3 to 5 minutes. Preheat broiler. Using a slotted spoon, place a ¼ of the mixture into each hoagie roll. Lay 1 slice of cheese on top of each roll. Broil 1 to 2 minutes until cheese is melted. Serve at once.

Variation: Low-fat or low-sodium beef base may be substituted.

Yield: 4 servings

The Frick Art and Historical Center, Owner
Susie Treon and Jacqueline Karkowsky, Chefs
Opened for business in the Spring, 1994.

This award-winning Café is located on the beautiful grounds of the Frick Art and Historical Center. The six-acre complex of museums and turn-of-the-century buildings is the legacy of Helen Clay Frick, daughter of industrialist Henry Clay Frick and his wife, Adelaide.

Raspberry Crostata

Pastry dough for
2 crostatas:
2 cups flour
¼ cup sugar
½ teaspoon salt
½ pound cold, unsalted butter
¼ cup cold water

Filling for 1 crostata:
¾ cup sugar, divided
3 cups fresh raspberries
Confectioners' sugar for dusting

To prepare pastry, mix flour, sugar and salt in a large bowl. Work butter into flour mixture with hands or a pastry blender until it resembles coarse meal. Add enough cold water to bring dough together into a ball, handling dough as little as possible. Cut dough in half; wrap each dough ball in plastic wrap. Chill at least ½ hour. Preheat oven to 425 degrees. Take ½ of the pastry dough (one chilled dough ball) and place on a lightly floured surface. Roll dough into a free-form circle, approximately 11-inches in diameter. Place on a baking sheet with edges. Sprinkle center of pastry with ½ of the sugar. Put raspberries into center of pastry leaving a 1½ to 2-inch border. Sprinkle berries with the remaining sugar. Fold dough border over berries, leaving a circle of berries exposed in the center. Bake for 25 to 30 minutes or until dough is golden brown. Dust with confectioners' sugar. To make the second crostata, repeat process of rolling out the dough and duplicate ingredients for the filling for one crostata. Serve warm or at room temperature.

Note: Remaining dough can be frozen for up to one month.

Variation: Other fresh fruits can be used; adjust the amount of sugar to the tartness of the fruit.

Yield: 4 to 6 servings per crostata

Tom Baron and Juno Yoon, Owners
Bill Fuller, Chef
Opened for business in November, 1995.

Casbah quickly established itself on the Pittsburgh dining scene with its award-winning menu. Diners relax and enjoy the ambiance while sampling Mediterranean cuisine with a focus on France, Italy and Spain. Middle Eastern and African cuisines lend a flavorful influence to Bill Fuller's creations.

Casbah Bread Pudding

Custard:
2 cups heavy cream
2 cups half & half
1 vanilla bean, cut lengthwise and scraped
12 egg yolks
¾ cup plus 2 tablespoons sugar
1 ounce orange liqueur

Pudding:
1½ quarts (1-inch cubes) lightly toasted ciabatta
2-3 cups diced fresh fruit, nuts, dried fruit or chocolate chunks (optional)

Combine cream, half & half and vanilla bean, with its scrapings, in a non-reactive pot. Bring almost to a boil. While cream is heating, whisk egg yolks and sugar together in a large bowl. Slowly whisk a ½ cup of the cream mixture into the egg mixture to temper. Gradually whisk remaining cream mixture into eggs, until totally incorporated. Add orange liqueur. Pass through a fine strainer. Allow to cool completely. Combine pudding ingredients in a large bowl; pour custard mixture over top. Mix and allow to soak for 1 to 2 hours. Preheat oven to 325 degrees. Place pudding in a 3-quart ceramic baking dish. Place baking dish inside a pan and fill pan ½ way up with water to create a water-bath. Bake for 1½ to 2 hours until pudding is set.

Yield: Approximately 8 servings

The following two recipes were donated by Marilyn McDevitt Rubin, a former food editor for the *Pittsburgh Press.* Now a columnist for the *Pittsburgh Post-Gazette,* her regular Sunday edition column has endeared her to Pittsburgh readers.

Very Good Salmon

2 tablespoons soy sauce
1 clove garlic, pressed
2 teaspoons fresh lemon juice
1 teaspoon sugar
¾ pound center-cut fresh salmon
    fillet, skinned and halved
4 teaspoons coarsely ground black
    pepper
2 tablespoons olive oil

Place soy sauce, garlic, lemon juice and sugar in a zip-top plastic bag; mix well. Place salmon in bag and seal. Marinate for 30 minutes in refrigerator. Remove salmon from marinade, drain and pat dry. Discard marinade. Press black pepper evenly onto salmon fillets. Heat olive oil, over medium-high heat, in a heavy skillet. Sauté salmon for 2 minutes on each side until crispy and fish flakes easily apart. Drain on paper towels; blot to remove excess oil.

Yield: 2 servings

Summer Couscous Salad

¾ cup water
½ cup couscous
Pinch of salt, and to taste
3 tablespoons olive oil
3 tablespoons safflower oil
3 tablespoons fresh lemon juice
Pepper to taste
¼ cup lightly toasted, slivered
    almonds
½ cup diced tomatoes
½ cup crumbled feta cheese
¼ cup finely chopped onion
1-2 tablespoons finely chopped
    fresh mint leaves, to taste

In a medium saucepan, bring water to boil. Stir in couscous and a pinch of salt. Remove from heat; cover and let stand for 5 minutes. In a medium bowl, stir oils and lemon juice together. Season with salt and pepper. Stir in couscous; let mixture stand for 2 hours in refrigerator. Add almonds, tomatoes, feta, onion and mint; toss. Serve chilled.

Yield: 4 servings

The following two recipes have been donated by Elaine Light, a Pittsburgh freelance food writer. Elaine's popular cookbook, *Gourmets & Groundhogs,* benefiting the Easter Seal Society of Punxsutawney, is now in its fifth printing.

White Pizza

8 ounces fresh spinach
½ cup olive oil
1-2 cloves garlic, peeled and chopped, to taste
⅛ cup cornmeal
Prepared dough for one pizza
½-1 teaspoon garlic salt, to taste
4 ounces shredded mozzarella cheese
4 ounces shredded Provolone cheese
4 ounces crumbled feta cheese

Preheat oven to 425 degrees. Wash spinach and remove stems; drain well. Heat olive oil in a sauté pan; add garlic and sauté until golden brown. Remove from heat. Remove 2 tablespoons of the oil from the pan; set aside. Add spinach to pan; toss to coat. Sprinkle cornmeal on a round pizza pan or free-form cookie sheet. Press out dough to desired thickness and place on pan; brush with reserved garlic-flavored oil. Sprinkle with garlic salt. Cover pizza with mozzarella and Provolone cheeses. Using a slotted spoon, place spinach on top of cheese. Bake 15 to 20 minutes until crust is golden brown and cheese is bubbly. Remove from oven and top with crumbled feta cheese.

Yield: 4 servings

Ultimate Crab Cakes

2 slices premium white bread, crusts removed
¼ cup heavy cream
1 teaspoon Old Bay seasoning
¼-½ teaspoon cayenne pepper, to taste
½ teaspoon freshly ground black pepper
1½ teaspoons Dijon mustard
1 teaspoon Worcestershire sauce
1 egg
2 tablespoons minced shallots or green onion
2 tablespoons minced green pepper
1 tablespoon minced fresh parsley
¼ cup mayonnaise
1 pound lump crabmeat, picked through
2 cups fine cracker crumbs
Butter and cooking oil for frying

Soak bread in cream. In a small bowl, combine Old Bay seasoning, cayenne and black pepper; set aside. Whisk mustard, Worcestershire and egg together in a large bowl. Whisk in dry seasonings; blend well. Add shallots, pepper and parsley. Stir in mayonnaise; mix well. Gently fold in crabmeat and bread. Drop large spoonfuls of mixture (3-inches round), one at a time, into cracker crumbs. Cover completely with crumbs; gently press into crumb mixture to coat all sides. Carefully scoop crab mixture out of crumbs using a slotted spoon or hands. Shake off excess crumbs; gently form into a cake. Place on baking sheet and finish patting into a cake form. Cover with plastic wrap and chill for at least 1 hour. In a large, heavy skillet, using 2 parts butter to 1 part oil, heated to moderate temperature, sauté crab cakes until golden brown on each side. Serve with lemon wedges, French fried parsley and tartar sauce.

Yield: 8 cakes; 4 servings

The following two recipes have been donated by Nancy Hanst, a Pittsburgh freelance food writer. Nancy's famous preserves are a part of many Pittsburgher's personal recipe collections.

Black Bean and White Corn Salad with Cumin Vinaigrette

3 cups dried black beans
1 tablespoon whole cumin seeds
¼ cup red wine vinegar, or to taste
1 teaspoon Dijon mustard
1-2 teaspoons kosher salt, to taste
½ teaspoon freshly ground black pepper
¾ cup light olive oil
4 Anaheim chilies
4 ears fresh white corn
1 bunch scallions, chopped
1 bunch cilantro, chopped

Rinse and pick over beans. Place in a large pot; cover with boiling water to 2-inches above beans. Cover pot and let beans soak for 1 hour. Bring beans and water to a boil; skim froth from top of water. Continue cooking until beans are tender, but not soft, approximately 1½ hours. Add additional boiling water to pot, as needed, to keep beans well-covered throughout cooking. Toast cumin seeds; grind using a mortar and pestle. Combine cumin, vinegar, mustard, salt and pepper in a small bowl. Slowly whisk in the oil. Pour mixture over the cooked, drained beans; set aside. Sear chilies over an open flame until evenly blackened; place in a closed paper bag for 15 minutes. Peel, seed and dice chilies. Cut corn kernels off cobs. Blanch kernels for 1 minute, chill in cold water; drain well. In large bowl, gently combine marinating beans with corn, chilies, scallions and cilantro. Adjust seasonings, especially vinegar and salt. Chill well before serving.

Variation: Substitute ground cumin (toasting step will be omitted). Substitute 2 cups frozen sweet white corn, which has been briefly thawed for no longer than 5 minutes.

Yield: 6 to 8 servings

Nancy Hanst Recipes, continued

Cranberry Crumble with Fall Fruits

Fruit Mixture:
1½ pounds fresh or frozen cranberries (unthawed), divided
1¾ cups granulated sugar, and to taste
2 teaspoons freshly grated navel orange zest
½ cup fresh navel orange juice
2 (8-ounce) Golden Delicious apples
2 (8-ounce) firm-ripe Bosc pears

Topping:
¾ cup rolled oats
¾ cup all-purpose flour
¾ cup firmly packed dark brown sugar
½ cup cold unsalted butter, cut into pieces

Whipped Cream:
1 cup chilled heavy cream
2-4 tablespoons minced crystallized ginger, to taste

Place a large sheet of foil on the middle rack of oven. Preheat oven to 375 degrees. Butter a 2½-quart shallow baking dish. To prepare fruit mixture, place ½ of the cranberries and sugar in a large, heavy saucepan. Cover and simmer, stirring occasionally, until sugar dissolves and berries burst. Remove from heat; stir in remaining cranberries, zest and orange juice. Peel and core apples and pears. Cut into ¼-inch thick slices; stir into cranberry mixture. Add additional sugar, to taste. Spoon fruit mixture into prepared baking dish. In a food processor, pulse together topping ingredients until mixture resembles pea-size crumbs (do not over process). Sprinkle topping over fruit mixture. Place dish on foil in oven. Bake for 50 to 60 minutes, or until topping is golden and filling is bubbly. Transfer to a wire rack to cool. To prepare whipped cream, in a medium bowl, beat cream until stiff peaks form; fold in ginger. Serve Crumble warm with ginger-flavored whipped cream.

Yield: 8 servings

Lee Deiseroth, Owner
David Indorato, Chef
Opened for business in 1978.

The Fluted Mushroom is the exclusive in-house caterer at the Benedum Center, Heinz Hall for the Performing Arts and the Mozart Room, all of which are located in downtown Pittsburgh's cultural district. The catering business is known for providing the elegant menus featured at many Pittsburgh parties and cultural events. The following recipe is one of their most requested.

Grainy Mustard Chicken Salad

3 whole skinless chicken breasts

Marinade:
Juice of 3 limes
½ cup olive oil
4 cloves garlic, minced
Salt and pepper, to taste

Dressing:
6 tablespoons balsamic vinegar
2 tablespoons white wine vinegar
½ cup plus 2 tablespoons olive oil
1 tablespoon whole grain mustard
Salt and pepper, to taste

1 pound steamed haricots verts or
thin green beans
1 pint cherry tomatoes, halved
½ cup slivered almonds, toasted

Arrange chicken in 9x13-inch baking dish. In a small bowl, mix all marinade ingredients together; pour over chicken to completely coat. Cover and marinate in refrigerator for at least 2 hours. Place all dressing ingredients in a carafe or 1½ cup container; cover tightly and shake well. Set aside. Stem, steam and cool green beans. Preheat broiler. Place chicken on a broiler rack; discard marinade. Broil until tender and juices run clear; let cool. Julienne chicken into ½-inch strips and toss with beans, tomatoes, almonds and dressing. This delicious salad is ideal fare for summer entertaining.

Note: Chicken breasts may be grilled instead of broiled.

Yield: Serves 6

Susan Parker, Owner and Chef
Opened for business in November, 1998.

This beautifully restored 1892 shingle-style Victorian house now caters to international guests from as far away as New Zealand, as well as those from the local Pittsburgh community. In the summer, guests can have breakfast on the brick patio while enjoying the ornamental pond and the owner's elegantly designed rose and perennial gardens.

Fraser-O'Loughlin Bed and Breakfast Decadent Egg Bake

1 dozen eggs
½ cup milk
½ teaspoon salt
¼ teaspoon pepper
1 tablespoon butter or margarine
8 ounces sour cream
12 slices of bacon, fried and
   crumbled
1 cup shredded sharp Cheddar
   cheese

In a large mixing bowl, beat eggs until frothy. Stir in milk, salt and pepper. Melt butter in a 12 to 14-inch skillet; coat pan evenly. Pour in egg mixture. Cook, without stirring, just until set but still moist. (With a smaller skillet, use a cover to aid in the cooking process.) Cool; stir in sour cream. Place mixture in a buttered 7x12-inch baking dish. Top with bacon and cheese. Cover dish and refrigerate overnight. Preheat oven to 300 degrees. Bake, uncovered, for 15 to 20 minutes.

Variation: Substitute 8 ounces of cooked sausage for the bacon.

Yield: 4 to 6 servings

Michael Hanley, Owner
Chris Madden and Pat Stoll, Chefs
Opened for business in December, 1996.

This lively little joint, adjacent to the University of Pittsburgh, features a casual fare menu with lots of personality. Regulars return for the brick-oven pizza and house brews, including their Pumphouse Pale Ale.

Rosa's Chicken Chili

¾ pound dried small red beans,
   such as pinto beans
2 quarts water
6 tablespoons olive oil
2 large onions, peeled and diced
½ cup peeled garlic cloves
8 small jalapeño chilies, finely
   minced
48 ounces canned stewed
   tomatoes, including liquid
5-6 bay leaves
1 (12-ounce) bottle beer
¼ cup ground cumin
¼ cup dried oregano
¼ cup mild chili powder
3 tablespoons Hungarian paprika
1 tablespoon unsweetened cocoa
   powder
½ teaspoon ground cinnamon
5 pounds boneless chicken thighs,
   skinned and cut into ¾-inch
   pieces
4 pounds boneless chicken thighs,
   skinned and ground coarse
½ cup yellow cornmeal
¼ cup salt, or to taste

Rinse beans; place in a large pot and cover with the water. Boil for about 1½ hours, until tender. Remove from heat and allow beans to rest in their cooking liquid; do not drain. In a large kettle, heat oil and add onions. Cook for 10 minutes over medium heat, until onions are tender and translucent. Add garlic and jalapeños to onions; cook an additional 2 to 3 minutes. Mash the softened garlic. Add stewed tomatoes, bay leaves, beer, cumin, oregano, chili powder, paprika, cocoa and cinnamon. Bring to a boil. Add chicken meat; stir well. Simmer 30 minutes, uncovered, just until chicken is cooked. Add beans and 1 cup of cooking liquid to chili. Heat to simmering, stirring constantly. Sprinkle 1 tablespoon of the cornmeal over chili, stir in; repeat with remaining cornmeal, being careful not to create lumps. Simmer for an additional 2 to 3 minutes; if the chili is too thick, add more bean liquid or water. Season with salt. Remove bay leaves before serving. Serve hot.

Yield: 2 gallons

Christine and James Dauber, Owners
Christine Dauber, Chef
Opened for business in 1983.

Located in a restored 1869 storefront, Le Pommier, (the apple tree), brought French country-style cuisine to Pittsburgh. With an extensive cellar of French wines, and a daily menu featuring fresh ingredients direct from the market, this lace-curtained restaurant is full of lovely surprises.

Filet De Saumon "en Papillote"

3 pounds salmon fillet, skin
  removed
Salt, to taste
Cayenne pepper, to taste
  (optional)
Zest of 1 lime, cut into threads
Fresh ginger, cut into threads,
  amount equal to lime zest

Sauce:
½ cup chopped shallots
½ cup port wine
½ cup fresh lime juice
½ cup reduced fish stock
3½ tablespoons heavy cream
12 tablespoons unsalted butter,
  chilled, cut in cubes

Slice salmon into escalopes (cut on diagonal) ½ to ¾-inch thick. Salt lightly; sprinkle sparingly with cayenne pepper. Cut 12 (12-inch) long squares of aluminum foil or parchment paper. Butter center of each square of foil. Place 3 slices of salmon on buttered portion of foil. Top with lime and ginger threads; seal fish in foil and refrigerate for at least 1 hour. Preheat oven to 375 degrees. Place salmon papillotes on a baking sheet. Bake 10 to 15 minutes. (If using parchment paper, baking is completed when papillotes puff.) Keep warm in a 180 degree oven until ready to serve. Prepare sauce while salmon papillotes are cooking. In a non-corrosive pan, boil shallots, wine, lime juice and fish stock until liquid is reduced to about a ⅓ cup; do not allow shallots to color. Add heavy cream. Return to a boil; whisk in cold butter. Place a ¼ cup of sauce, per serving, on a warmed plate. Open papillotes. Place 6 slices of salmon on top of sauce if serving as a main entrée; 3 slices if serving as a first course entrée.

Note: Prepare salmon for baking at least 1 hour in advance.

Yield: 6 main entrée or 12 first-course servings

Joseph and Jennifer Mico, Owners
Joseph "Pino" Mico, Chef
Opened for business in March, 1994.

This family-owned and operated business offers much more than pizza. The following recipe was brought to America from Reggio Calabria (Italy) by Pino's mother, Angelina, more than thirty years ago.

My Mother's Garden Tomato Salad

3-4 Roma tomatoes, cut in 1-inch pieces
1 medium celery rib, sliced thinly on the diagonal
1 small sweet red onion, finely chopped
1 roasted red pepper, sliced in thin strips
1 cup roasted red potatoes (recipe follows)
1 teaspoon shredded fresh basil
Your favorite Italian vinaigrette
4 pepperoncinis
Salt and pepper, to taste

In a large mixing bowl, combine tomatoes, celery, onion, red peppers and potatoes. Toss with basil and vinaigrette. Season with salt and pepper. Garnish serving plate with pepperoncini. Accompanied by Italian bread, this is a great summertime salad!

Variation: Substitute vine-ripened tomatoes, if available.

Yield: 2 servings

Roasted Red Potatoes

3-4 small red potatoes
¼ cup olive oil
½ teaspoon chopped garlic
¼-½ teaspoon salt, to taste
½ teaspoon ground black pepper
½ teaspoon chopped fresh oregano
½ teaspoon chopped fresh basil

Preheat oven to 350 degrees. In a small saucepan, cover potatoes with water; bring to a boil. Simmer 5 to 7 minutes; drain. Cut potatoes into 1-inch cubes; spread evenly on a baking sheet. In a small bowl, mix olive oil with all of the seasonings; drizzle mixture over potatoes. Bake 10 to 15 minutes, or until lightly browned.

Yield: 2 servings

Lawrence A. Poli, Jr., Owner
David T. Conley, Chef
Opened for business in 1921.

At this Pittsburgh dining legacy, Lawrence, Jr. and Joseph, II, are third generation owners and operators. Along with their mother, Dolores, they strive to maintain the excellent reputation that has rated their establishment as number one in seafood for seventeen consecutive years.

Lemon Sole Italiano

4 (6-ounce) lemon sole fillets
8 tablespoons butter, divided
Salt and pepper to taste
1 medium zucchini, seeded and
    diced
6 plum tomatoes, diced
1 small red onion, diced
1 medium green pepper, diced
½ cup sliced black olives
2 cloves garlic, minced
¼ cup white wine
Chopped parsley to garnish

Preheat oven to 350 degrees. Place fillets in a shallow baking dish. Top each fillet with 1 tablespoon of the butter; season with salt and pepper. Bake for 10 to 12 minutes. While fish is baking, place remaining butter into large, hot skillet. Add zucchini, tomatoes, onion, green pepper, olives and garlic. Sauté until tender. Add white wine and reduce slightly to a sauce consistency. Season with salt and pepper. Place fish on individual serving plates; spoon topping over fillets and garnish with parsley. Serve immediately.

Yield: 4 servings

Paul Carrozzi, Owner
Richard Carrozzi, Sr., Chef
Opened for business July 1, 1959.

A trip to Pittsburgh's Strip District would not be complete without a visit to Roland's. Situated in its present location for 39 years, Roland's has been in the Strip for a total of 55 years. Dine on the wrought iron balcony and gaze down Penn Avenue at Pittsburgh's skyline.

Red Prima Vera Sauce

18 ripe tomatoes
6 cloves garlic, chopped
8 basil leaves, chopped
1 large onion, chopped
⅓ bunch parsley, chopped
1 tablespoon olive oil
1 (16-ounce) can tomato puree
3 ribs celery, chopped
½ head of cauliflower, chopped
1 head of broccoli, chopped
2 carrots, chopped
½ red pepper, chopped
½ green pepper, chopped
1 small zucchini or yellow squash, chopped

Place tomatoes in a large pot. Cook over medium heat until broken down, about 10 minutes. In a medium skillet, sauté garlic, basil, onion and parsley in olive oil. Strain tomatoes and return to pot; add spice mixture. Stir in tomato puree. Cook over low heat, stirring occasionally, for 2 to 3 hours. Add vegetables and cook for an additional 20 to 30 minutes. Serve over your favorite pasta.

Yield: 8 to 10 servings

The Prime House
Greentree

Interstate Hotels, Owner
John Smith, Chef
Opened for business in 1986.

The Prime House features continental cuisine and offers seasonal entrées along with traditional fare. The following recipes offer delicious gourmet versions of two traditional American dishes.

Meatloaf

1 onion, diced
½ bunch celery, diced
1½ tablespoons minced garlic
1-2 tablespoons butter
1 cup milk
5 eggs, beaten
1 loaf of bread, trimmed and cubed
1½ tablespoons ground black pepper
1 tablespoon dried basil
½ tablespoon Worcestershire sauce
5 pounds ground beef

Preheat oven to 350 degrees. In large skillet, lightly sauté onion, celery and garlic in butter; set aside to cool. In a large bowl, whisk milk and eggs together. Soak bread in milk and egg mixture. Mix well. Add pepper, basil and Worcestershire to the skillet. Add skillet contents to bread mixture; combine with ground beef (do not over mix). Shape into a loaf; place in baking or loaf pan. Bake for 1 hour, a ½-inch from top of oven, to an internal temperature of 160 degrees.

Yield: 12 servings

(continued)

Garlic Roasted Smashed Red Skin Potatoes

5 pounds red skin potatoes
1 pound butter, softened
½ cup sour cream
2 tablespoons chopped roasted garlic (see note)
¼ cup chopped scallions
Salt and pepper, to taste

Boil potatoes in large pot of lightly salted water until fork-tender. Do not overcook. Drain and place in a large mixing bowl. Add butter, sour cream, garlic and scallions to bowl. Smash together using back of a large spoon. Do not over mix. Season with salt and pepper.

Note: To roast garlic, remove any loose skin from garlic bulb. Slice across top of bulb to just expose cloves. Place on a small baking sheet. Preheat oven to 400 degrees. Place baking sheet on top rack of oven and roast for 20 to 30 minutes, until tender when pierced with fork. Cool. Individual cloves will easily squeeze out from skins.

Yield: 12 servings

Larry Umenhofer and Jim Andrachek, Owners
Bill Ehlert, Head Brewer
David Achkio, Chef
Opened for business June 6, 1997.

The Strip Brewing Co. is located in the heart of Pittsburgh's Strip District and is housed within an 80-year old former wholesale business building. Customers can enjoy the numerous complex brews which are mastered there. The creative menu includes many selections that feature an in-house brew as an ingredient.

Roasted Tomato Hefe-Weissen Soup

6 large ripe tomatoes
1-2 tablespoons olive oil
2 tablespoons butter
1 tablespoon julienned shallots
1 tablespoon minced garlic
1 banana pepper, seeded and diced
1 bell pepper, seeded and diced
2 ribs celery, diced
½ quart heavy cream
1 tablespoon chopped fresh
    cilantro
1 tablespoon chopped fresh basil
½ quart hefe-weissen beer
1 teaspoon crushed red pepper
    flakes
Salt and pepper, to taste

To roast the tomatoes, wash and remove stems. Preheat oven to 500 degrees. Slash skin on bottom of tomato with large X. Place stem side down in roasting pan. Drizzle a small amount of olive oil over the skins; roast for 20 to 30 minutes. Place tomatoes in a closed paper bag until cool; remove tomato skins and discard. Set tomatoes aside. In a medium to large saucepan, melt the butter. Add the shallots; sauté 7 to 15 minutes. Just before shallots caramelize, add the garlic, banana pepper, bell pepper and celery. Cook until vegetables soften, about 5 to 10 minutes. In a separate saucepan, scald the cream. Add roasted tomatoes, cilantro and basil to the saucepan with the vegetables. Cook over medium heat until tomatoes break down, about 5 minutes. Add hefe-weissen and simmer for 3 minutes (do not reduce). Add heavy cream and red pepper flakes; simmer for 10 minutes. Season with salt and pepper.

Note: Hefe-weissen is a German-styled wheat beer brewed with 50-percent wheat malt. The clove-like and banana flavors are derived from the use of a specific strain of yeast. The Strip Brewing Co. offers Wüggleundstrip, their in-house brewed hefe-weissen.

Yield: 4 servings

Paul Kyros, Owner
Diane Plank, Chef
Opened for business in 1957.

The Tin Angel is known for its elegant, candlelit dining and features an enchanting view of the "Point" where Pittsburgh's three rivers meet. The continental cuisine and dramatic views are the background for many a romantic evening at this sky-high location.

Clam Dip

2 (8-ounce) packages cream
** cheese, softened**
1 (8-ounce) can minced clams,
** drained**
10 dashes Worcestershire sauce,
** and to taste**
4 dashes Tabasco, and to taste
¼ teaspoon onion salt, and to taste
¼ cup cream

Combine all ingredients in a large bowl; mix well (add additional cream, if needed, to thin). Taste and adjust seasonings. Place in a 2-cup serving bowl; cover and refrigerate until use. Offer as a dip for crudités. In the summer heat, its flavor seems only logical; in the winter, it stirs memories of hot sunny days at the beach.

Yield: Approximately 2 cups

WQED, which began broadcasting in 1954, was the first community-owned public television station in the country. Chris Fennimore, programming director, contributed the following WQED Baked Mashed Potato recipe. Nancy Polinsky, a freelancer and co-host of WQED cooking specials, contributed the WQED Pound Cake recipe.

WQED Baked Mashed Potatoes

8 tablespoons butter, divided
½ cup bread crumbs
6-7 large potatoes
½ cup milk
½ pound mozzarella cheese, cubed
3 tablespoons grated Romano cheese
⅛ pound hard salami, minced
¼ teaspoon salt, or to taste
⅛ teaspoon pepper, or to taste

Grease a 3-quart casserole with 1 tablespoon of the butter. Coat the sides and bottom with bread crumbs; set aside. Peel potatoes and cut into 1-inch cubes. Boil until tender and drain well. Preheat oven to 350 degrees. In large mixing bowl, mash potatoes. Add 6 tablespoons butter and the milk. Whip until smooth. Add mozzarella, Romano and salami; stir to blend. Season with salt and pepper. Spoon potato mixture into prepared casserole. Dot with remaining 1 tablespoon of butter. Bake 1 hour or until top is golden brown. The salami is what makes these potatoes "the ultimate!"

Yield: 8 servings

WQED Pound Cake

1½ cups butter, softened
1 (8-ounce) package cream cheese, softened
3 cups sugar
6 large eggs
1½ teaspoons vanilla
3 cups sifted cake flour

Preheat oven to 325 degrees. Butter and flour a 10-inch tube pan. In a large mixing bowl, add butter, cream cheese and sugar. Beat to a creamy consistency. Add eggs, one at a time, beating well after each. Add vanilla and flour; mix well. Spoon batter into the prepared pan. Bake for 1 hour and 15 minutes. Check cake with a cake tester. If necessary, bake cake for an additional 15 minutes (do not overbake). This is an old recipe from a WQED supporter's Grandmother!

Yield: 10 to 12 servings

A

Appetizers

Apples

Artichokes

Asparagus

Avocados

B

Bananas

Chicken

Chili

Chocolate (also see Candy, Cookies and Bars, Desserts, and Pies)

𝒫

S

Salad Dressings

Salads

Sauces and Marinades

Turkey

U

V

Veal

W

Water Chestnuts

Z

Zucchini

Sacred Heart Elementary School PTG
325 Emerson Street
Pittsburgh, PA 15206

Please send _____ copies of *The Heart of Pittsburgh*   @ $17.95 each

Plus postage and handling   @   2.50 each

                                                                    Total $20.45   each

Pennsylvania residents add 7% sales tax of $1.26 for each book

Name _____

Address _____

City _____ State _____ Zip _____

Make checks payable to Sacred Heart Elementary School PTG

- -

Sacred Heart Elementary School PTG
325 Emerson Street
Pittsburgh, PA 15206

Please send _____ copies of *The Heart of Pittsburgh*   @ $17.95 each

Plus postage and handling   @   2.50 each

                                                                    Total $20.45   each

Pennsylvania residents add 7% sales tax of $1.26 for each book

Name _____

Address _____

City _____ State _____ Zip _____

Make checks payable to Sacred Heart Elementary School PTG